The Burning Bed

by Faith McNulty

The Burning Bed

Harcourt Brace Jovanovich
New York and London

87816

To Peggy Brooks

Contents

Author's Note

Francine Hughes was charged with the death by fire of her husband, Mickey Hughes, in 1977. Had it occurred a decade earlier, the facts underlying the crime would probably never have been widely known, but in the seventies there was a new willingness to listen to a story such as hers. By the time she went to trial her case had become a cause célèbre.

The Hughes case is a classic example of chronic marital violence, and for this reason Mrs. Hughes agreed that her story should become a book. I read records of her trial and talked to many of the people concerned. Mrs. Hughes wrote down her recollections and discussed them with me over many hours. We agreed that in telling her story, truth is of the essence. Nothing fictional has been added.

There is, of course, something missing. No one can speak for the man who was her partner in tragedy. What he thought and felt can never be known. As I wrote I had a further frustration. I found that what Francine Hughes experienced is, in the fullest sense, indescribable. At times she would say, "There just aren't any words to tell you how I felt." Nonetheless, I believed that I understood. I hope the reader will feel the same.

—F. McN.

The Burning Bed

The Crime

EX-WIFE HELD IN FIERY DEATH

—Lansing State Journal

March 25, 1977

"As far as I'm concerned . . . this is a typical murder case. There is nothing unusual about it."

—PETER HOUK

Chief Prosecutor, Ingham County, Michigan

"The best personal advice I could have given Mrs. Hughes is that, while I don't know the answer, the alternative is not to commit murder."

—LEE ATKINSON

Assistant Prosecutor, Ingham County, Michigan

"Family violence is a common problem and a critical one everywhere in the United States. It occurs at all income levels and among all sorts of people. What happened in Dansville could have happened anywhere. There was a pattern of continuous trouble at the Hughes' residence over quite a few years. These episodes became progressively worse. This is not unusual. In my experience these situations between husband and wife end in one of two ways: the parties divorce and get out, or it will terminate in death."

—KENNETH PREADMORE

Sheriff of Ingham County, Michigan

Testimony of Sergeant Edward Nye of the Ingham County Sheriff Department at the trial of Francine Hughes in Ingham County Circuit Court, Lansing, Michigan, October 25, 1977.

Questions are by court-appointed Defense Attorney Aryon Greydanus.

Q. What is your profession, sir?
A. I am a police officer.
Q. What department?
A. Ingham County Sheriff Department.
Q. How long have you been so employed?
A. Ten years.
Q. Were you on duty, sir, on the evening of March the ninth, 1977?
A. I was.
Q. Had you been on duty earlier in the day, sir, when there was a domestic call to an address on Grove Street, Dansville?
A. Yes, I was.
Q. Were any arrests made at that time?
A. No.
Q. Have you been involved in responding to domestic calls yourself, Mr. Nye?
A. Yes, I have.
Q. On how many occasions, would you estimate?
A. Numerous times. I have been on hundreds of them.
Q. Hundreds?
A. Yes. Hundreds.
Q. Is it true that the police have problems dealing with domestic situations?
A. There is not much you can do.
Q. Not much you can do? Do you sometimes take one of those persons to jail when you find the situation to be aggravated?
A. Not unless there is an assault.
Q. An assault?
A. An assault that takes place in your presence—while the police officer is on the scene.
Q. So the only time that you will take one of those persons to jail is when you actually see them hitting someone else in your presence?
A. That is correct.

Q. What about if you found someone who was badly beaten by someone else but didn't actually see that other person strike them? Would you take them away?

A. No.

Q. What if you heard someone threaten to kill someone else? If you heard him say that he would kill her as soon as you, the police, left the scene, would you take them to jail then?

A. No.

Mr. Greydanus: That's all I have. Thank you, officer.

From the testimony of the defendant, Francine Hughes:

Francine Hughes: Well, I don't know how it started or anything, but he began hitting me. The kids were outside. He told them to stay out. I remember he was pulling my hair and he was hitting me with his fist and he had hit me on the mouth and my lip was bleeding. . . . Then I got away from him and ran around the dining-room table. He picked up some stuff and threw it at me and hit me on the ankle. I think it was a glass bird.

Defense Attorney Aryon Greydanus: Did you try to get help?

Francine Hughes: I yelled to my daughter, Christy, to call the police because I was afraid. . . . Before the police came he ripped up all my schoolbooks. They were schoolbooks from the classes that I took at Lansing Business College. He ripped them up and threw them all over the living room. Then he made me pick them up. He made me burn them. He made me put them in the burning barrel where we burn our trash and burn them up. Then he said he was going to take the sledgehammer to my car, smash up my car so that I wouldn't be able to drive to school any more. About that time he realized the police were going to come. He went in the living room and sat down.

Aryon Greydanus: The police hadn't been able to do anything for you in the past; isn't that correct?

Francine Hughes: What they could do, they did. Their hands were tied. . . .

Aryon Greydanus: What happened after the police left, Francine?

Francine Hughes: The kids were at the front door hollering they were hungry. And they were cold. I let the kids in. I just tried to stay quiet. Move quietly. Not say anything. Walking on eggs, because I didn't want him to start up again. I had the kids wash and we sat down to eat. None of us had eaten all day. I remember the salt on the food stinging my split lip where he'd hit me. The kids were trying to be quiet and I was trying to be quiet. Then Mickey came into the kitchen. He got a beer from the freezer and started yelling at me all over again. He pounded the table and the kids' milk spilled. It was dripping on the floor. The kids jumped up and started crying. Mickey made the kids go upstairs. Then he picked up the plates and dumped all the food on the floor. [Witness is crying.]

Aryon Greydanus: What did Mickey say after he dumped the food on the floor?

Francine Hughes: He said, "Now pick it up!"

Aryon Greydanus: Did he say it just that way, Francine?

Francine Hughes: No. No. He cursed me and said, "Now clean it up, bitch!" So I started to clean it up. He went into the bathroom. While he was in there I got it all cleaned up—broken glass, food, milk. Mickey came back and asked, "Do you have it all cleaned up?" I said, "Yes." So he took the garbage can and dumped all the stuff back on the floor again and he said, "Now, bitch, clean it up again." I got down on the floor to start picking up again. I was crying. I don't remember what he was saying, but he took a handful of food and started smearing it on me, on my back, smearing it into my hair, and yelling things at me, saying, "If you think things were bad before, they are going to be worse now." Then he was hitting me again and I backed into a corner. I crouched down and covered my head with my hands. Finally he quit and I just sat there.

Aryon Greydanus: What did Mickey say to you while you sat there crouched in the corner?

Francine Hughes: He said he was going to the bedroom with his beer to watch TV and he wanted me to fix something to eat and bring it to him.

Aryon Greydanus: He went into his bedroom and then what did you do?

Francine Hughes: I fixed him something to eat.

Aryon Greydanus: What happened next?

Francine Hughes: He finished eating. He hollered for me to come into the bedroom.

Aryon Greydanus: Did you go into the bedroom?

Francine Hughes: Yes.

Aryon Greydanus: And when you came in what did he say?

Francine Hughes: He said, "How about a little?"

Aryon Greydanus: What did that mean?

Francine Hughes: He wanted to have sex.

Aryon Greydanus: Did you have sex?

Francine Hughes: If I refused I knew he would start again. . . .

Aryon Greydanus: How did you feel?

Francine Hughes: I felt awful.

Aryon Greydanus: What happened after that, Francine?

Francine Hughes: I got dressed and told the kids they could come downstairs now; that their dad was asleep. They said they weren't hungry anymore so we sat together in the living room and watched TV. During that time I was thinking about all the things that had happened to me . . . my whole life . . . all the things he had done to me . . . all the times he had hurt me . . . how he had hurt the kids.

Aryon Greydanus: What did you decide to do?

Francine Hughes: I decided that the only thing for me to do was to just get in the car and drive. . . . Just go. And not let anyone know where I was at. Just leave everything and never, never turn back.

Supplemental Crime Report   March 9, 1977
by Jeffrey J. Simons, Gate Guard
Ingham County Sheriff Department

At approximately 2046 hours, one lady, with kids, arrived in a blue Ford Granada, Lic. #PVY-992. She was hysterical. Said she thought she murdered someone. I phoned the desk for assistance and returned to the vehicle, when she then said that she set the house on fire and her husband was sleeping in the bedroom. I then phoned dispatch and advised of a possible fire in Dansville on Grove Street. Assistance then arrived at the gate.

The Ingham County Sheriff Department is on the outskirts of Mason, Michigan, a small town and county seat near the center of the state. Sheriff Kenneth Preadmore commands a large, well-equipped force of deputies who provide police service throughout Ingham County. Their beat is a wide area of farmland and scattered towns. Like other modern police forces, the Ingham County deputies deal with every manner of accident and emergency as well as crimes that range from petty offenses to murder. They dispense law and order at the most basic level. Their headquarters is a large, flat-roofed building that also houses the county jail. The building and its parking lot are enclosed by a high, wire-mesh fence and there is always a guard on duty at the entrance.

At 8:46 on the evening of March 9, 1977, Sergeant Edward Nye had just come into the lobby of the jail when the telephone operator, Patricia Moore, told him to get out to the gate shack quick; Jeff Simons needed help with a hysterical woman. As soon as Nye left the lobby he could hear the sound of sobbing, loud enough to carry across the parking lot. A light blue Ford sedan, lights on and engine running, stood in the driveway. As he reached it he could see by the glare of the lights from the parking lot that the driver was a woman. Her face was buried in her hands, her body jerking convulsively. Beside her in the front seat was a young girl, perhaps twelve years old. Nye glanced in the back and saw the white faces of two younger children.

Nye turned to Simons and asked what was going on. Simons told him that so far he'd been unable to find out what the problem was. Nye leaned into the car. "What's wrong?" he asked. "Can we help you?"

The woman took her hands from her face and gripped the wheel. Nye noticed her knuckles whiten as she struggled to speak. But she only sobbed more loudly. The child in the front seat spoke. "He's been beating my mother for years," she said.

"Who has?" Nye asked.

"Her husband," the girl replied.

Suddenly the woman forced out words. "I did it! I did it! I did it!" she cried out, ending with a strangled scream.

"Did what?" Nye asked.

"He was sleeping and I set the bedroom on fire."

"You mean it's burning now?"

She answered, "Yes," and buried her face in her hands.

Lieutenant Albert Janutola, the deputy in charge of the desk that evening, heard himself paged and hurried out to the gate, accompanied by Deputy Jerry Hidecker. Janutola reached the car in time to hear the girl in the front seat say something about her mother being beaten. It crossed his mind that the woman had come to the police seeking help. Then he heard her say, "I did it! I did it! I did it!" and tell Nye she had set a fire. Janutola took over the questioning and asked the woman if she was sure her husband had been asleep. She said, "Yes."

The car's engine was running, and the automatic shift in Drive. The car inched forward as the woman's foot slipped spasmodically on the brake. Janutola pulled open the door and leaned in to shut off the ignition. As he did so the woman pressed something into his hand. It was a screw cap—the top of a container. Janutola got a whiff of a familiar odor and brought the cap to his nose. The smell was gasoline.

"Did you throw gas on him?" Janutola asked.

"No," the woman sobbed. "I threw it around the bed."

The girl in the passenger's seat broke in, begging to use the phone. She explained that her little brother, Dana, was at the house of a neighbor. She wanted to call her grandmother and tell her to look for the boy. "If he comes home and sees the house on fire," the girl said, "he might go crazy and try to go inside."

Janutola told the woman and children to get out of the car. He gripped the woman's arm and led her across the parking lot. "Oh God, he must be burning," she sobbed as they entered the lobby of the jail. She blinked helplessly in the bright lights. Janutola saw that she was young, of medium height, wearing black slacks, a turtleneck sweater, and loafers but no stockings. In spite of her matted hair, reddened eyes, and haggard face, Janutola noticed that she was "Not all that bad looking." As the woman stood, trying to control her sobs, Janutola sized her up with a practiced eye, unclouded by sympathy. Thirteen years as a police officer had long since dried up compassion for the perpetrators of violent crimes and the woman's admission of arson had quickly transformed her in his mind from victim to criminal.

Janutola told the children to sit down on a bench in the lobby and they silently obeyed. The eldest, who had done the talking, was a pretty girl with curly brown hair. Her brother, a little younger, was a thin boy in horn-rimmed glasses who looked terrified. A bewildered little girl of about six clung to his hand. She cried out in protest as her mother disappeared, escorted by detectives down a corridor.

Within moments of the arrival of the blue Ford and Gate Guard Simons' call, the dispatcher at the Sheriff Department had gotten in touch, by radio, with a police car cruising near the scene of the reported fire. Deputies Bruce Havens and Richard McDowell were on the outskirts of Dansville, where they had just finished writing up a traffic violation, when they received the order to investigate a fire on Grove Street in Dansville. Two or three minutes later they drew up before a modest white frame house surrounded by a grassy yard. At the rear of the house a red glow lit up the darkness and illuminated clouds of dense, dark smoke billowing from a single-story ell. Havens called in a fire alarm and jumped out to join McDowell in the yard, where he was coping with two hysterical people—a tall middle-aged woman and a smaller man. "Both subjects seemed to be extremely emotionally upset," Havens later wrote, in the dispassionate prose of his crime report. "They advised us there were people inside the building and insisted we go in immediately to get them out." Havens went back to the car and told the dispatcher that there might be "subjects" inside the building; he and McDowell would try to go in.

Havens followed McDowell through the door of a glassed-in porch at the front of the house. They opened the inner door into the house and encountered a wall of seething, acrid smoke. McDowell, who had been a fireman before becoming a police officer, noted that the smoke came within six inches of the floor. He told Havens there was no possibility of making it into the building without protective equipment. He slammed the door and the two men returned to the yard.

Now Havens and McDowell had their hands full with the two "subjects." The woman screamed that her son and possibly her grandchildren were in the house and that if the officers were too cowardly to save them she would go in herself. She ran toward the rear of the building. Havens followed and grabbed her, telling her it would be suicidal to go in the house. She twisted and fought in his grasp, screeching that he was not doing his job.

Meanwhile, the other "subject" had run to the front of the house and was struggling to open the front door. As McDowell reached him, the man smashed a pane of glass in the door. Air rushed into the building, feeding the flames. The windows of the room behind the porch, where the fire was centered, glowed with brilliant light as flames shot to the ceiling. McDowell caught the cursing, sobbing man in a practiced grip and wrestled him away from the door. He ordered him not to try again. Now more people had appeared in the yard. Havens ran to the police car, picked up the mike, and called for reinforcements.

Fortunately, at that moment, fire trucks and cars rolled up—both the Dansville Fire Department and the Ingham County Fire Department had responded—and firemen swarmed out, pushing back the crowd of bystanders and unloading equipment. They pulled their hoses to the rear of the house, pouring water through the windows into the burning room.

As John Fairbank, a volunteer with the Ingham County Fire Department, drove up in a tanker truck, he could see flames shooting out of the lower windows at the back of the house. He jumped out of the cab. A sheriff's deputy ran up to him and told him there might be children trapped on the upper floor. A bizarre recollection flashed across Fairbank's mind. He had been in this house before. At Christmas time, playing Santa for the Lions' Club's festivities, he had visited neighborhood homes in which there were children, this house among them. While Fairbank strapped on a Scott Air Pack, he tried to recall the layout of the house. At that moment, a distraught young man rushed over, told Fairbank he was a member of the family and described the way to find the stairs to the upper bedrooms where the children might be.

Inside the house Fairbank found himself enveloped in smoke so dense it seemed as though his eyes were closed. He turned left, touched a wall with his groping hand, and followed it until he touched a stair rail. He mounted a few steps and felt fiery heat penetrating his clothes. The blackness above was total. He turned and groped his way back to the outdoors. Then, unwilling to give up, he looked about for someone to help with a lifeline. All the firemen were busy at the rear, so Fairbank plunged into the scorching darkness within the house a second time, and again was driven back. He made a third try, using a new strategy: crawling on the floor and cutting straight across the living room to save time on the way to the stairs.

"It was so smoky you couldn't see the floor," he later testified. "I started up what I now knew was the stairs to the second floor. In the excitement I hadn't put on my gloves or my helmet. I kept going up the stairs until the heat was burning my ears and the top of my head and my hands. I couldn't go any further. I had to come down. I was down in the living room again and I heard somebody call me. It was Fire Chief Don Gailey who yelled, 'I think we have something over here.' I crawled to where his voice came from. We did have something. There was a man lying on the floor. I'd missed him when I came through. It was still very smoky, I couldn't see, but I could feel him. He was naked. Gailey was beside me. We hollered to the paramedics, but it was too smoky for them to come in, so we grabbed the victim to pull him out onto the porch. When I took hold of his ankles the skin came off in my hands. We went outside and got a rope. With that we were able to pull him out onto the porch."

By the time this task was finished, the firemen had extinguished the flames in the bedroom and the heat inside the house had subsided to the point where Fairbank was at last able to go up the stairs. The upper bedrooms, though filled with smoke, had not been burned. He made a quick search and to his relief found no one there.

Meanwhile Deputy McDowell, who was a paramedic as well as a policeman, had gone into the glassed-in porch and knelt beside the body of Mickey Hughes. He checked for vital signs, pulse, respiration, or pupil response, and found none. He came out and told Deputy Havens the victim was dead. Havens informed the dispatcher at the Sheriff Department that the ambulance could slow down; a detective should be sent to the scene.

Donovan Hughes, twenty-seven, youngest brother of Mickey

Hughes, lived a few blocks from his parents and brother. Earlier in the day his father, Berlin Hughes, had telephoned Donovan to say that one of Mickey's children had come over and used the telephone to call the police because Mickey and Francine were fighting. Berlin told Donovan there were two police cars in front of Mickey's house right then.

"I'm not gonna bother with it," Donovan had told his father. "The police can take care of it. I'm just gonna stay away and not get involved." He hung up. That evening, after dark, the telephone rang again. It was his mother, Flossie Hughes. Crying hysterically, she told Donovan that Mickey's house was on fire and Mickey was in it.

Donovan dashed out of his house and ran to Adams Street. His parents' home occupied the corner; next to it on Grove Street was the house in which Mickey and Francine lived. Donovan found the area jammed with police cars, fire engines, and spectators. Searchlights lit the scene and tinted huge clouds of smoke. Donovan sprinted across his parents' yard to the burning house. For a moment he stood dazedly among the spectators; then, seeing a fireman preparing to go in the house, he ran to him and explained the layout of the rooms. He heard a woman scream and turned to see a policeman holding his mother pinned against the side of the garage. She was fighting and struggling in his grasp. Donovan ran to them. "It's my mom," he told the deputy. "I'll take care of her." The policeman let her go. Moments later Berlin Hughes, the other "subject," gray-faced with shock, ran to his wife and son. "They found Mickey," he gasped. "Dead. He's laying on the porch. And *she* did it. The cops got her at the jail right now. Fran burned him alive!" He covered his face and leaned, shuddering, against the wall.

Lawrence Hughes, another son, who had reached the scene a few minutes after Donovan, joined them. He had just seen his brother's body. Tears were streaming down his face. Donovan said, "We better take Mom and Dad inside." Flossie Hughes was moaning, "Don't let them do an autopsy on him. Please!" The two young men led their parents into their house, where Berlin collapsed sobbing across the kitchen table while Lawrence called a doctor. Then the brothers telephoned the other Hughes sons, Dexter and Marlin, who were out of the state, to tell them of the incredible tragedy that had befallen the family.

When the woman, now known to be Francine Hughes, had been brought into the lobby of the jail with her children, Lieutenant Janutola and Detective Richard Fitzgerald led her to an empty office in the detective department. Seated in a straight chair beside a metal desk, she pressed her hands over her mouth as she struggled for control. From time to time she managed a few words between sobs. "Have they found him yet?" she asked. "Oh God, is he dead? Have they found him?" She raised her head, and looked at the men staring down at her—more deputies had come into the room by now—but no one answered. Then she asked about her fourth child—a boy named Dana. Crying harder, she tried to explain. "I couldn't wait . . . I tried . . . we waited and waited . . . where is he? Will somebody try to find him?"

Janutola told one of the men to get in touch with Sergeant Nye, who had by now arrived at the scene of the fire, and instructed him to look for the missing boy. Also, because it is considered desirable to have a woman present when a female suspect is questioned, Janutola sent for the telephone operator. Patricia Moore offered Mrs. Hughes coffee, which she refused, and urged her to pull herself together and tell them exactly what had occurred.

While the officers waited for the woman to calm down, a deputy took Detective Fitzgerald aside and quietly informed him of events at the scene of the fire. Sergeant Nye had called in to report that the fire was under control and a body had been found in the burned-out bedroom on the ground floor. It was almost certainly the Hughes man, but he hadn't yet been positively identified. Fitzgerald left the room and called Lieutenant Harry Tift, head of the department's homicide squad. He told him that a homicide had occurred and the suspect was in custody. Then he picked up a Miranda Rights form and returned to Mrs. Hughes. He asked if she would be able to understand it. She nodded and he read it aloud, pausing after each paragraph to ask if she had fully understood. Each time she said yes and when he finished, she obediently signed her name. Lieutenant Tift arrived and took over. It would be his task to ascertain exactly what had occurred and to gather evidence to support the criminal charge that would later be brought against Francine Hughes.

Tift, a small, sharp-featured man in his late fifties, regarded the suspect with no more sympathy than Janutola had felt. In his experience it is not uncommon for murderers, especially females, to show emotional disturbance immediately after the crime. He asked Francine Hughes to tell him what she had done. Instead, she began to pour out a story of being beaten, food thrown on the floor, garbage rubbed in her hair; of being afraid she would be killed. One of the deputies interrupted to tell Tift that there had been a "domestic disturbance" at the Hughes home earlier in the day. On checking the records it had been discovered that there had been a call from one of the Hughes children; two officers had gone to the house and restored calm without making an arrest. Tift nodded. He himself recalled the name Hughes and that the man had a record of violence and minor law-breaking.

As she told her story Mrs. Hughes referred to Mickey Hughes as her ex-husband. Tift asked her whether they were married. She explained that she had gotten a divorce six years before, but that they had continued to live together.

"Has he been beating you all that time?" Tift asked.

"Yes."

"Why didn't you throw him out?"

"I couldn't. He wouldn't go."

Tift shrugged and turned to other questions. He and the officers who were listening heard the woman's account of what had happened that afternoon without surprise. The details struck them as a bit more extreme and disgusting than in the average wife-beating case, but in other respects quite ordinary. Nevertheless, they listened attentively to the story the woman struggled to tell because what had happened that day was important as evidence; the beating provided a motive for the crime of murder.

Part way through her story Mrs. Hughes asked if she could go to the bathroom. Pat Moore took her by the arm and led her out into the corridor, where the woman caught sight of her children, still sitting in the lobby, and tried to run to them. Pat Moore grasped her arm and pulled her away. "Don't, it will just make things worse," she said, and steered her down the hall. When they reached the

The Burning Bed

restroom they found the door locked. The two women stood waiting while a deputy fetched a key. Pat Moore took care to recall everything that the suspect said. Any utterance by Mrs. Hughes was now potentially useful as evidence against her. In a report Pat Moore wrote:

"While we were waiting for the key the suspect stated, 'He must be dead! My God, what have I done!' The suspect kept trying to hold back her crying, but every once in a while a little cry would come out. I told her to think of her kids and try to calm down. She said, 'Oh my God, my kids! Now they'll have nobody! I have destroyed their lives!'"

A deputy brought the key. In the restroom Mrs. Hughes washed her hands and Pat Moore noted that after washing them she brought them to her face as though smelling them, then washed them again and smelled them again. It struck Pat Moore as possible evidence that the suspect was trying to wash away a telltale odor reminding her of her guilt.

When Pat Moore brought Mrs. Hughes back to the detective room she was more composed and answered Tift's questions coherently. A deputy interrupted Tift to tell Mrs. Hughes that her son, Dana, had been found. A neighbor was bringing him to the jail. Mrs. Hughes said, "Thank God," then asked if she could telephone her mother and ask her to come and get the children. Tift said she could and Pat Moore took her to a phone in another room. At the end of the call Mrs. Hughes asked if she would be allowed to speak to her mother when she arrived. She was told she could not. She handed her purse to Pat Moore, saying, "Please give this to Mom. She'll need it for the kids." Pat Moore gave the purse to the desk man, and brought Mrs. Hughes back for further questioning by Tift.

In the hour since Mrs. Hughes had surrendered, the detective room had become a busy place. Phones were ringing and deputies coming and going. Tift didn't immediately notice that the suspect had been brought back. He called to one of the men, saying that he had sent for a dentist to check the victim's teeth.

"A dentist?" Mrs. Hughes cried. "Why are you doing that?"

Tift turned to her. "Because the man is dead. We have to confirm who he is."

She cried, "Oh my God," and crumpled in her chair.

Tift seated himself at a desk with a typewriter and asked, "Are you ready?"

Mrs. Hughes raised her face—tears were again sliding down her puffy cheeks. She looked bewildered. "Ready for what?" she asked.

"Are you ready," Tift repeated, "to make a statement? To tell exactly what you did."

Mrs. Hughes stared as though she didn't understand.

"I've been trying to tell you," she said. "What more do you want?"

"I want a statement," Tift said. "On paper." When she hesitated he gave her a slight smile. "Come on," he said. "You might as well. You've already admitted everything anyway."

The woman dropped her head and stared into her lap in silence.

"Come on, Francine," Tift urged. "Let's get it over."

Mrs. Hughes found her voice. "Maybe," she said, apologetically, "I ought to talk to a lawyer. Can I see a lawyer?"

Tift yanked the paper out of the typewriter and motioned to a deputy. "Book her and take her upstairs to reception," he snapped. "You," he said to Mrs. Hughes, "are going to be charged with murder."

As soon as the Hughes woman had been taken away, Tift turned to the second stage of his evening's work—securing the evidence that would be required by the prosecutor's office if and when the case went to trial. Lieutenant Janutola gave Tift the cap that Mrs. Hughes had pressed into his hand and wrote a detailed description of it so that he could later identify the incriminating object . . . "metal with a white plastic covering. On the plastic was printed, TURN, CLOSE, OPEN, SQUEEZE, with arrows."

Tift dispatched Detective Fitzgerald to Grove Street to act as medical examiner, and Detective Clinton Chadwell to photograph the scene of the homicide. He called the Fire Marshal's Division of the State Police and talked to Sergeant Onnie Selin, who agreed to meet him in Dansville later that evening. He reached Ingham County Prosecutor Peter Houk at his home. He told Houk he had a murder case that looked like first degree; a woman had burned up her husband with apparent premeditation. Houk decided to come to the Sheriff Department immediately.

When Houk arrived around ten o'clock, Tift filled him in on

events so far; then the two men made the ten-minute drive from Mason to Dansville, retracing the route Francine Hughes had taken in her frantic flight. On Grove Street they found the fire extinguished. A few firemen and several Ingham County deputies were still there, holding back the last bystanders. Tift had ordered a round-the-clock guard on the house to protect whatever evidence it might contain. Fire Department searchlights illumined the white clapboard facade of the house, the trampled grass in the yard, the heat-scorched shrubbery around the glassed-in porch, and reflected off the dark windowpanes of the children's bedroom upstairs. Except for the smoke-darkened window frames and an ugly black hole where flames had eaten through the sidewall and roof of the bedroom in which Mickey Hughes died, the house was intact. The windows of that room were filled with light from portable lamps. Detective Onnie Selin was working there when Tift and Houk arrived.

As Tift stepped onto the porch he "observed the body of a Caucasian male" (as he described it in his report), "nude and lying face up on the floor." Detective Selin greeted the two men and told them he had picked up a number of items that could be useful as evidence: samples of burned bedding, carpet, and so forth.

They surveyed the ruined bedroom. It was a shambles of fallen plaster and twisted pieces of furniture. The skeletons of two single beds stood side by side, their bedding burned away and their frames distorted. Facing them, a TV set had somehow survived. Smoke had darkened its screen so that it stared at the beds like a blinded eye. Several windows were broken. A cold night wind swept through, stirring the ashes, and an acrid smell filled the air.

Selin had found that the south bed was more completely consumed and heat-twisted than the other. Beneath it some of the floor had burned through, making a hole into the cellar. The carpet had been destroyed in the vicinity of the beds, but was intact near the walls. The ceiling and upper section of the walls were more heavily burned than the lower. A double door leading into the living room was also burned at the top. Selin concluded that the fire had started under the south bed. The charred wood of the remaining floorboards showed that the fire had started on the surface and burned down, ruling out any possibility that it had started in the cellar, where accidental fires often begin. The fact that the walls and doors had burned from the top down also indicated that the fire had started on the floor. Heat and flames, Selin pointed out, rise. When the mounting flames touched the ceiling they folded back and burned downward.

Selin said the fire must have been intense and burned rapidly. He pointed to a metal clothes basket that had melted into the floor. He ruled out an explosion preceding the fire because the broken windows showed patterns typical of heat fracture rather than blast. Selin told Tift he had been able to detect the smell of gasoline when he first entered the room. On his way into the living room he had found a one-gallon can of Coleman Lighter Fuel lying on its side just inside the living room. The cap was missing. Selin had shaken the can and found a small amount of liquid inside. Smelling it, he concluded that the can contained gasoline. The can and the samples of charred debris would be labeled and forwarded to the Michigan Department of Public Health Crime Laboratory for further analysis. Selin told Tift and Houk he felt sure gasoline had been used to start the fire. His investigation added up to a confirmation of Francine Hughes' account of what she had done. If she later attempted to deny it, the prosecutor had the physical evidence to refute her.

Lieutenant Tift returned to the Sheriff Department, where Detective Nancy Kalder, was interviewing the two older Hughes children. Francine Hughes' mother, a small, plump woman in her fifties named Hazel Moran, had arrived and, though it was now after midnight, had been told she could not take the children home until they had given an account of events leading up to their father's death.

Kalder first talked to ten-year-old Jimmy. The little boy tried to hold back tears and his answers came reluctantly.

"Okay, Jim," the detective began, "could you tell me what you know about things that happened today? About the argument that your parents had earlier this afternoon?"

"Well, my dad ripped up my mom's schoolbooks and made her burn them."

"Do you know why he did that?"

"Uh-uh. No."

"What did she say while she was burning them?"

"I don't know."

"Where did she burn them at?"

"In our burning barrel. In the yard."

"Is this why the police were called today . . . because of this incident?"

"Uh-uh . . . they were called out there because my dad was beating her up."

"Do you know why he was beating her up?"

"No."

"What was he saying?"

"He wasn't saying nothing while he was beating her up."

"Does this happen quite frequently?"

"Yes."

"Do you know why?"

"No."

"How often would you say they get into a fight?"

"Probably every other day."

"What does your mother have to say about all that?"

"Nothing. She just cries."

"Does your father work at all?"

"Uh-uh . . . no."

"Does your mother?"

"No."

"But she goes to school?"

"She ain't going to be going any more."

"Did she tell you that?"

"No, but she probably can't because her books are gone."

From Kalder's point of view Jimmy's most significant answer concerned the gasoline can that Detective Selin had found by the bedroom door. Kalder asked the boy if gasoline had been used to set fire to the house.

"Well, she had, uh, asked me what the combination to the garage was. My dad had taught it to me . . . and so she asked me to tell her, so I told her. I didn't know what she was gonna do. After she went to the garage she came back in the house and I went by the back door and . . . there was a can of oil, or something like that, sitting there."

"What did the can look like?"

"Well, it was square and had a handle on it . . . in front of the handle it had a lid and it said 'Fuel' on it."

"Do you know what is usually kept in that can?"

"Fuel."

Detective Kalder turned to Christy Hughes. Unlike her brother, she was tearless and self-possessed. She willingly told the detective details of the events she had witnessed that day. "Daddy come in the kitchen and he was mad because Mom was cooking TV dinners. He grabbed her arm and she says, 'Don't, Mickey. Don't.' And, uhm, he grabs her arm and bends it up behind her back and is hurting her and she bends over like trying to get away." Christy jumped up to demonstrate. "And Daddy hits her in the face and then hits her on the head. . . ."

Kalder moved on to the episode of the burned books. "Did she burn them herself? Did she pour anything on them?"

"I don't know. I seen the smoke and I asked her what it was. She said, 'Daddy made me burn my schoolbooks.'"

"Do you know why he did that?"

"Yes, I guess this is the reason; because he, he didn't want her having no fun. He noticed, he realized that she was . . . you know . . . that her spirit was coming back . . . and she was really happy and all because she got to go to school . . . he realized that and got mad, I guess."

"Okay, so what happened after that?"

"I was outside. He sent us outside because I was screaming, like usual, saying, 'Stop, Daddy, stop! Stop!' Stuff like that . . . screaming my head off 'til I was hoarse. Mom yells, 'Christy! Go call the cops!' I take off running over to Grandma Hughes' house. When he realized what I'm doing he stops beating her and when the cops come he's sitting down. Then, when they leave, he starts up again."

"And what happened then?"

"He sends us kids up upstairs."

"And when you came down?"

"I see fish patties and peas and potatoes sitting on the stove and I realize he's ate, and he's in the bedroom sleeping. Usually after he eats he's all relaxed and he snores."

Kalder skillfully questioned Christy about her mother's behavior just before the fire, trying to establish the time at which her father had gone to sleep and how much later her mother had set the fire.

"We sat in the living room for a half an hour . . . I don't know . . . yeah, we sat there for a long time waiting for Dana, my little brother."

"Did you observe anything unusual sitting by the door when you came out of the house?"

"Uhm. Hold it! Yeah!"

"What?"

"There was a, uhm . . . I don't know . . . a little thingy, with a . . . a gasoline can . . . I thought it was something that Dad had brought in."

Christy told how her mother had led her and Jimmy to the car, carrying little Nicole, the six-year-old, and then gone back to the house. A moment later she returned to the car and scrambled into the driver's seat. "She started the car as fast as she could . . . we . . . we took off."

"What was she saying?"

"She was saying, 'Oh my God. Oh my God . . . my God.' I was thinking like, 'Daddy's chasing us . . . it's just Daddy chasing us.' But Mom keeps saying, 'Oh my God,' and keeps looking back at the house . . . and really crying. She was just breaking up and everything. I say, 'Mom, what's the matter?' And she says, 'I burned him! I burned him!' She was frantic. . . ."

"Whose idea was it to come to the police?"

"Mine and Mom's both. I felt as soon as we can get somewhere safe, the better we are. So I say, 'Go to the police, Mom. . . .' She drives sixty miles an hour and I says, 'Mom, you're scaring me. Slow down.' She slows down and we get here, and I say, 'Oh Mom, finally we're here.'"

As the interview ended, Mrs. Moran, Francine Hughes' mother, who had sat listening while the children were interviewed, tried to put in a word in her daughter's defense. "I know she has tried to make a good home for those children. I do know that. It's awful hard sometimes. I practically went through the same thing with my marriage and it's hard. But I do know Francine is a good mother. And I do know that she is a good girl."

Kalder asked Mrs. Moran if she had anything further to say. Looking anguished, Mrs. Moran shook her head. "I don't know," she said helplessly. "I don't know. I can't think of anything. I'm just . . . just all mixed up."

On the morning following the fire, Lieutenant Tift went to the prosecutor's office to discuss the next step in the Hughes case with

Chief Prosecutor Houk and Assistant Prosecutor Lee Atkinson. In the administration of justice the most crucial decisions are often made at the earliest stage. A police officer can decide on the spot whether a traffic violator receives a lecture or a summons. A detective gathering evidence in a homicide case has no formal authority to determine what the charge will be, but his informal opinion is frequently taken into account by the man next in the chain of decision—the prosecutor—who has considerable latitude in deciding what charge to bring. He may consider a death justifiable homicide, which usually results in the case being dismissed, or bring any of an ascending scale of charges, from manslaughter or second-degree murder to the most serious of all—murder in the first degree.

In the view of the three men discussing Francine Hughes' fate, she had obvious motives for killing Mickey Hughes with "malice aforethought." Tift knew that calls to quell violence at the Hughes' home were a familiar story at the Sheriff Department. Christy's first words at the gate of the jail were, "He's been beating her for years." It would not be difficult to prove that Francine Hughes had reason to hate her ex-husband and wanted to get rid of him. Everything she had told the police after her surrender about the horrors of her life with Mickey Hughes could bolster the case against her.

The manner in which Mickey Hughes died had been made clear not only by Francine's admission, but by the findings of Detective Selin and the accounts given by the children. Most damning of all were the statements made by the children that after their father had gone to sleep their mother had deliberately searched for gasoline and then waited for a period of time before setting the fire. This interval could be considered time in which to premeditate the act of murder.

What about mitigating circumstances? Self-defense, the heat of passion, a hitherto blameless life, unbearable provocation? When there are such considerations prosecutors often bring a lesser charge, but Houk and Atkinson did not see the case of Francine Hughes as meriting leniency. Atkinson made out a warrant for first-degree murder and, for good measure, added a charge of felony murder, based on the fact that she had committed arson, a felony, resulting in a death.

When Tift returned to the Sheriff Department, he ordered Detective Nancy Kalder to get Mrs. Hughes ready for a trip to District

Court, where she would be arraigned. Kalder found her lying on
her bunk, half-awake. She looked haggard and sick. Kalder had
brought her clothes. Mrs. Hughes got up, dazedly, as though still
unsure of where she was, and obediently changed from prison
sweatshirt and slacks, modestly turning her back as she did so. She
was silent as Kalder took her down to the lobby, but when Kalder
snapped handcuffs on her wrists, Mrs. Hughes pulled back with a
look of shock. "Do I have to wear these?" she asked. "I'm not going
to run away!"

"Sorry," Kalder said. Mrs. Hughes looked at her wrists and tears
slid down her cheeks. Kalder patted her shoulder. "Buck up," she
said cheerfully, "the first time's the worst!" The two women got
into the back seat of a police car. Mrs. Hughes huddled in her seat
in withdrawn silence. Glancing at her, Kalder noticed blue and purple bruises mottling her face and thought, "The poor thing looks
like the wrath of God, and no wonder! She sure had a rough night!"

At the courthouse Kalder took Mrs. Hughes to an empty room to
await her turn. Suddenly the prisoner seemed to waken to the reality of her surroundings. "What am I supposed to say?" she asked in
apparent panic. "What do I tell the judge?"

"What are you talking about?" Kalder asked. Her sympathy for
the woman did not prevent her remembering that any admissions
made by the prisoner might later be useful to the prosecution.

Mrs. Hughes began to cry. "I know I did it and I'm guilty," she
whimpered. "I just don't know what I'm supposed to say. . . ."
Kalder had no time to reply. A court attendant beckoned her to the
courtroom. She hastily gave Mrs. Hughes a piece of Kleenex and
waited while she mopped her eyes. Later, Kalder reported Mrs.
Hughes' admission, "I know I did it and I'm guilty," to Lieutenant
Tift.

There were several arraignments that day before Judge Robert
Bell and the small room was crowded with spectators. The parents
and brothers of Mickey Hughes sat on the right of the aisle. On the
left, as far distant as possible, were Mrs. Hughes' mother and sisters
and her four children. Judge Bell read the charges and asked Mrs.
Hughes if she wanted the court to appoint an attorney to defend
her. She said yes. Bell set the date of her next court appearance for
March 21—ten days hence.

Outside the courtroom Mrs. Hughes was allowed a moment with

her mother and children. They hugged each other and wept. Then Detective Kalder took her to the police car. On the trip back to the jail she cried silently, and was still crying when Kalder returned her to her cell.

The case of Francine Hughes excited only a moderate amount of interest among the men at the Sheriff Department. Domestic quarrels are frequent and police heartily dislike dealing with them. When a policeman is called to the scene of a wife-beating he knows he is walking into a situation that is volatile and dangerous—so dangerous that the Ingham County Sheriff Department makes it a rule to send *two* deputies on domestic calls. More police are killed dealing with "domestics" than with any other type of crime, including holdups, burglaries, and bank robberies. Burglars and robbers, when caught, are often sentenced and taken out of circulation at least for a while, but wife-beaters almost never are.

It is an axiom in police work that beaten wives seldom bring charges against their husbands. The reasons are various: fear of retaliation, loss of income if the husband is sent to jail, the stigma that children will have to bear as the episode is made public and their father is branded with a criminal record. A less apparent but sometimes equally compelling reason is a lingering emotional tie; in spite of their quarrels there may still be a sexual bond between husband and wife. If, after a beating, the victim does not sign a complaint, the police can take no further action. Thus what police consider the futility of their task adds bitterness to their attitude. As they see it, they risk their lives intervening in a domestic fight only to have the ungrateful victim return to her abuser and the ugly situation occur all over again. A woman who continues to live with a chronic wife-beater—a man the police regard as a low form of life, slightly above pimps and molesters of children—inevitably loses dignity and claim to decency in the eyes of the police. "If a woman doesn't like being beaten, why doesn't she leave?" they ask, even though they are aware of the difficulties that often stand in the way. "Why would a decent woman go on living with a bum like that?"

More often in domestic fatalities it is the husband who kills the wife, but even so there was nothing unusual in a wife having killed her husband. It was the way in which Mickey Hughes met his death that struck the men as a particularly atrocious form of homicide. What sympathy there had been for Francine Hughes when she arrived sobbing at the jail evaporated as soon as the officers learned what she had done. "If she had picked up a knife and stabbed him, I could understand it," several men said. Her story of suffering and abuse explained her act, but did not alter the fact that she had taken the life of a man who was helpless at the time. Lieutenant Tift believed the circumstances plainly showed that Francine Hughes had premeditated the crime. He saw it as an open-and-shut case of murder in the first degree.

On Saturday, March 14, a service for Mickey Hughes was held at a funeral home a few miles from Dansville. The room was crowded with mourners. Mickey Hughes' four brothers, good-looking, dark-haired men, and their wives were there, and his sister with her children. His brothers wept as their mother clung to them. She expressed not only sorrow, but fury, at her son's murder, saying she hoped that her former daughter-in-law would go to prison for the rest of her life. The victim's father wanted quicker vengeance. His thin, sallow face was a mask of misery and bitterness.

By the following Monday the case of *The People* vs. *Francine Hughes* had begun to move through the legal process that would culminate in her trial. The presiding judge of the Ingham County Circuit Court chose an attorney to represent the defendant. His name was Aryon Greydanus. He was thirty-one years old, and had only recently entered private practice in Lansing.

A murder case, even one that isn't too promising, can be helpful in a young attorney's career, and Greydanus was glad to get the assignment. He went to the jail that evening. When Francine Hughes was brought in for their conference he thought her nice looking, but unremarkable. She was dressed in prison garb—a gray sweatshirt and blue cotton trousers. She had thick curly brown hair cut short, dark brown eyes, even features, and fair skin. Her expression was a mixture of fear, misery, and despair.

Greydanus talked to Mrs. Hughes for three hours, listening with increasing shock to her account of beating and abuse. When he got home he told his wife, Rosemary, "You're not going to believe your ears. What that woman lived through year after year is simply incredible."

"Do you mean that he beat her for *years*? Why didn't she just go away?"

"She couldn't," Greydanus said. "She was too scared. He had her convinced that wherever she went he'd find her and kill her." Greydanus paused, reviewing in his mind the story he'd just heard from Francine Hughes. "He probably would have, too. She was in a real bind. She could get killed if she tried to leave the guy and she was going to get killed if she stayed. He was getting closer to it every day."

On March 21, Francine Hughes was again brought in handcuffs to District Court. This time Aryon Greydanus was there to meet her. So was a young prosecutor named Martin Palus, whom Houk had assigned to her case. Palus presented a string of witnesses—firemen, deputies, the pathologist who had performed an autopsy on Mickey Hughes, and the Hughes children—to show that *The People* had grounds on which to try Mrs. Hughes on the two counts of murder—felony murder and murder in the first degree—with which she had been charged. At the end of the hearing Greydanus asked for bail, arguing that Mrs. Hughes was not an ordinary criminal. Judge Bell said that though he regretted it, he felt unable to grant bail in a first-degree murder case. He suggested, however, that Greydanus take up the matter with the judge who would preside over her trial.

That judge proved to be even less sympathetic. When, some days later, Mrs. Hughes was arraigned before Circuit Judge Michael Harrison, Greydanus again asked for bail. Judge Harrison listened stonily and denied the request. "After all," he added rhetorically, "what kind of woman would burn up her husband?"

Judge Harrison's question haunted Greydanus. It indicated the feelings that Francine Hughes' crime was likely to arouse. On the face of it her act seemed horrible, cruel, inexcusable. In order to have any hope of persuading a jury to see it differently, Greydanus knew he would have to answer the question "What kind of woman . . . ?" and show that it might be any woman trapped in the situation Francine Hughes had described when he talked to her at the jail.

Francine Hughes spent eight months in jail awaiting trial. During that time Greydanus visited her regularly, drawing out the story of her life. He enlisted a psychiatrist and a clinical psychologist to give their appraisal of her mental and emotional condition. She herself found it difficult to understand what she had done, and tried, by searching her past, to find answers that would ease her burden of guilt. She wrote an autobiography beginning with her earliest memories. She wrote it in her cell in pencil on a lined tablet, covering dozens of pages with a neat, graceful script.

Beginning

This is Francine's earliest memory: She is about five years old. The scene is somewhere out in the country, probably on one of the muck farms—vast onion fields—where her mother and father worked after they first came north from Kentucky to Michigan. Francine remembers a cold, starlit night in October, close to Halloween. In the afternoon the family had piled into their car and gone to town on a shopping expedition. Francine's mother bought the children, Francine and her older brother and sister, warm coats to face the cold winter ahead. Francine's was a beautiful blue with a red lining, and a red hood and mittens to match. While her mother shopped with the children, her dad and her uncle went off on errands of their own. It was dark and cold when the family assembled and got back into the car. Her father and uncle were noisy and cheerful—overflowing with generosity. They'd bought a big bag of candy, peanut-butter kisses wrapped in orange-and-black Halloween paper, for the children. Her mother rationed out a few of the candies to each child and kept the rest with her in the front seat. Francine remembers riding in the back seat of the old car that vibrated and rattled over the road, feeling snug between her brother and sister, with the sweet candy melting in her mouth and the boxes of new clothes and other bundles piled under their feet.

While her father drove, he and Uncle Press passed a bottle back and forth between them. They laughed often and sang bits of songs. Francine knew they were drunk—she could smell the familiar, strong fumes—but it didn't bother her. Liquor was grown-up candy. It was very late when they finally lurched up a rutted farm road and stopped in front of their small frame house. The children were drowsy and the candy taste had long disappeared from their mouths. Francine's mother told them to hustle into the house to escape the icy wind. Sleepily Francine followed the grown-ups. The packages—coats, candy, and all—were left in the car.

In the morning, when she woke, the first thing Francine thought of was the coats and the candy. She doesn't remember how she learned what had happened—whether her mother told her, or if she and her brother went outside and made the discovery themselves—but in the night the car had burned up. One of the men must have left a lighted cigarette smoldering in the upholstery. Francine and her brother climbed inside the blackened skeleton of the burned-out car and poked through the bitter-smelling ashes. The coats had turned to blackened shreds, but in a crevice Francine found one piece of candy.

Until she was in prison Francine was not aware that she possessed this memory. Then, at Greydanus' urging, she searched far into her past, and told him about this and other scenes from her childhood. She told about the burned coats with puzzled disappointment, but no anger. "I didn't think about it being anyone's fault . . . about Dad and my uncle being drunk. I didn't think about how hard Mom and Dad had worked to buy the coats or about what we'd do without them. I guess Mom got us others second-hand. But I remember how bad I felt about the candy." It did not seem to strike her that her first memory concerned being deprived of what was rightfully hers by a drunken man whom she trusted to love and protect her.

Francine's father, Walter Moran, was born in Pike County, Kentucky, and married Hazel Fleming in 1938 when she was fourteen, he twenty-five. In the 1930s and '40s many poverty-stricken Kentucky people heard of better lives up north. From the mountain hollows of Kentucky to the flat croplands of central Michigan was an enormous social leap, but a highway distance of only 250 miles. All it took was a jalopy and enough money for gas at fifteen or twenty cents a gallon.

The city of Lansing in Ingham County, Michigan, is surrounded by miles of farm country. The area offered both seasonal farm work and factory work. Penniless arrivals from Kentucky got their first foothold in the farm labor force and then, with luck and new sophistication, graduated to better-paid jobs in factories. In Ingham County, several small towns—Stockbridge, Mason, Williamston, and Dansville—were heavily settled by what are politely called "southerners." Their children joke about being "hillbillies," but there is some reality in the jest. Customs and attitudes from the Kentucky mountains still color their lives. Michigan hillbillies know how to cook southern food and sing mountain songs. Less tangible elements of mountain culture survive in their behavior; women are expected to be strong, hard-working, and submissive, and men masculine. Masculinity often implies domination.

Walter Moran was over six feet tall, with blue eyes and a rugged face that suggested Irish ancestry. Hazel was small-boned and trim with a fine nose and a heart-shaped face, a pretty girl. Walter was literate. He had been through three years of grade school. Hazel had had only one year, and, until her husband taught her, could not read or write. Walter and Hazel Moran's first years in Michigan were spent working on farms and living in houses that their employers provided free. Wages in the onion fields were thirty to fifty cents an hour. For a while Hazel as well as Walter worked in the fields; then Hazel began to take jobs as a waitress. It was easier work for a lightly built woman who was often pregnant to boot. Hazel's first two babies died in infancy. Her first child to survive was Joanne, born in 1942. Robert Lee was born two years later. The family moved often. When Francine was born in 1947 the family was living on a farm outside the town of Stockbridge. "Francine" was an unusual name for that time and place. Hazel Moran was listening to the radio, thinking about the coming baby, when she heard a French chanteuse named Francine. Hazel was struck by the glamor of the name and decided that if her child was a girl she would be Francine.

Francine remembers her earliest years as her happiest. She was pleased with herself and loved to please others—to receive compliments. Describing herself as a child she wrote: "I remember having thick, pretty hair. Everywhere I went everyone commented that I was so pretty—so smart—such a nice child. I tried to live up to this; to do everything just right. When Mom had company I would be very polite and try to be a hostess. I had a coloring book and I remember working with crayons and trying to do it perfectly—no smeary places around the edges. Then I'd show the book to the grown-ups and everyone would say, 'My, doesn't she color good to be just five!'"

About this time the family lived in the country on what is now Old Ann Arbor Road outside of Jackson, a small city south of Lansing.

"It was a very small house for all the kids Mom had. Downstairs was the kitchen. Upstairs there was a living room and two bedrooms. We had an outhouse and washed in the kitchen sink. In summer we'd take our baths in a washtub in the yard.

"Mom used the same tub to scald chickens in. I can see her sitting out in the yard in the sun, plucking them. That night we would have the best fried chicken. Mom had a garden up on a hill above the house. She'd go to her garden and pick tomatoes. Everything she made tasted so delicious.

"I remember going barefoot a lot in the summer and how much I loved it. I *loved* going barefoot. Mom would tell us to put our shoes on. I hid them under the porch because I didn't want to wear them. My feet felt so good without them. I remember loving things about nature. The feel of the grass under my feet and the greenness of it and the wetness of it. Mom let us play outside in the rain. It seems that the summer rains we used to have were warm. I loved the warm summer rains. We played like ducks, sitting in mud puddles and running through the water that poured off the roof.

"We—Joanne and Bob and I—were wonderfully free. There were so many places to play—an apple tree by the chicken yard had a tire hung in it for swinging and low branches for climbing. We roamed in cornfields. We went on hikes and picked berries. We found abandoned orchards and ate green apples, eating around the wormholes.

"Those memories of being so happy in the country have meant a great deal to me—especially in prison. Even though I was a small child I got from it a feeling I've never forgotten—a feeling of closeness to nature, closeness to life. The way I feel close to God is touching and seeing and even tasting and feeling the things that He created. I have gone out in the spring and this feeling would come over me—just overwhelm me. The first garden I ever had was in Dansville where I lived the last years with Mickey. It is the only happy memory of Dansville that I have. After I planted the garden I would go out *every* day hoping that something green had come up. I remember stooping down and picking up warm soil—warm from the new spring sun. When I did that, felt the soil, and smelled it and looked up at the sun, I felt such great peace. Just for a few seconds. It seemed a long wait for the seeds to come up, but when they finally did I yelled to the kids, 'The garden's up!' They got really excited, too. They helped me all that summer. Maybe my harvest wasn't too great. The plants were a little spindly and the bugs got some, but it didn't matter. I wish that someday I could live in the country and try to find that feeling again."

Francine started school while the family was living in the house on Old Ann Arbor Road. It was a two-room school and her memories of that are also happy. She was exceptionally good in the early grades—a champion speller, and when she competed with an older boy for top honors, she won. "I wanted those gold stars so bad." She also remembers looking across the room at the second-graders—where the desks were bigger—and thinking, "I'll never make it."

Her brother Bob sat with his class on the far side of the room. "One day I came to school without my milk money. I had been out sick when it was collected and so I hadn't paid. That day I would have to go without milk. At lunchtime Bob saw I didn't have any milk. He got up and brought his milk and set it down on the table in front of me and walked away without a word. I never forgot him doing that. It was chocolate milk, too."

When Francine was three her mother had another daughter, Diana Lynn. A boy, David Lee, was born when Francine was five. Hazel Moran's last child, Kathleen, was born when Francine was eight. About this time Walter began to drink and to gamble. Hazel had to work longer hours at her waitress jobs to make ends meet. She brought home leftover food and this was often all they had. As Francine recalls it, the food was good, but she was aware that there was shame attached to eating "leftovers."

Meeting other children at school also made her realize that her family was poor. "I met a girl who lived down the road on a big farm. Her family seemed really affluent. The farm was beautiful. This child was a pretty girl, chubby and rosy-cheeked and friendly. I can't remember her name, but I knew we hit it off. When she invited me to her birthday party, I was thrilled. Then I realized I didn't have a present to take. I had only one 'nice' dress and I couldn't find it. It seemed like I couldn't go without a present and a proper dress. I sat down and cried.

"Mom and Dad were at work. My older sister, Joanne, asked me what was the matter. When I told her she said, 'Well, let's find your dress and then we'll look for a gift.' We searched around and found the dress in the clothes basket. I ironed it myself and put it on. Then Joanne and I went down to my uncle's gas station a little way down the highway. My uncle gave me some candy to take to the party. So I was able to go after all. My friend seemed to be pleased with the gift and pleased that I had come, but even so I felt some-how unhappy—as though I wasn't as good as she was. We played together only a few more times.

"The dress I wore to the party had been given to my mother by a lady who lived in a trailer park nearby. It had belonged to her daughter. It was a white dress, with blue flowers on it and a big sash. I loved it. Unfortunately the daughter went to my school. One day I wore the dress to school and the girl told everyone I was wearing her old cast-offs. I was so ashamed that I cried about that, too."

When Francine was eight, life in the country came to an end. Walter Moran switched from farm work to a job in a factory. The family moved to a rented house in Jackson. Jackson then was a medium-sized town of working-class families supported by factories making automobile parts. It is old, as Michigan towns go, and known for its trees that shade the yards surrounding almost every house. Most of its homes were built around the turn of the century and are modest frame houses, quite like New England houses of the same vintage. In Jackson the Moran family had the luxury of indoor plumbing and paved streets for the first time. Francine, how-ever, felt lost in her new school. It was large and impersonal. Mak-ing friends was not as easy as it had been in the two-room school. To make her problem worse, the family moved often, from one rented house to another, probably (she now surmises) because of difficulties in meeting the rent, and each move usually meant that Francine had to start again in a new school.

Factory work may have meant a better income for Walter Moran, but the deadly monotony wore him down. As he drank and gam-bled ever more heavily Francine became aware of her mother's anxiety and that her father's irresponsibility was darkening the life of the family.

Francine remembers her father thus: "My dad was very tall and big in every way; he had big hands and a big voice. He didn't yell a lot. His voice was firm. When he told us kids to do something we knew we had to do it. There wasn't any arguing or asking 'why?' His face was ruddy and he had reddish blond hair. His eyes were the kind of blue that you see in a deep, blue river. All through the week he usually worked hard and didn't drink. When he was sober he was very quiet. He came home, read the newspaper and watched the news on TV, or played solitaire at the kitchen table. He hardly said a word. He'd maybe grunt if you asked him something. I think now that he was very depressed when he was sober. Then, when Friday night came, he'd get drunk. If Mother didn't catch him in time all our grocery money would be gone. She would have to go to the place he worked on Friday afternoon to make sure she got the money.

"Sometimes Dad would stay away all weekend drinking and playing poker. He'd bet everything we had. He lost all his fishing gear. We had an old black car. He gambled that away. One night when I was about nine, Mom got me up out of bed and told me to come with her. We went to the corner gas station and found my dad standing at a pinball machine with piles of dimes stacked along the side. He was drunk. My mother cupped her hand and brushed all the dimes into her hand and dropped them into her purse. Watching, I was scared, but I knew she was doing it because she had to. Dad got angry, but he let her take the money and we went home. I don't know why she took me with her. Perhaps she figured he wouldn't fight with her if I were there.

"I seldom saw a fight between Mom and Dad. They tried to keep their fights to themselves. Sometimes I heard them arguing at night when we kids were supposed to be asleep. They might get loud, but not really violent. Money was always the problem. At the end of his life, when his drinking was totally out of control, Dad did beat my mom. By then I had left home. Mom was ashamed and said very little about it, but my sister told me he hit her so hard that blood spattered the yellow paint in the kitchen. A couple of times my sister called an ambulance.

"I was never frightened of Dad drunk or sober. When he was a little drunk he'd be more inclined to talk to us. He'd be jolly and tell us tall tales. He told us about the time back in the Kentucky hills when he went into a cave where a bear was sleeping and he reached in and grabbed the bear by the tail and pulled him out, wrong side out! He wasn't ugly or mean with us when he was drunk. He'd just be happy and silly and then go to bed.

"The only sign that I had a hidden fear of Dad was a recurrent dream I had concerning him and my little sister Kathy. I adored my baby sister. Mom let me take care of her when she was little. I remember putting on her coat—it seemed so tiny—doing up the buttons, putting on her bonnet, and taking her outside to play. This is the nightmare. In the dream she'd be wearing her coat and bonnet, and we'd be walking together. Then I'd see my father coming down the street. As he came closer he would get bigger and bigger. As he lifted his feet they seemed huge. I would see these huge feet approaching and I had a terrible fear that he would step on little Kathy and squash her."

At about this time Francine's father was sent to jail for a short term. Once a week their mother sent Francine and Bob to the jail, a few blocks from the house, to bring their father cigarettes and candy bars. Francine did not know what to make of the episode. It was strange that this powerful man was dependent on her for cigarettes and candy. Not until she was grown up did she learn what he had done. Desperate over gambling debts, he had stolen tools from the shop where he worked, and been sentenced for petty larceny.

Walter died in 1966 when he was fifty-three. By then Francine had left home. Looking back, she is sorry she never knew her father better. "He was intelligent and knew he could have done much more with his life, but he was trapped. Growing up in Kentucky and coming to Michigan with so little education was a terrible handicap. While he was still young and wanted to have fun, he had the responsibilities of a wife and six children, all saying, 'I'm hungry now! . . . I need a place to live now!'"

Family loyalty was a strong element of Francine's Kentucky heritage. Among the desperately poor the loyalty of kin is often the only defense against disaster—loyalty and pride. Francine's mother told her there were two sorts of people in Kentucky, the proud poor and the shiftless poor. *Her* family was proud.

Francine's grandmother, her mother's mother, was raised in the mountains of southeastern Kentucky. Her name was Susie Robinson. Her first marriage ended violently. Her husband was having an affair with a woman who was also the sweetheart of his cousin. Susie saw her husband take his pistol, mount his horse, and ride up the hollow toward the cousin's cabin. She heard shooting. Shortly after, the cousin rode down to her cabin and told Susie he had shot her husband to death. Susie picked up her three young children and moved to the tiny coal-mining town of Martin, Kentucky, where she married a man named Fleming and bore three more children. Francine's mother, Hazel, was the youngest.

Hazel's childhood was grimly poor. She told Francine some of her memories: how she began to work as a small child, doing domestic chores for families that were better off. She washed quilts on a scrubbing board, earning ten cents apiece. With the money she bought fabric to make her clothes for school. She had only two dresses that she washed and wore alternately. She had no shoes. Going to school barefoot was uncomfortable, but worse, it was a humiliation. The kids who had shoes made fun of her. She was glad to leave school after only one year.

One way the family kept its pride was with cleanliness. The floor of their cabin was bare wood. It was scrubbed every day and the more it was scrubbed the whiter it became. Susie instilled in her daughter Hazel the lesson: "No matter if you have only one pot and one dishrag . . . keep them clean!" Hazel, in turn, impressed this on Francine.

"Mom taught us very young to do everything around a house and I helped her gladly. It was instilled in me that this was what a woman did. It never occurred to me that there was anything else for a woman to do. As I look back on my childhood I was always doing housework. Where were my brothers? What did they contribute? Almost nothing. I didn't question whether it was fair. It didn't even enter my mind."

Francine was a child who loved to be loved. She felt sure of her mother's love, but it was, after all, spread thin among six children. Francine briefly felt the warmth of a special love from her other grandmother, who moved up from Kentucky to live with her daughter Myrtle. From time to time Grandma Moran stayed with Francine's parents and made Francine her favorite. "I'd sit on her lap and she'd rock me and talk to me. I loved her so. She felt so soft, so warm. I felt very close to her. I used to go downtown and buy her these cards that when you opened them up the girls' skirts would fan out. I would write 'to Grandma with love' very carefully on the cards. She kept everything I gave her, even a ball of aluminum foil I'd collected. She'd take me in her room and we'd look at her things. She had lots of pretty belts . . . one was woven and had a gold buckle. She had a gold locket that opened. She told me some day she would give it to me. I didn't realize what that meant.

"Soon she was dying and she told my Aunt Myrtle that she wanted me to have the locket. Then she died. My aunt gave it to me. I held it in my hands for a moment. I was ecstatic to have it and I was heartbroken too. Mom took the locket and locked it up in a cabinet for safekeeping. After Grandma died I was so sad for so long that the family worried about me. I missed her so! I would think about her and tears would run down my face. One day I was in the bedroom—feeling so bad—and I heard the grown-ups talking about me. Someone said, 'It isn't normal. Maybe we ought to take her to the doctor.' I was shocked. I said to myself, 'Don't let them see that you're sad any more or you'll have to go to the doctor!' So I kept my sadness to myself and little by little it went away."

Francine never saw the locket again. It disappeared from the cabinet, and its loss was never explained.

Francine's mother depended on her a good deal to take care of the two youngest, David and Kathy—to "watch them," as Francine says. This led to the first truly traumatic event in Francine's childhood. The family was living in Jackson, in a rented house a block or two from Michigan Avenue, the busiest thoroughfare of the town. On a summer day Hazel was washing clothes in the kitchen.

"I was supposed to be watching David. David was a cute little kid. His hair was so blond we called him 'Cotton Top.' He was about three. I can see him now in his overalls . . . his fat little tummy. Anyway I was keeping an eye on him, and hanging clothes with Mom, when someone passing by stopped and told us there was a clown at a gas station down the street giving away free balloons—a publicity stunt to draw customers to the gas station. Mom said I could take David to see the clown. I walked along, hanging onto David's hand. I was full of pride that Mom trusted me with my brother. I was very careful when we crossed Michigan Avenue. At the gas station the clown gave David a helium-filled balloon. I brought him home and we showed Mom the balloon. Then I went back to helping Mom with the laundry. I must have forgotten about David for a while. Without anyone noticing, he wandered out of the yard and down the street, trying to find the clown and get another balloon. The first we knew of it was when a girl came riding down the street on a bicycle and yelled to Mom, 'I think your son has got hit by a car!'

"Mom ran down the street to Michigan Avenue. She was barefoot. I was running after her. I could hear her crying out, 'Oh my God, my baby! My baby!'

"We got up to the corner of Michigan Avenue. There was a crowd of people, police, sirens, horns blowing. I couldn't see through the crowd, but I could hear Mom screaming. I squeezed past the legs of the people and got up beside her. She was hysterical. An ambulance had just taken David away. Mom was crying so hard she probably didn't know what she was doing, but she grabbed me and shook me and she yelled, 'It's your fault. You should of been watching. I told you to watch him!'

"David lived, but he was badly hurt. He'd been dragged under the car. Both arms were broken. One ear was half torn off and had to be sewn back on. We found out later that the man who hit him was drunk.

"David was in the hospital a long time. Nobody said any more about it being my fault but every time I looked at him I felt a terrible guilt. I loved him more than ever. At home he was in bed for weeks and everyone waited on him hand and foot. I felt so sorry for him. He was such a little child and so miserable with casts on both arms. I remember how bad I wanted to do things for him. I nursed him a lot. He recovered, though he still has a silver bolt in one arm. Now he works in a factory and still lives with Mom."

Years later psychiatrists who examined Francine suggested that this episode, which aroused so much love, pity, and guilt, made her overly sensitive to the suffering of others—especially, and fatally, Mickey Hughes. In prison she was given psychological tests. "My score on 'empathy' was practically off the graph. Too much for my own emotional well-being. I remember in my childhood having very strong feelings for people. Kids can be cruel to other kids. I found that out in the Jackson schools. I was strong and I learned to stand up for myself, but I hated to see the weaker ones tormented. I used to try to take them under my wing, protect them.

"There was a skinny little girl in my school; kids picked on her. She didn't have any friends. It made me mad to see her picked on so I befriended her. At first I did it out of pity; then we became real friends. Her name was Barbara. I played at her house after school. We had nice times. She was very quiet, a contrast to what I was. After a while my family moved, I went to a new school, and we drifted apart. At Christmas, when it was snowing out and everything was like a Christmas card, there was a knock on our door. I opened it and Barbara was standing there, smiling. She had found our new house and come all this way to give me a present. She had made a huge Christmas tree cookie for me. It was a foot high, decorated with green frosting and beads. I'll never forget opening the door and seeing her holding out the cookie and saying 'Merry Christmas.' I felt as though I'd been rewarded a hundred times over for anything nice I might have done for her."

As Francine moved on through grade school, her awareness of social differences grew. An inner uneasiness, the feeling that had first been aroused by the birthday party at the farm, now came quite often. Paradoxically, she was a leader. She had vivacity, liveliness, a talent for clowning and fun that attracted friends. The friends she chose, and felt comfortable with, were those in the same economic bracket as her parents. The girls who had better clothes, who gave off an aura of greater security and prosperity, made her feel alien. "I just felt I couldn't fit into their world."

Francine's parents were not churchgoers, but friends took Francine to religious services and religion filled an emotional need for a child who loved order, discipline, and the thought of virtue rewarded.

"Because I went to church with a series of friends I went to several different churches—Baptist, Methodist, Catholic. I liked them all, but I loved best the churches that had beautiful music and flowers and sermons about being kind and good. I liked looking at the women dressed up. Some held little handkerchiefs and even gloves. They wore perfume and smelled like flowers."

Francine won a prize for signing up the most children to go to Vacation Bible School. She enjoyed reading Bible stories and learning verses. She memorized the names of the books of the Bible and can still recite them. She continued to go to church until she started junior high. Then religion was swept away with a great many other aspects of her childhood.

In the grade school in Jackson there were fewer gold stars for Francine. In large crowded classrooms teachers didn't seem to notice her. She read more fluently than most and did her math with ease, but received no particular praise. Her confidence that she was brighter than other children began to fade, and with it her incentive to study. It was replaced by another feeling: that because of her responsibilities at home and her increasing awareness of her family's problems she was more mature than her schoolmates. She felt set apart, increasingly estranged, looking forward to the bell ringing, the moment of release.

"School didn't seem related to real life. To me my 'real' life was my dream life. I loved to play pretend. I had a Mexican girl friend, Rosie, who lived down the street. One day we went up to Mom's closet and looked at her clothes. We dressed up in long dresses and high heels, put on lipstick and necklaces and went for a walk down the street. I thought I was so beautiful. I felt like a queen! People looked at us and smiled. It didn't occur to me we were funny."

Movies and TV were Francine's biggest source of information about life. "We had a TV with a very small screen. We kids sat on the floor, Indian fashion, and watched 'The Mickey Mouse Club.' I loved that show! Annette Funicello was my ideal person. I thought she was beautiful and charming and everything I would want to be."

Francine began to go to movies regularly—Roy Rogers, Elvis Presley, Tarzan filled her head with romance. Going into the movie theater was a luxurious experience. "I remember going into the dark, full of the delicious smell of popcorn. Tiny lights along the aisles were so pretty. The rugs, the seats, the thick curtains—to me everything seemed like it was velvet."

Francine shared a bedroom with her older sister, Joanne. As Joanne became adolescent she began to wear clothes that Francine admired for their femininity. "Joanne had a skirt called a can-can . . . a crinoline with layers of ruffles of pink and blue and yellow. I would put it on when she wasn't there and sit on the bed and look at it, all fluffed up around me, and dream that I was dancing in a ballroom."

At fifteen Joanne was going out with boys. Ten-year-old Francine was embarrassed when she surprised Joanne kissing a boy in the kitchen. At sixteen Joanne was married. Her young husband was a "southerner"—a truck driver by trade. From time to time Joanne and her husband and the baby born within a year of their marriage would come back to stay with Hazel and Walter. Francine fell in love with the baby. She looked into the basket and thought it was the most beautiful baby she'd ever seen.

"When I held him I would want to smother him with kisses. His skin was so soft, his eyes so blue. I'd bathe him and play with him, and smell that sweet, clean baby smell. He'd smile and look happy and that would make me feel good."

It became apparent that Joanne's married life wasn't working out. Francine knew her sister was struggling to survive. "Her husband was too young," Francine says in retrospect. "Any boy of twenty wants to play and sow wild oats." Francine remembers the moment when she first saw Joanne's life as grim and sordid. Joanne had a second child soon after the first. Unable to pay the rent, she brought her babies to her parents' home. "There was a crib in the living room. I overheard Mom and Dad saying that Joanne's husband was a bum. He came to the house drunk and there was an argument. While it was going on the little boy was standing up in the crib crying. My heart went out to him. I was only a kid, but I was old enough to know this was no way for a little child to start life; that something was very, very wrong."

As it does with many girls, the onset of adolescence brought confusion into Francine's life. "One day I would try to act like a teenager and the next day I'd be climbing trees, going exploring down by the Grand River. Maybe even in the same day I'd do both things; fix myself up and be clean and neat for a while and then shed it all and go play in the dirt. I loved playing out at night in the summertime; hide-and-go-seek, or throwing a ball in the street under the lights. My tenth summer was the last where I was really carefree like that. I remember being barefoot; running through hoses in the heat of the day; going in for lunch and then back out; playing with the neighborhood kids; going in for dinner and going back out again and playing until dark, being just filthy. Mom would say, 'Time to get in the bathtub!' She'd put two kids in at a time—me and Diana Lynn—I'd look down at my arms, all streaked where I'd eaten a Popsicle or something and it had dripped, and thinking, 'Gee, I didn't know I was so dirty.' I'd get all scrubbed up and climb in between cool sheets."

At eleven Francine was less satisfied with her life—and especially herself. She was growing. She felt awkward and was embarrassed by the size of her hands and feet. She often crossed her arms to hide her hands. She wore a size eight shoe and her brothers teased her . . . "Why don't you just buy the boxes and leave the shoes behind?" She pretended indifference, but wanted to cry.

Walter Moran watched the teasing and finally intervened. "From now on," he told Francine, "if someone says something about your feet, just tell them it takes a better foundation for a church than it does for a shithouse!"

Francine laughed and the laughter swept away her shame. There was also a happy feeling that her father had cared enough to come to her rescue. In Francine's family life there was seldom any overt expression of inner feelings, and small demonstrations were important.

Francine kept her deeper feelings to herself. For a long time she wasn't aware that emotions *could* be put into words—in books perhaps, but not in real life. As she grew older and her emotions more complicated, the gulf between her daily life and her inner life grew wider.

Her parents were of little help in making the transition to adolescence. Walter Moran had conservative views; a woman was a good woman or a tramp. Sometimes Francine's mother did housework for richer families who gave her clothes. One summer day she put on a pair of shorts an employer had given her. Walter scowled and told her to take them off; he wouldn't have his wife looking like that. It was a hot day and she didn't change, but went outside to water the grass in the yard. Her husband followed and soaked her with the hose, not playfully but grimly, and she cried. Francine watched the episode, absorbing the idea that it is indecent to show your body. The lesson was reinforced when her mother brought home matching outfits for Francine and Diana Lynn. They were short shorts with halter tops. The little girls were ecstatic as they put them on. It was a Saturday and their father was at home. He glanced up as his daughters appeared and threw down his newspaper in anger. "Go back upstairs and put your clothes on," he ordered. The outfits were not worn again.

Sex wasn't acknowledged in the Moran household. When Francine was quite small she asked her father where she had come from. He told her what his mother had told him: "You were shit on a stump and the sun hatched you out." Neither he nor Francine's mother ever told her the truth.

"I learned about sex from the other girls and from sex-education courses in school. We were shown films in the fifth and sixth grade that tried to explain it in childish terms. Even so they were somewhat above my head because I knew so little to begin with."

Hazel never told Francine that she would menstruate. Francine learned about it at school, but still, at twelve, was emotionally unprepared. "I was in the bathroom when I realized it had begun. I was scared and shocked. I called to Mother and told her. She told me to wait. Then she opened the door and tossed me a Kotex and a belt and went away. I called to her, 'Mom, what am I supposed to do?' She said, 'Put it on!' I said, 'How?' She said, 'You might as well learn for yourself. You're going to have to do it for the rest of your life.'"

At eleven Francine had begun to work. She did housecleaning and baby-sitting for a neighbor who had four children. Eager to demonstrate her skill, Francine made the house and the children cleaner and neater than either had ever been before. The next year she waited on tables at a restaurant. Her mother let her keep her earnings as pocket money, though she sometimes had to borrow a dollar or two that Francine was proud to lend.

In the autumn of 1960, after her thirteenth birthday in August, Francine entered the seventh grade at Hunt Junior High, and began a year of changes in her life that were both exciting and frightening. She experienced for the first time a feeling of independence from her parents—a delicious sense of freedom that sometimes turned to a nameless fear. She felt as though she were swimming, alone, into deeper water. In fact, the distance between herself and her parents was widening, almost beyond calling distance.

At junior high Francine found the atmosphere quite different from that of her previous schools. Among the girls there was an emphasis on beauty and clothes. Francine found that a larger proportion of girls and boys were from wealthier homes. Resentfully, she assumed that the girls who dressed well were snobs. She remembers thinking scornfully: "You may have more material things than I do, but I have a deeper sense of life."

Subconsciously Francine was struggling to overcome the feeling that she bore the stigma of poverty. She had always been a cooperative and obedient student, eager to please her teachers. Now she felt hostile and estranged. Academically she was very capable, but there was little incentive to study. On the contrary, fellow students disliked those who outstripped them. Francine loved reading, loved words, and could have shone in her English classes, but didn't dare. "I would look up words in the dictionary and want to use them in my speech, but I knew if I did everybody would think I was putting on airs."

Feeling out of things, Francine didn't join in extracurricular activities and rejected sports because they conflicted with her ideal of femininity. "I had always loved to run. At Hunt they were starting a girls' track team and asked me to join. I thought it wasn't the right thing for a girl to do. I pictured a boy in a track suit, his legs bulging with muscles. I didn't want to look like that so I refused.

"It shows how I'd changed in a year or two. When I was a little girl running was my sport. I ran and ran. I ran races with boys and always won. 'Want to race?' I'd ask any new kid. I loved the feeling of running. I ran home from school, timing myself. The teacher released us at five minutes of twelve. The lunch whistle blew at twelve. I would try to run the eight or nine blocks home in five minutes. It was an obstacle course; people to get around, streets to cross. Lots of times I beat the whistle. Then, suddenly, that sort of thing was over for me. I began to try to excel in the only other thing open to me, that seemed natural for me—being feminine."

Francine's transition from child to adolescent was completed when she had her hair cut. Her long, thick hair, gleaming with reddish light, had been an important psychological element of her childhood. Her grandmother had lovingly brushed her hair and adorned it with ribbons. Her mother had shown her how to braid it. Everyone had praised it. Her hair was a symbol of Francine, the well-loved child. When her hair was cut she felt transformed. The "bubble cut" was in fashion and Francine came home looking six inches taller, leaving her childhood behind on the beauty-parlor floor. For days she was fascinated by the mirror; she put on makeup to highlight the transformation. Walking down the street she thought that people looked at her in a new way—especially boys.

A few days later, in school, the haircut brought Francine a new friend. A girl with big dark brown eyes and a cute turned-up nose came over to her and said, "Hi, I love your hairdo. It looks really great." Francine smiled back and thanked her. The girl said her name was Sharon Taylor. "How would you like to come to my house after school?" Sharon asked, friendly as a puppy. Francine said she'd like to very much. Sharon's father worked in the same factory as Francine's father and her house, a two-story clapboard house similar to the Morans', was on the next street. The two girls became fast, devoted friends. It was the most intimate friendship Francine had ever had, and the most fateful. Within two years Sharon Taylor would fall in love with a boy named Bill whose best friend was a boy named Mickey Hughes.

As Francine made friends at school she began to stop at a drug-store where groups of teenagers hung out. She would spend an hour or two in this heady atmosphere, electric with adolescent contact, drinking Cokes, playing the jukebox, learning to show off, and making her first experiments in the art of flirtation.

Walter Moran discovered Francine's visits to the drugstore, and saw the scene differently from Francine. Inarticulate as always, he was harsh and ugly as he told her that only tramps went to the drugstore. He demanded she promise never to go there again.

Francine was astonished. She argued that the kids at the drug-store were nice kids and whatever they did was perfectly innocent. She had never before argued with her father and he had never punished her harshly. She was unprepared for what happened next.

Her father took off his belt. "Tramps and whores," he shouted. "That's who goes to that place! You ain't goin' there no more! You better promise!" The injustice of it overwhelmed Francine's fear. Faced with her first beating, she cried and argued but refused to promise. Walter grasped her in a powerful hand and began to whip her. Francine remembers thinking: "Why is he doing this to me?

He has no right to make me promise. I haven't done anything wrong."

Francine's mother intervened, crying, "Walter, stop it!" Francine twisted loose and ran upstairs. Her father followed. He cornered her again and raised the belt. Though she was terrified Francine heard herself crying out, "I'm not a tramp! And I'll never promise!" After a moment her father's arm dropped. He turned and went downstairs.

Alone, Francine cried for a long time. She had no idea why her father had behaved as he did. It seemed bitterly unfair. "I knew I wasn't a tramp—whatever that was. I knew I was only a thirteen-year-old kid and I couldn't see why he thought it was wrong for me to have Cokes and play the jukebox with the other kids. I lay there thinking I'd run away, tie sheets together and climb out the window. While I was planning it I got under the covers. I got sleepy and that was how it ended. I never gave my promise and I kept on going to the drugstore."

During this time Francine's relations with her mother were also changing. "I had always felt that Mom was my rock and my strength. Now I was doing things on my own. It was a shock to realize that what I did away from home was my own responsibility. I knew my mother had struggled to raise me, but that soon it would all be up to me. This comes to everyone, but to me it came pretty young."

Francine's need to be close to someone was filled by Sharon Taylor. "I had never had a friend like her before. I'd had playmates, but Sharon was more than that—a confidante. It meant being able to spend the night at each other's houses and whisper secret things that no one else was supposed to know; being up at midnight when everyone else was asleep; talking and painting our fingernails and listening to sweet, romantic music on the radio."

Suddenly both girls wanted terribly to be attractive. Francine became painfully self-conscious. She was tall—five-seven—and her burgeoning figure embarrassed her. "I felt too big in every direction, clumsy and knock-kneed. I desperately wanted to cover these defects and transform myself from an ugly duckling to a swan." Clothes were a means of transformation; Francine and Sharon became intensely interested in them. They spent after-school hours window shopping. One day they fell in love with a blouse in Wool-worth's window.

"We thought, 'Wouldn't it be neat for us to have matching blouses!' We shared everything else!" The blouses were pullovers with slanted stripes of purple, blue, and green. They cost $2.98 each, and as the girls walked across town—walking was one of their pastimes—they discussed how to earn the money. They passed a Dairy Queen and Francine spotted an envelope lying on the ground. She found five dollars inside. Happily, there was no name on the envelope. "We couldn't believe our fortune. It was as though fate wanted us to dress like twins. We had a dollar so we rushed back to get the blouses. Then we rushed to Sharon's house and put them on. Each of us told the other how cool she looked."

The blouses raised the girls to a new plateau of what they considered sophistication. "We got a sickening pale lipstick that was 'in' that year. We wore it with black stuff on our eyes. To top it all off we got a friend to dye our hair with streaks of blond in the front. When we put the whole thing together—the streaked hair, the blouses, the makeup—we thought it was terrific."

At fourteen Francine got what she considered a truly glamorous job—usher in a movie theater. She loved going backstage in the theater, and putting on a burgundy-colored uniform. "I was a different person as soon as I put on the uniform. I felt gracious and important as I led people to their seats with my flashlight. I'd watch the movie and eat popcorn and enjoy the atmosphere of luxury: the velvet carpet, the artwork on the walls, Michelangelo-type pictures with fleecy clouds, cupids, and gold vine leaves everywhere. It all seemed lovely."

At about this time she began to think about her future life. Some of the possibilities that passed through her head were teacher, nurse, secretary, stewardess. All of them seemed impossibly beyond reach.

"I had lots of thoughts, ideals, feeling about life that I never voiced for fear of being silly. Sometimes I felt different and smarter than the kids around me, but I wanted to be part of the group, so I kept quiet. I assumed that the women I admired, teachers and nurses and secretaries, came from a richer background than mine; that a life like that wasn't for me. Girls in my group didn't talk about careers; they talked about getting married and having kids, so I daydreamed about that. I'd picture a home in the suburbs, children who were perfect students, a husband who was kind and loving, a life that was tidy with no big anxieties. In my heart I knew even this much wasn't reality, but it seemed more within reach than any other dreams I had."

Romance was an element in Francine's fantasies, but not sex. Sex frightened her. She thought of it as something that inevitably occurred in married life, but until then was fraught with peril. She had absorbed from her mother and girl friends the conviction that virginity must be sacrosanct before marriage. A girl who went too far became "used goods" that no other man would love or respect. Francine felt no physical desire. Her idea of romance was "what you would see in a Tony Curtis movie—roses and candle-lit dinners."

At junior high Francine and her girl friends didn't "date." They met boys by going to the places they knew boys would be—the drugstore, the movie house. "If you sat on a park bench with a boy, that was a date. We didn't go to movies *with* boys. We went knowing they'd be there. There was one boy I used to sit with pretty often. We'd sit staring at the screen and out of the corner of my eye I would watch his arm sneaking around the back of the seat. My heart would pound while I wondered what to do if he actually put it around me. I'd think, 'This is silly pretending to be a man and a woman with his arm draped around me, when actually we're only kids.' I'd get up and go to the bathroom or something to get away. Looking back I wonder why I had to make an excuse. Why didn't I have the nerve to tell him to quit?"

During the summer that she turned fifteen Francine and Sharon began to go to the Pleasant Lake Pavilion, a teenage heaven about ten miles out of town, where young people danced the cha-cha, the bop, and the Bristol stomp. Sometimes there were guest musicians, such as Jerry Lee Lewis, but mostly the patrons danced to a jukebox whose multicolored lights glowed hypnotically in the dimly lit room. A girl didn't need a date to go to the Pavilion. Boys and girls milled around, drinking Cokes, at the edge of the dance floor, pairing up to dance and then separating. Between sets couples went outside. As they left, the ticket taker marked the backs of their hands with a stamp visible under ultraviolet light. Francine remembers the romance of standing by the shore sharing a cigarette and looking at the stars and the house lights reflected in the dark waters of the lake.

At Pleasant Lake Francine and Sharon met a boy named Darryl. He was fifteen, too young to drive, but he had friends with a car, and he introduced the girls to the thrills of motorized dating. "We spent summer evenings bombing around town, yelling at other kids, having a terrific time." On a certain evening Francine and Sharon were sitting in the back seat. Darryl was between them. Sharon was a little in love with Darryl and he had his arm around her. Suddenly he turned to Francine and looked deep into her eyes.

"Are you thinking what I'm thinking?" he asked.

"I don't know," Francine said, "what are you thinking?"

Darryl bent down and kissed her.

Francine remembers: "I saw stars! I went all to pieces inside— not because of the kiss—the physical part meant nothing—but because he'd chosen me! Of course I felt guilty about Sharon, but as it turned out she didn't blame me. For a little while Darryl and I pretended we were in love. He gave me his ring. He kissed me a few times on the shore at Pleasant Lake. Then the summer ended and we forgot the whole thing."

Francine was now a very pretty fifteen-year-old. She had a heart-shaped face, thick curly hair, and dark brown eyes fringed with heavy lashes. Her nose was tilted at a saucy angle and she had an enticingly dimpled smile. But her looks didn't satisfy her. She yearned to be more fragile, delicate, and ladylike. She fought to keep her weight down. But no matter how insecure she felt, her vitality and sense of humor were irrepressible. She covered her awkwardness with jokes as though she refused to take herself seriously. Francine had a natural flair for comedy and clowning, for the quick, teasing remark that could puncture pretense or turn embarrassment to laughter. She used it to attract boys and to keep them at arm's length. She and Sharon felt the same way about boys. They wanted to be with them and at the same time evade heavy advances. Half shy, half show-off, Francine usually found herself the leader of any group, the life of any party.

Suddenly Francine's teenage social life was blossoming. She was not attached to any particular boy, but on Friday and Saturday nights she and Sharon dressed up in ski pants, mohair sweaters, and pointed flats, and got together with five or six other boys and girls, sometimes driving around in cars, sometimes playing records at the home of whatever set of parents was willing to tolerate it. On a certain Friday evening during winter vacation Francine's parents went out, leaving her to mind the younger children. Sharon came over and a girl named Beverly arrived, bringing several boys and girls Francine had never met before. One of them was Mickey Hughes. He was a tall, very slim boy with thick black hair and dark blue-green eyes. He was eighteen, a year or so older than most boys Francine knew, and he carried himself with an aloofness, an air of worldliness that made him instantly attractive.

"All the kids were bombing through the house, acting crazy. The girls were hiding in the closets. Before she hid, a girl would say, 'If you find me you can kiss me,' or something like that. Then there'd be a lot of giggling and scuffling. It was all silly and fun. But Mickey didn't take part in it. I can see him standing in the kitchen, smoking. The way he carried himself struck me as more manly, more mature—the way he held his cigarette, the way he combed his hair. He smiled and was polite, and a little disdainful, too, as though he were saying, 'It's okay for you to play games because you're just kids, but it doesn't interest me.'" Francine was so impressed she stopped giggling and accepted a cigarette from him. She smoked it with what she hoped was nonchalance.

At their next meeting Mickey Hughes was less suave. Francine and Sharon were at a friend's house one evening when Mickey arrived with a friend—Bill Hensley, a blond boy Francine and Sharon thought very good-looking. It was a school night and near the curfew hour set by Francine's mother. Mickey and Bill offered Francine and Sharon a ride home. On the way Mickey parked the car and tried to kiss Francine. She resisted. He was persistent and their struggle went on for several minutes. In the back seat Sharon was wrestling with Bill Hensley. Finally Mickey gave up in disgust and started the car, and dropped the girls off at their street. They walked home so that Mrs. Moran wouldn't know they had been in a car. Francine and Sharon told each other that Mickey and Bill were creeps.

Francine and Mickey met for the third time late that spring at the Pleasant Lake Pavilion. Francine and Sharon were together. Mickey asked Francine to dance. He was having a good time and his smile lit up his face. After a minute or two of small talk he asked Francine if she'd like to go out with him the next Friday. The invitation was tossed out casually—as though her answer made little difference. Francine, who had had few real "dates" in her life, said, "Okay, why not?" She tilted her chin flirtatiously. "What have I got to lose?" Mickey suggested that Sharon come along as a date for Bill, who stood on the sidelines watching. At the end of the dance, Mickey squeezed her hand. "See you Friday," he said and walked off into the crowd. Francine said "Okay," and wondered if he meant it. Long after, Mickey told Francine he had invited her only because Bill had bet him a dollar she wouldn't accept.

On Friday Sharon and Francine dressed for the evening not sure how they would spend it. Uncertainty added spice to their weekend fever. "We were always preparing for something terribly exciting to happen. We didn't know what, but we had great expectations." Sharon came to Francine's house and the two girls discussed the possibilities. Sharon had agreed to go out with a group of boys and girls from a nearby town and told them to pick her up at Francine's house. Who should she go with? Francine said she wouldn't go out with anyone unless Sharon went along. Finally they decided to let fate settle the problem; they would go out with whoever arrived first.

The first to arrive were Mickey and Bill. The girls got in Mickey's car and he drove to McDonald's for hamburgers and Cokes. Then they parked, listening to the radio, talking, and engaging in some light necking. "Mickey didn't try any heavy stuff and neither did Bill. It was cozy and exciting. The dark car was like our own little world—the four of us. Every time someone said something we'd all giggle as though it was the world's funniest remark. Every time Mickey tried to kiss me I'd light another cigarette instead. When they took us home I felt okay about the date. At least it hadn't been a disaster, like the first time I'd been in a car with Mickey. On the other hand I wasn't in love either. But Sharon was. From that night on she was mad about Bill."

Mickey and Bill showed up the next weekend and the next weekend and the next. Their dates repeated the pattern set on the first evening: driving around, hamburgers and Cokes, parking, cigarettes and soft music, giggling and kissing. Francine learned that Mickey lived with his parents in Dansville; that they, too, were from Kentucky. Mickey had left school at sixteen. His parents had promised him a car if he would finish school. He had the car, but had never fulfilled the promise. He was working as an orderly at a nursing home. His job and his car made him seem rich. He had freedom and pocket money that boys still in school didn't have and he concentrated all his attention on courting Francine. Sometimes he and Bill took Francine and Sharon to the Pleasant Lake Pavilion, where they danced to Frankie Valli and the Four Seasons. A song that Francine loved was "Kisses Sweeter Than Wine." After she had been there a few times with Mickey, the other boys seemed to pick up some secret signal. No one else asked her to dance. Mickey had Francine all to himself.

Mickey took Francine to his home in Dansville, a half-hour drive from Jackson. The Hughes family lived on Adams Street, a tree-shaded street of small houses and ample yards, in an old frame house, neatly kept and much like the one in which Francine's family lived. Francine remembers her future mother-in-law's appraising stare as Mrs. Hughes looked over her son's new girl friend. Francine was wearing a bouffant hairdo and heavy makeup. She had thought she looked wonderful until she saw the expression on Mrs. Hughes' face: a half-smile that seemed to say "this girl will do anything to please a man." Mrs. Hughes was a tall woman with straight, handsome features and strong coloring—white skin and coal-black eyes. She had a direct gaze that was disconcerting. She talked freely in a way Francine recognized as "old-fashioned Kentucky mountain" talk, but her husband was silent. He was smaller than she. His skin was sallow and his eyes a strange, murky blue. Francine thought he had a sour, disagreeable face. She sensed that Flossie ruled the roost in the Hughes home. At the time Francine didn't particularly care. She had no inkling that her life would ever be entwined with theirs.

The spring semester, Francine's last in junior high, was an academic disaster. She wasn't keeping up with her classes. Her mother didn't let her go out with boys on weeknights, but when dinner was over and the dishes done Francine would skim through her homework and walk to Sharon's house. Sharon wasn't much interested in school either. The two girls discussed their love lives. Francine didn't think she was in love with Mickey. Sharon was sure she was in love with Bill, but wasn't sure he loved her. There was no lack of drama in either affair.

Summer began and Mickey's ardor increased. Francine's feelings were confused. Mickey had told her that he loved her. No one else had ever said that. She found she loved being loved, but felt a deep uneasiness about what obligations might go with it. She found her feelings flickering and elusive. She had many emotions, but nothing she could identify as love. Sometimes she found Mickey terribly appealing and attractive; at other times she wished he would leave her alone and let her return to a simpler life. Their playing at sex— this was the first serious necking she had ever experienced—both excited and frightened her. She was terrified that she might slip and violate that ultimate taboo—giving herself before marriage.

Alone with Sharon, Francine happily reverted to being a teenager. The Jackson County Fair was held in August. Sharon's house overlooked the fairgrounds. Francine remembers how one night, after dark, she and Sharon made a batch of popcorn and climbed up on the roof. Perched there, eating popcorn, they could see the bright lights, hear the grandstand speakers and the music from the rides. The sidewalk below them was crowded with people going to the fair. Francine and Sharon felt giddy with fun and excitement, calling out teasing remarks to the people below, and doubling up with giggles as their victims looked about in vain for the source of the catcalls. When that palled they began rolling popcorn kernels down the roof, betting on whose kernel would win the race to the edge. Francine had more fun that night than in a dozen dates with Mickey, but she knew that in truth her childhood was coming to an end. She felt in limbo. Playing at being a child was just as unreal as playing at being a woman. That August she became sixteen.

Mickey was a sexually experienced young man. He told Francine of the sexy goings-on during the night shift at the nursing home, and about a previous job at a resort where an older woman crept into his room at night. He continually pressed Francine to sleep with him. On this point it was easy for her to be resolute because the rules were clearly defined in her mind. Furthermore, she didn't really want to.

"I wanted our relationship to be just a boy friend and girl friend sort of thing. I liked the four of us—Bill and Sharon and Mickey bombing around and having a good time—McDonald's, the lake, playing records at Sharon's house. I liked Mickey. He had a good sense of humor. He was good-mannered when he wanted to be. He was intelligent. Though he had quit school early, he had a lot of information about the world that impressed me. But I had no deep feelings about him. If he had disappeared I wouldn't have missed him. Lots of times when he pressed me too hard I'd tell him to go away—to leave me alone. But he wouldn't. He came back and back and back. He was so persistent I began to feel this terrible responsibility of having somebody love me so much. I began to tell him I loved him because it seemed so cruel not to. Sometimes I felt it was true, but I knew in my bones that it was not."

As Mickey's passion grew hotter he no longer wanted to share dates with Bill and Sharon. He took Francine out alone and there was no respite from the intensity of his desire for her.

During the summer Francine made several attempts to get away from Mickey. When she refused to talk to him on the phone he came to the house. His calls and visits caused embarrassing commotions. Francine's mother and father were disapproving, but did not directly forbid her to see him. To avoid involving her parents, Francine went to the door when Mickey arrived and her weak refusal to see him would be quickly overwhelmed. Once Francine went to stay with Joanne to hide from Mickey. Sharon found her and pleaded for Mickey: "He's sitting alone, listening to records. He's crying." Francine melted.

When, after weeks of ardent persuasion, Francine still refused him sex, Mickey began to talk about marriage. Francine received the proposal with a chill of fear. She had seen the dismal consequences of Joanne's early marriage. Mickey had taken her to visit his older brother, Dexter, whose wife, Cleo, was fourteen when they married. They had two children and it was clear they were struggling to survive. Cleo was a beautiful girl, a year or so older than Francine, and Francine liked her, but their home was far from Francine's fantasy for her own future. It was more nearly a dreary replica of her parents' home, of the drab poverty she had dreamed of escaping.

Reluctantly, with foreboding, Francine found herself more and more deeply enmeshed with Mickey Hughes. Instead of the fun they'd enjoyed a few months before, now they spent hours in his car, talking far into the night.

"I told him again and again I wanted to wait. If we still loved each other later we could marry then, but he wouldn't listen,

wouldn't take no for an answer. Somehow he made me feel guilty
and responsible for him. I didn't know what I had done to make
him love me so much, but since I had done it, I felt to blame. As a
child I always wanted to be good. I couldn't bear feeling to blame
for anything. I guess the way I felt in this situation was an extension of that childish fear of doing wrong. But here was a situation
where I couldn't do anything right. If I slept with Mickey, like he
wanted me to, that would be wrong. But he kept telling me how I
was making him suffer by not having me, and I didn't want him to
suffer. When I suggested we separate for a while, he'd say, 'No, I
can't bear it. I can't be away from you. I love you so much. I want
to marry you.' I looked at this man who loved me so much and . . .
I don't know really what I thought . . . but I felt a great need—a
duty—to fulfill his love. I thought he really loved me. No one had
ever loved me like that. It was a very powerful thing."

In September 1963, Francine entered the tenth grade at Jackson
High School. It was bigger than Hunt Junior High and she felt
even more estranged. Sharon was also at Jackson High and also
disliked it. Quite often the girls played hookey. Sharon's parents became concerned and for a while drove Sharon and Francine to
school to see that they got there. Rebelliously, the girls went in the
front door and out the back. Francine told her parents that she was
thinking of leaving school. They urged her to keep on, but without
any great conviction. The older children, Joanne and Bob, had both
left school at sixteen. Higher education, especially for women, was
an idea far removed from her parents' lives; possibly they saw no
more use in it than Francine herself did at that moment.

"I remember the day I quit. It was in October, about six weeks
into the fall term. All those weeks I'd felt restless and too emotionally churned up to study. On the one hand I had teachers treating me like a kid, making me stand in line and raise my hand to
speak. On the other I had this grown man (I thought) telling me he
loved me so much he'd die if I didn't marry him. I felt confused,
pressured, confined. I wanted freedom. I made the decision impulsively, while I was sitting in math class. The teacher was going on
and on and I didn't understand a thing. It suddenly seemed clear to
me that nothing in school had anything to do with me. When class
was dismissed I put my books in a locker in the hall and picked up
my coat. Sharon was in a classroom across the hall. She saw me and

came out and asked, 'Where are you going?' I said, 'I'm quitting!' She said, 'Wait for me.' We left together."

Though she did not consciously plan it, Francine believes now that leaving school led inevitably to another fateful decision—to give in to Mickey. Again, it was a spur-of-the-moment decision that had been a long time in the making. It took place in the back seat of his car parked in a cornfield. She will always remember the eerie sound of the rustling stalks. Suddenly Francine was tired of resisting. "I didn't fight him off. I just let it happen." As the act took place her initial excitement turned to dismay. "It wasn't good. It hurt and I felt dry inside. I didn't know what to expect; not even the basics, like what semen was. I remember a feeling of being used, of giving something I really didn't want to give. I did it to please him. He was so crazy about me. But I wasn't prepared for how bad it would make me feel. I was immediately afraid I was pregnant. I knew nothing about birth control and he didn't use any."

When it was over the first thing Mickey said was, "Now you don't have to marry me if you don't want to."

Francine thought, "Oh my God! I *do* have to marry him! I do! I've given him my body. I've given him everything. I'm *his*."

In the days that followed she felt so guilty she thought there must be some outward sign. She wondered if people could tell by looking at her that she had had sex; perhaps by the way she walked, or the look in her eyes. She told her parents that she wanted to marry Mickey. They protested, but not very firmly. Neither did Mickey's parents object.

Once Francine had agreed to marry Mickey, a load seemed to lift. The prospect of being married became happy and exciting. Mickey, too, was delighted, though he was none too pleased that Francine refused to have sex again until after the wedding. She still felt deeply ashamed of her lost virginity. Whenever she felt doubts about her coming marriage she would remember that it was too late to change her mind. She no longer had a choice.

She began to look ahead and think, "Maybe it will be okay. Maybe I can make things different from the bad marriages I've seen." She felt she had "higher ideals" of marriage and resolved that she and Mickey would try harder. She had confidence in herself as a housekeeper. She would be thrifty, tidy (clean and proud

as her Kentucky grandmother had taught her), and if she and
Mickey had children they would be loved and protected and raised
in a loving home. All her life she had heard such sayings as "Life is
what you make it" and "Love conquers all." Francine believed
them and vowed to make them come true. With such a shining goal
it was easy to put down flutterings of doubt as she wondered if
what she felt for Mickey was really love. If it wasn't love, she
thought it must be because of some failing in her. Perhaps the full
realization of love would come after marriage.

Francine was so concerned with her own feelings that she had
little insight into the personality of the boy she was marrying. In
the weeks before their marriage there were two incidents that dis-
turbed her. Not knowing what to make of them, she brushed them
aside. First, Mickey quit his job. Francine was astonished. He gave
no particular reason except that he was tired of it. When Francine
pressed him as to how they would live when they were married, he
airily promised that he would find another job soon. And in the
meanwhile, he assured her, they could always stay with his folks.

Francine blamed herself for the second episode. Mickey's
brother, Lawrence, was engaged to Bill Hensley's sister, Lillian. A
wedding shower for them was being held in the Town Hall in
Dansville. That night Francine and Sharon went to Dansville with
Mickey and Bill. When they got to the Town Hall, the girls spotted
several of Mickey's and Bill's former girl friends going to the party
and refused to go in. The two boys went in, leaving the girls to wait
in Mickey's car. After a while Francine and Sharon got restless.
Pique added to their boredom. Francine, who knew only the rudi-
ments of how to drive a car, decided to practice driving around
Dansville. She started the car and zoomed around the block. As she
drove back by the Town Hall she saw Mickey and Bill coming out.
A teasing impulse made her floor the gas pedal and the car took off
in a rush. In the rearview mirror she saw Mickey waving and running after her. Francine drove two blocks to Adams Street and
brought the car to a screeching halt in front of the Hughes house.
She and Sharon ran inside and hid behind the stove. Shortly,
Mickey and Bill slammed in after them. The girls' giggles gave
away their hiding place and they ran out the door. Mickey caught
Francine on the sidewalk. He grabbed her by the front of her
blouse with a yank that pulled off the buttons. His fingers closed

around her neck in a tight grip. What shocked Francine most was the rage in his eyes. He said, "Don't you *ever* take my car."

Francine said, "It was only a joke," and burst into tears. Mickey's face softened and his hand dropped away. Francine knew she was wrong to have taken the car. Mickey had a passion for cars; this one was his most treasured possession. She apologized and Mickey kissed her. Francine erased from her mind the shock of his hands on her neck, the buttons popping off her blouse, the glitter in his blue-green eyes.

A few days later Francine and Mickey went to a jewelry store in Jackson to buy wedding rings on credit. Since Mickey was out of work, his mother went with them to co-sign the loan. They bought matched gold bands for ninety-three dollars, payable in monthly installments.

Francine and Mickey were married on November 4, 1963, in the Dansville Methodist Church. She was sixteen, he eighteen years old. Francine wore a short white dress. Mickey wore a suit. Their families attended. Lawrence and Lillian stood up beside the bridal couple.

"I was scared to death. All I could think of during the ceremony was that I was closing a chapter in my life—too soon. I looked at Mom and I saw uncertainty and regret on her face. When it was over I tried to tell her not to worry—that I would be all right, that she had done the right thing. I was reassuring her when I was the one who needed reassurance, and thinking that I wished she had said no. I have had thoughts like that throughout my life, not blaming my mother exactly, but wishing she had been a little stronger and said, 'No! You're not getting married.' Maybe it would have stopped me. I was not prepared emotionally or physically for any of the things that were going to happen to me in the next three or four years. I was still growing up and living in my dream world, my teenage world."

The newlyweds went back to the Hughes home in Dansville for their honeymoon. For a few days they could have the house to themselves. The Hughes family was in Kentucky attending the marriage of seventeen-year-old Lawrence and his fifteen-year-old bride.

Trying

Dansville is a village of fewer than five hundred inhabitants lying among flat, fertile farmlands east of the highway that connects Jackson, where Francine was raised, and Lansing, the capital of Michigan. You can walk from one end of Dansville to the other in ten minutes. The streets end at the edge of cornfields and pastures. The houses are old frame houses, purest Americana, some quaint and cozy, others run-down and decrepit, depending on the owner's style. There are many tall trees that shade the yards during the hot days of summer and in winter sigh and bend in the cold winds that sweep off the open fields. The business section of Dansville consists of a few frame or brick buildings at the intersection of Route 36 and Jackson Street. There is a gas station on one corner, the Dansville Grocery on another. The grocery has checked curtains in the windows and signs for "Beer, Wine, Orange Crush" over the door. Next to it are the Township Fire Department, the library, and the Town Hall, all housed in one white frame building. Across the street at the Crossroads Inn quick meals are served at a counter and more sociable ones at Formica-topped tables. There are apt to be more men than women in the place—men dressed in work clothes, heavy boots, jeans, and sweatshirts. They eat and smoke and drink coffee, gossiping and joking through their lunch breaks and after work. When the place is crowded they fill the room with a male presence that lets a visitor know that this small section of the United States remains a man's world dominated by "breadwinners." Some of them earn very good money in the factories in Jackson or Lansing, but people here are also accustomed to earning less. Life is geared to that.

Flossie and Berlin Hughes still live at the corner of Adams and Grove next to the house in which their son died. Flossie Hughes is a woman who gives an impression of uncommon strength and intense feelings. She stands straight and has a commanding presence. Her hair is gray, but her brows are still dark. Her years in middle America have not modified her regional Kentucky speech or her habit of chewing tobacco. She was born in a mountain town called Crockettsville and raised in the slightly larger town of Jackson, Kentucky. Her father served in the First World War and afterward was a farmer. "We had a good childhood life," she says. Flossie married Berlin Hughes in Marshallsville, Kentucky, in 1938. She was sixteen, he seventeen. Berlin had a less fortunate childhood. His father was killed in a mine cave-in when Berlin was three years old. His mother, a woman of Cherokee blood named Patient Yates, went to work for a man named Will Hall. He helped Patient Yates raise her children, but he was hard on Berlin and his brothers.

Berlin and Flossie Hughes came to Michigan in 1939. Berlin worked in the fields and operated heavy machinery. The family lived precariously, moving often as Berlin went from job to job. They went to Kansas and then on to California looking for a better life, but failed to find it. They returned to Michigan in the sixties and settled in Dansville.

Flossie bore six children: first a son, Dexter, and then a daughter, Estafaye, and four more boys—James, nicknamed Mickey, Lawrence, nicknamed Wimpy, Marlin, and Donovan. Flossie ruled the household with a strong will and a volatile temper. Her children, especially the boys, were her pride and joy. Berlin taught them to be tough. "He let us know that if you come home from school with your shirt torn from a fight you better have some buttons off the other guy's shirt in your pocket," Wimpy recalls. Besides an ideal of toughness, Berlin brought from the Kentucky hills the concept of a family loyalty superseding all else.

Quarrels among the boys were not tolerated. If they fought, Berlin took off his belt and forced them, on pain of a beating, to sit on the floor in a circle, holding hands, until their anger subsided. Only when they had kissed each other in forgiveness were they allowed to get up. "Maybe it seems strange to be forced to kiss your brother," Wimpy says, "but we sure as hell come to love each other an awful lot." The three middle boys—Mickey, Wimpy, and Marlin —only a year or so apart in age, were the closest of all.

Flossie's family was a handsome one. Dexter and Marlin and Donovan grew to be big, powerful, good-looking men. Wimpy is shorter, but has his mother's features and vitality. Mickey was tall, and as a youth, extremely slim, like his father. He also had his father's Indian features—a strong jaw and long, narrow eyes that were an unusual color.

By the time Mickey met Francine, the Hughes boys had already sown many wild oats. Girls, cars, and good times occupied most of their thoughts. Mickey and Wimpy had quit school and moved through a variety of short-term jobs—farm worker, gas-station attendant, dishwasher, and nursing-home orderly—earning enough to finance their pleasures. The Sheriff Department knew them as cocky, troublesome juveniles, quick to start fights and sass cops. Mickey's first recorded arrest, for disrupting the peace, was in March 1963, soon after he met Francine. Schoolmates and neighbors of the Hughes boys were aware that if you had trouble with one Hughes, you had better prepare to take on all of them. The fierce loyalty of the old Kentucky clans lived on in the Hughes family, transplanted intact from the backwoods hollows to the quiet streets of Dansville, Michigan.

When Francine had envisioned her coming married life she had looked forward to having her own home to take care of and make beautiful. She had also imagined marriage would bring peace of mind; the blessing of the church and the privacy of their own bedroom would put an end to the struggle over sex. It didn't work out that way. Ten days after she and Mickey were married, the Hughes family returned from Kentucky. Mickey's younger brothers, Marlin, fifteen, Donovan, twelve, and an adopted child, Vicky, eleven, the daughter of Flossie's deceased sister, were still at home. The elder Hugheses slept in a downstairs bedroom. To accommodate the newlyweds, Vicky moved out of her upstairs bedroom to share an adjoining bedroom with the boys. The two rooms were connected by an open doorway so that privacy was impossible. Francine was horribly embarrassed by making love in such close quarters. It didn't bother Mickey and he was persistent in his desires. The nights became whispered struggles, Francine saying, "No, no, please, everybody will hear us," and Mickey persuading and insisting. To make it worse, Francine had what she describes as "a lot of hang-ups" derived from the prudery of her early training. Though she would respond initially to Mickey's lovemaking, it wasn't until several years after her marriage that she was able to enjoy sex completely.

Instead of spending her days in the nest-building she had anticipated, Francine spent them helping Flossie with the housework. She was trying to be part of the Hughes family, to like them and make them proud of their daughter-in-law. They took her in generously enough, but she was always conscious that she and Mickey were a burden in the overcrowded house. Francine desperately wanted a place of their own. Mickey, on the other hand, was quite satisfied. He continued life as before—looking for work in a desultory fashion, and spending his days as he pleased. The only difference since his marriage was that he now had Francine in his bed at night.

Francine discovered that in the Hughes home the boys were kings. Flossie petted and pleased them. If one of them suddenly wanted a clean shirt, Vicky was ordered to iron it. Their misdeeds were looked on with indulgence. Flossie expected a great deal of the girls, but she always softened when one of her boys was involved.

A few weeks after the wedding, Mickey's temper flared for the first time since the incident with his car. The issue was jealousy. He began to complain that Francine's clothes—clothes she had worn before they were married—were too sexy, too provocative, and designed to attract the attention of other men. Francine was bewildered. She told Mickey that her clothes, her sexy appearance, everything she did and felt, were for him.

Francine often wore a pair of black ski pants and a blouse tucked in at the waist. Mickey said the costume was too revealing, and told her to wear the blouse hanging loose. One day, while Mickey was out looking for a job, Francine rebelliously tucked in the blouse while she worked around the house. Just before he came home she pulled it out. Mickey noticed that the blouse was wrinkled. Francine admitted she had been wearing it tucked in. Mickey grabbed her by the arm and yanked her up the stairs and into their bedroom. He pushed her down on the bed and pulled off the ski pants. Swearing furiously, he ripped them to pieces. Francine was numb with shock. Too surprised to be angry herself, she protested that she had meant no harm, that she loved only him, that he mustn't feel jealous. After a moment Mickey calmed down and took her in his arms. Francine wept while her mind seethed with confusion. She told herself she had done nothing wrong, but at the bottom of her mind the voice of guilt reminded her that she could have avoided the scene if she'd worn the blouse loose as Mickey wanted her to. She was also humiliated. Their voices and scuffling must have been audible all over the house.

Before they went to sleep that night Mickey apologized. He said he was sorry; that it had happened because he loved her so much. He even cried a little. Francine forgave him and vowed to be more careful. She was relieved that when she came down in the morning no one in the family made any reference to the incident. It almost seemed as though it hadn't happened.

Francine had few clothes and needed to replace the ski pants. With Flossie she went shopping in Lansing and by good luck found a pair of pedal pushers for a dollar. They were very pretty; the fabric was printed with lavender flowers and green leaves and she bought a lavender top to match. She thought glowingly of how becoming the new outfit was, how attractive she would look for Mickey. At home she rushed upstairs to put it on. She was wearing her hair long. She brushed it and arranged it in a new style. The total effect was stunning. She waited eagerly for Mickey's coming, looking forward to the admiration in his eyes. She heard the front door open and turned, radiant with expectation:

"He came in and stood staring at me. I said, 'Hi, Mickey,' and then I saw this horrible look come over his face. He leaped at me and grabbed me by the front of my blouse. He said, 'Where did you get that?'

"I said, 'Mickey! Let go! What's the matter? I got it in Lansing . . . at K-Mart . . . I went with your mother.' . . . Mickey tore at the blouse until it ripped. Then he ripped off my pedal pushers and threw the pieces on the floor. He said, 'There! I'll bet you never wear *that* again!'"

Nearly naked, Francine fled up the stairs. In her flight she passed Flossie in the hall, watching in silence.

After a while Mickey came upstairs to where Francine lay sobbing on their bed. He was calm but self-righteous. He said he was sorry, but that the episode was Francine's fault because the outfit had looked "too good" on her. He wasn't sorry he had ripped her clothes. He was sorry that the whole thing had happened, that she had provoked him. He told her she would have to learn that he was boss.

With bitter hurt, Francine thought, "I did it all for you and you ruined it. I was only trying to be a good wife. It wasn't wrong to look pretty before we were married. Why is it now?" But, again, Mickey's accusation filled her with guilt. Hadn't he warned her only a week before? Did he sense that she hadn't truly given him all her love? This was a secret Francine kept deeply hidden. She was ashamed that she didn't love Mickey in the fullest sense, as a good wife should—and she wanted above all to be a good wife.

As Francine wept, Mickey's anger subsided. She became conscious that the whole household—Flossie, Berlin, the two younger boys, and Vicky—must have their ears tuned to what was happening upstairs. Embarrassment forced her to stop crying. She got up and dressed in an old sweater and skirt. Mickey kissed her, ran a comb through his hair, glanced blithely in the mirror, and went down to the supper Flossie was preparing. In the bathroom Francine tried to erase the signs of her crying. Then she joined the family already at the table. No one said a word to her as she sat down. Again, it was as though the incident had never happened.

Mickey was making no progress in his quest for work. Berlin, who counted every penny and berated Vicky for using too much hot water when she washed her hair, began to remind Mickey that it was time he made a home for himself and Francine. Mickey would say sulkily that he was doing his best and promised to repay his parents when he got work. Money was a constant source of friction in the household. Francine came to dread Friday nights, when Berlin came home with his paycheck and he and Flossie invariably fought over its allocation. As tension mounted Francine longed to leave.

Mickey precipitated their departure when he flew into his most violent rage yet. There had been visitors during the afternoon, and everyone had sat drinking coffee and talking. One of the guests was a man Francine had never met before. She remembers him only as "the man with big hands." Later, in their bedroom, Mickey suddenly accused Francine of "looking" at the man. Francine realized Mickey had worn a stormy look ever since the visit and was puzzled; then she remembered the visitor's huge hands. She told Mickey, "I was only looking at his hands; I never saw anyone with such big hands." Mickey's fist shot out and knocked her over on the bed. She struggled up, fighting to defend herself, at the same time pleading with him to stop, to listen to reason. His face was furious. "I'll teach you not to look at other men, you whore," he said, and hit her again. This time Francine fought back.

The noise was clearly audible downstairs. Berlin yelled upstairs to Mickey to "knock it off" and then came upstairs himself. Mickey turned on his father, cursing, telling him to mind his own business. Francine ran downstairs. Berlin and Mickey followed.

Now Mickey and his father stood shouting at each other; Berlin was asserting that Mickey would have to behave himself while under his roof; Mickey became wilder and more abusive. When he broke a chair and threatened his father, Flossie telephoned the police. Mickey was still hot with fury when the deputies arrived. Flossie let them in and he turned to face them belligerently. One of them put a hand on Mickey's shoulder and Mickey instantly swung at him. Seconds later Mickey was under arrest. Cursing his parents, Francine, and the deputies, he was led away.

Francine had witnessed the scene with shock. Tearfully she called her mother and asked if she could come home to spend the night. Berlin drove her from Dansville to Jackson. For the first and almost the last time, Mickey's parents blamed Mickey, rather than Francine, for what they called "the racket" that had taken place. Berlin told her he was prouder to have Francine as a daughter than Mickey as a son.

Hazel greeted Francine with few questions and Francine was grateful. It would have been difficult to explain how a jealous quarrel had set off such a scene. Already Francine felt guilty that she had stared at the man with big hands, and even worse about burdening her mother. "My leaving had made things easier for Mom . . . one less mouth to feed. I didn't want her to feel she had to take me back. I didn't want her to worry. So right then I started making as little of the episode as possible. I began to cover up what had happened . . . how bad it really was."

The police booked Mickey for assault and battery, then released him. Within hours he arrived at the Morans' house. He was calm and had little to say. He kissed Francine and hugged her. That night Francine's younger sister, Diana Lynn, moved in with little Kathy. Mickey spent the night with Francine in what had once been her bedroom. Before they went upstairs Mrs. Moran made her position plain. She told Mickey, "You can stay here for a little while, but that's all. You get a job . . . you get an apartment and you take care of your wife." Mickey accepted the ultimatum quietly.

During the couple of weeks the newlyweds stayed at the Morans', Mickey was pleasant, polite, and sunny to everyone. Kathy, who was eight at that time, remembers how much she liked her brother-in-law. She called him "Mickey Mouse." He joked and played with her. He went out daily looking for work and Francine went apartment-hunting. He found a job at a factory in Jackson, a monotonous job finishing small auto parts. Francine found a small apartment on Stewart Street, only five blocks from her parents' home.

The apartment was an "efficiency." The couch slid out and became a bed. There was a small dining room, a kitchenette, and a bath shared with another tenant. It was far from the dream home of Francine's fantasies, but she felt it was something to build on. Perhaps this tangible symbol of married life would transform them into instant adults. She brought over their wedding gifts—a few pots and pans, ashtrays, lamps, a vase of plastic flowers.

Mickey seemed happy. Francine cooked him good breakfasts and he went to work cheerfully, while she stayed home, cleaning the apartment over and over to make sure everything was perfect.

Within a few weeks a fight exploded without warning when she and Mickey were driving to a shopping center.

"We had gotten a car. Mickey's old one had collapsed. My dad co-signed for a 'fifty-seven Chrysler. It cost us a hundred and twenty-five dollars. I was sitting beside Mickey, looking out the window, and apparently he thought I was looking at a fellow, just some unknown man, standing on the street. Without a word Mickey hauled off and hit me across the face."

Francine said, "My God! What did you do that for?"

Mickey's eyes were glinting with rage. He said, "I'll teach you to look at guys that way! You know how you were looking!"

"I wasn't, Mickey! I wasn't!" Francine cried and buried her face in her hands. Sobbing, she defended herself. Mickey drove on, saying nothing. Francine became quiet. "Oh God," she thought. "I've done it again. I've got to be more careful!"

In the months that followed Mickey hit Francine again and again on similar pretexts. Almost anything might trigger his jealousy—if she were gone too long at the store, went to see a girl friend or her sisters, mentioned a boy she might once have flirted with. Each time Francine was taken by surprise, as though she had stumbled over something in the dark. She became apprehensive of any situation that could pose a risk.

"If anybody came to the apartment while he was away I'd be nervous, wondering if I would dare tell him and afraid that if I didn't he might find out and be even madder. Beverly, a girl I used to hang around with, and her sister stopped by one afternoon. He wouldn't believe they just came in, saw the apartment, and had some coffee. When I told Mickey, he was sure we had gone out, running around and meeting guys. Sometimes he got upset over a thing like that and sometimes he didn't. I never knew what would set him off, so I was scared to do anything. I hardly dared leave the house.

"When he would hit me it wasn't just the pain of the blow that hurt. It was the emotions that flooded over me. My chest would hurt. My heart ached. Tears came pouring out. I couldn't stop them. Usually Mickey stayed angry until I quit crying. I would try to stop; to be real quiet and do nothing that would start him again. I would sit there wondering what it was all about. Then he would begin to feel sorry. Little by little he'd apologize, saying that it would never happen again. He'd say, 'I love you. I just can't stand you looking at other men.' I'd say, 'I don't look at other men. I don't want anybody else. I just want our marriage to work.' Then he'd kiss me and we'd make up. I wanted to believe him so badly."

Between episodes of anger and violence there were intervals of fun and companionship in which Francine rebuilt her hopes for a workable marriage. Even at his best Mickey was touchy, arbitrary, and intensely selfish, but Francine was too unsophisticated to at-

tach such labels to his behavior. She told herself that she must learn
to be a wife—that a wife must bend to her husband's wishes and
thus make a happy home. She and Mickey began to weave a bond
between them. They went shopping, discussing what to buy with
his meager paycheck. Mickey would gallantly pick up the bags of
groceries and carry them into the apartment. They went to movies,
visited Bill and Sharon, who were now married and living with
Sharon's parents, or went to see Mickey's brother Dexter and his
wife Cleo. Mickey seemed to share Francine's nest-building ambi-
tions. They would discuss future plans. Francine hoped that someday they might have a place in the country, and then her spirits
would soar. They were still only sixteen and eighteen years old and
enjoyed life like any teenagers—or almost did.

After a few months in the efficiency apartment Francine found
they could rent a larger apartment next door. It had a separate bedroom and a living room, dining room, and kitchen. She was quite
thrilled when they moved in. To help pay the rent, Francine persuaded Mickey to allow her to work part-time as a waitress at a restaurant a few blocks away. Francine loved going to work. It filled
her idle time and allayed her feeling of isolation.

Mickey soon became suspicious of Francine's activities at the restaurant. When he came home from work he would ask what she
had done that day. As she told him he would question her sharply,
picking up any small discrepancy, insisting on a complete list of the
people she had seen and an account of what they said. Actually her
days were uneventful, filled with routine work. During the eight
hours Mickey was at work Francine did the laundry and ironing,
cleaned the apartment, and put in her hours at the restaurant.
Mickey worked the second shift and she picked him up at eleven in
the evening at the Tumble Finish Factory.

One night, unusually tired, Francine lay down to rest before
picking him up, and fell asleep. She awoke, terrified by the sound
of someone battering down the bolted door. Mickey burst in, furious. "What have you been doing?" he demanded. Francine tried to
tell him that she'd accidentally fallen asleep, but Mickey raged on.
He had imagined that she had a man in the bedroom with her.
When he found no one he blamed her for causing him to get
worked up. As punishment he decided that henceforth he would

take the car to work. Thereafter Francine could not drive anywhere without him.

A few weeks later Mickey brought Francine's restaurant job to an end. With her earnings Francine had bought herself a few new things, including a brassiere with stretch straps. When Mickey saw her put it on he made an angry face and said that it allowed her breasts to bounce. Defiantly Francine replied that there was nothing wrong with the bra. She finished dressing and went to work. She was busy serving dinner customers when Mickey came into the restaurant. The look on his face made her heart sink. He walked down the aisle between the tables and grabbed her arm. He said, "Get your things. You're going with me." Francine protested that she couldn't leave in the middle of a rush hour. She had begged the restaurant owner for the job. It would be the height of ingratitude to walk out without warning.

"You're coming with me," he repeated grimly. "If you don't you'll wish you had of."

Francine looked around at the crowded room and decided it would be better to leave quietly than have a fight right there. She picked up her coat, whispered to her employer that there was an emergency at home, and left with Mickey. At home he ripped the offending bra off her body and tore it to shreds. Then he beat her. Francine hit back as best she could, but it only maddened him more. Not until she lay on the floor, sobbing and begging, did his anger cool down. Once he was calm Francine dared say nothing that might start it up again. When he told her he didn't want her to work anymore, she agreed. "I was willing to do anything to keep peace. I thought if I did, this phase would pass; Mickey would get over it and we could live a normal life. When we had fights I yearned to go home and stay there, but I knew there was no turning back. When I got married it was final. I had shut the door on my teenage life."

After a few months' work at the Tumble Finish Factory Mickey became restless at his job. He had heard from friends in Kansas about better pay and opportunities there. Sharon and Bill were still close friends with Mickey and Francine, and Bill caught Mickey's enthusiasm for a move to a new frontier. At first the girls were dubious, but allowed themselves to be persuaded that a better life full

of fun and prosperity awaited them in Kansas. Mickey promised
that his Kansas friends would house them all until he and Bill
found jobs and living quarters. Francine and Sharon packed their
clothes into Mickey's car and the four set off in high spirits.

Soon Francine's optimism began to ebb. She had never been out
of the state of Michigan. "We drove, and drove and drove endless
miles . . . I couldn't sleep in the car and we didn't have money for
motels. Mickey would say, 'Why don't you just lay down and go to
sleep, Fran,' and I would try, but I couldn't, so I was awake for the
whole two days. Mickey and Bill took turns driving. I was afraid
the driver would get groggy and we'd have an accident. It was all
scary—not knowing where we were going or what we were going to
do when we got there."

When they arrived at the home of Mickey's friends, it was obvious that four guests were too many. Bill and Mickey's first day of
job hunting was fruitless. Francine and Sharon became instantly
homesick. "I felt terrible in this strange place, miles from my family, sponging on strangers."

After another jobless day the men were discouraged, too. They
had arrived penniless and their hosts' cordiality was becoming
strained. Mickey borrowed twenty dollars and the two crestfallen
couples drove home to Michigan. Having given up their apartment
as well as Mickey's job, Francine and Mickey returned to the
Hughes home in Dansville.

Luckily Mickey found a new job. It was in a factory in Williamston—a small town about fifteen miles north of Dansville. He and
Francine moved into an apartment over a hardware store nearby. It
was a dark, gloomy place with no windows in the back room. Francine was intensely lonely. She had no friends to visit, no telephone,
no TV, nothing to do except housework. She was dependent on
Mickey for all her pleasure and companionship.

"I would try to clean everything up, and with him gone, there
wasn't anybody to mess things up. The dishes amounted to a couple
of plates, forks, coffee cups, a frying pan. You could do those in ten
minutes, and you could sweep the floor, dust, and do everything
that needed to be done in an hour. Sometimes I would sit there all
day with nothing to do, not daring to go out, for fear he would get
jealous. Sometimes I would sneak out and just sit on a park bench
and look at the birds."

One day, on a furtive outing, Francine dropped into a drugstore and bought some nail polish. When Mickey came home he instantly noticed her painted nails. He asked how she had gotten the polish. She told him she had gone for a walk. Mickey said he didn't think she needed to go for walks. Francine began to pour out her unhappiness—how she hated the idleness, the loneliness, the gloomy high-ceilinged apartment. Mickey was unsympathetic. Francine protested she had the right to go for a walk if she chose. The scene ended in a beating.

When Francine had surrendered to helpless sobbing, Mickey dropped his hands and left the room. After a fight their reconciliation followed a standard pattern:

"I'd be crying. He'd leave the room. For a while nobody would say anything. Then I'd get up and wash my face. Mickey would be quiet. He'd sit in the living room pretending to read. After a while he'd say, 'Fran, come here.' I'd say, 'No. I don't want to.' He'd say, 'Come here. I want to talk to you. I want to tell you I'm sorry.' I'd say, 'No. I don't want to hear it. You're not sorry. You've done it before. "Sorry" doesn't mean anything.' He'd say, 'Fran. Please come here.' His voice would be getting very soft and apologetic. I'd get up and sit down a distance away from him. Silence again—him not knowing what to say and me not knowing what to say. I'm just sitting there, thinking, 'What's this all about? What am I doing here? Where am I going?' I'd feel so exhausted and confused I couldn't think straight. I'd just be wondering what to do. Then Mickey would start saying he was *really* sorry; that he loved me. When he did that I would cry again, wondering why, if he loved me, why did he do it in the first place? Then I'd think about whatever it was I had done that had set him off and resolve not to do it again. I thought maybe jealousy was normal in a young married man; that if I could make him believe I loved him he would get over it.

"Sometimes things seemed to be working out as I hoped. Mickey would be nice and loving for weeks. I'd begin to feel secure and then, wham, he'd get mad over some tiny thing, and let me have it. I'd have a black eye, and my feelings would be all torn up again."

The factory at which Mickey worked was only a few blocks from their apartment and he often came home for lunch. One morning Sharon and Bill dropped in and the four had lunch together. Afterward Bill and Sharon planned to go to Jackson. Francine saw a

chance to visit her mother; Bill and Sharon would give her a ride
both ways.

Mickey objected. "There's no sense in it. You don't need to go.
What do you want to go up to Jackson for?"

"I haven't seen Mom in a long time," Francine said. "I'd just like
to see her, that's all. I've got nothing to do here."

Mickey scowled. "You don't need to go to Jackson to look for
something to do, and you don't need to see your mom."

Suddenly Francine rebelled. "I just couldn't stand Mickey's eter-
nal domination one more minute. I picked up my coat and started
for the door. I said, 'I want to see Mom and I'm going, no matter
what you say. I don't care!' That did it! Mickey pulled back his fist
and floored me. Bill and Sharon stood there, looking amazed. The
two of them were very upset and embarrassed. I got up and ran
into the bathroom to cry. Bill and Sharon left in a hurry. Then
Mickey beat the living hell out of me. He stayed home from work
and we fought all afternoon."

This was the worst beating Francine had had yet. Her face and
body were covered with bruises. The next morning when she got
out of bed she ached all over. In the bathroom she looked at her
swollen face with horror. The whites of her eyes were shot with
blood. They looked ghastly against a background of puffy purple
bruises. Mickey took one look and turned away. He had almost
nothing to say. She cooked his breakfast in silence. He ate in silence
and went to work.

"When he had gone I sat there thinking, 'My God, what are you
letting him do to you?' I'd go and look at myself in the mirror. I
looked so terrible that tears would begin to trickle down. I thought,
'I've got to get out of here. I can't take this anymore; the beating,
the living in prison. He won't let me go anywhere, he won't let me
do anything, even have any friends. I'm a prisoner!' Finally I got
enough determination to go out to a pay phone and call Mom. My
brother, Bob, answered. I told him I had to leave and asked him to
come for me. Within an hour I was packed up. When Bob saw my
face he didn't have to ask what had happened. I remember how humiliated I felt, arriving at Mom's with my face beat up and my
boxes and bundles standing on the doorstep. Mom said, 'My God,
what happened to you?' I don't know what I told her. I really didn't
have to explain."

An hour after Francine arrived at her mother's, Mickey came home from work, discovered her flight, and followed her to Jackson. He banged on the Morans' door. When no one opened it he began to yell, "What the hell do you think you're doing! God damn it, you come out here, I want to talk to you!" Francine refused to open the door, although Mickey's yelling made her cringe as she thought of the neighbors listening. She shouted through the door, "Mickey, go away. Leave me alone. Can't you see you've done enough?"

Mickey left, but he didn't leave Francine alone. He telephoned constantly. Sometimes Francine hung up on him. Sometimes she took the phone off the hook. As soon as it was back in service Mickey rang again. After several days of siege everyone's nerves were frayed. Francine was miserable and embarrassed. Finally her mother advised her to talk to Mickey and settle matters one way or the other.

"When I picked up the phone, every fiber in my body was warning me not to go back, but the moment I heard his voice, soft and pleading, I wanted to forgive him and try again. He was begging, 'Please come back to me. I love you so.'"

Francine held out a few days more, but her stay at home was increasingly uncomfortable. Her father had nothing to say about her situation. (It would have been difficult, since his own episodes of violence were becoming more frequent.) Francine's mother suspected what Francine herself did not yet know—that Francine was pregnant—and hinted that Francine should not be hasty about ending her marriage. Francine knew she couldn't stay with her parents, but the prospect of striking out alone was too frightening to consider. She was no match for the forces pushing her to go back to Mickey. She doesn't remember how long she resisted—only that eventually he came to the house, she opened the door, and he took her in his arms. She felt a surge of relief that the struggle was over. Mickey kissed her tenderly. His strange, narrow eyes were alight with triumph.

Francine packed her things and Mickey jubilantly put them in their car. Francine said goodbye to her parents and she and Mickey started off. Only then did she discover that during the crisis Mickey had quit his job and given up their apartment as well. He explained that he'd been too upset to go to work and so hadn't paid the rent. He drove Francine back to his parents' home in Dansville.

Francine's flight to her mother was in the spring of 1964. Francine and Mickey had been married for six months and Francine was indeed pregnant. She became certain of it shortly after she returned to Mickey. She had prayed it wouldn't happen, but beyond douching she had done nothing to avoid it. The only other birth-control method she knew of was condoms, which Mickey refused to use.

"I knew it wasn't right for two teenagers to bring a child into the world when we could barely support ourselves. We were still staying with Berlin and Flossie when I found out. I told him, 'Well, you know, I'm pregnant, Mickey,' in a really scared tone of voice. He looked at me in surprise. He said, 'What's the matter? Don't you want my child?' He was overjoyed."

Flossie and Berlin were less pleased at the prospect of another mouth to feed. Mickey had been in no hurry to find work. Francine realized that he was happy to be back with his mother and to have them both waiting on him. But when his parents found Francine was pregnant they nagged him to do something. Mickey found a job at a lumber yard in Mason. He and Francine rented an apartment nearby.

The new apartment was sunny and pretty, and, after her first dismay at being pregnant, Francine felt a lift to her spirits. She believed that giving Mickey a child of whom he could be proud would quiet his jealousy, and they could begin real married life. Already Mickey seemed changed—truly grateful to have her back, and much in love with her. Francine found herself responding. At night she lay in his arms feeling loved and protected and thought, "This is what marriage can be."

The coming child gave purpose and focus to their lives. At last Francine had a foundation on which to rebuild her hopes. "As I carried the baby and felt the stirring of life, it became a joy to me. I thrilled with anticipation. I began to prepare. I wanted everything to be perfect. Mom had a shower for me, and Joanne gave me a bassinet with a ruffled skirt. I had baby clothes neat and folded in the drawers five months ahead of time."

Mickey's earnings at the lumber yard were small. When he brought his paycheck home the cupboard would be almost bare. After he and Francine had gone shopping, paid the rent, and put gas in the car, there would be little money left. Cleo, the wife of Mickey's oldest brother, Dexter, had a job and offered to pay Francine to do the ironing for her household. Since this was work Francine could do at home, Mickey agreed. Each day, after she had cleaned the apartment, Francine ironed clothes and watched TV. Mickey had used a tax refund to buy her a set.

"It was a struggle to make ends meet. We were eating beans, but I was willing to make sacrifices. I thought, 'At last we're really trying, and if we work together things will get better.'"

They didn't. As Francine swelled with pregnancy, Mickey's mood changed. His temper was short and he complained about any flaw in her housekeeping.

"He wasn't so jealous anymore, but he found other things to get mad about. If he came home and found the trash hadn't been emptied that day, or some other little thing I'd forgotten, he'd have a tantrum. He wanted his dinner cooked, the floor mopped, the bed made, clean clothes all the time. I had to wash by hand. If I left anything undone he'd get mad, and say I was a slob. 'Can't you keep the house cleaner than that?' he'd yell. I would defend myself. We'd argue and yell at each other, but he didn't hit me. I think he was afraid he'd harm the child."

Just before their first anniversary, when Francine was in the seventh month of pregnancy, Mickey came home one Friday and made a sudden announcement. "Fran," he said, "I just can't do it any more. I can't take care of a wife and child."

Francine was stunned. "What am I supposed to do?" she asked. Mickey shrugged. He was busy packing his clothes. "You can always go to your mom," he suggested.

"Mickey!" Francine wailed. "You can't *do* this! You mean you're just going to walk out and leave me flat?" Mickey didn't answer. He took his suitcase down to the car, and returned for some other possessions. Francine stormed, but Mickey remained calm. He told her he now realized that their marriage had been a mistake; he wasn't old enough to settle down. He left with his paycheck in his pocket. After the door had closed Francine threw her heavy body on the bed and cried in utter despair. She thought of cutting her wrists, but the unborn baby stopped her. She could kill herself, but not her child.

At last she calmed herself enough to think of what to do next.

The rent was due that day, there were no groceries to speak of, and she had no cash. There was no alternative but to leave the apartment and go to her mother's.

"I called Bill and Sharon and they came over and helped me pack up. The apartment was furnished, so there were no heavy things. On our way to Mom's in Jackson I asked Bill to go through Dansville and down Adams Street. Mickey's car was parked in front of his mom's house. Just as we drove by, the door opened and Mickey came out with a girl. He didn't see us. I looked back and it was obvious they were together. They were laughing and talking as they got in his car. The emotion I felt then was . . . well, impossible to describe. I was so hurt, so jealous, so betrayed. I cried in front of Bill and Sharon. I thought of all I'd given up for Mickey; how I'd exchanged my happy teenage life to be his wife and have his child; how much I'd suffered and how hard I'd tried. I'd done it because he loved me so much and begged so hard. It seemed totally unbelievable that he would just suddenly walk away from it all and drop me for some other girl."

When Francine arrived at her mother's home, her response was not comforting. She immediately asked who was going to pay the doctor's bill? The hospital bill? What was Francine going to live on? "Aren't you going to make him pay child support?" she demanded. "You're going to need things for the baby." Francine felt overwhelmed. "I felt like saying, 'Gosh, Mom, I don't know. I'm only seventeen; how am I supposed to know these things!'" Francine's father had nothing to say. He listened in silence while the women talked.

After a few days, Francine swallowed her pride and called Mickey at his mother's house. "I said, 'Hey, we've got this child that's coming into the world, and it's not only my responsibility; it's yours, too. There's going to be doctor's bills and hospital bills. Until I can work, you've got to help.'

"Mickey acted as though it was none of his affair. When I insisted, he got belligerent. He said, 'I don't have to pay anything. If you get anything out of me, you're going to have to *make* me pay.' I said, 'If that's how you feel, then okay, but I think that since it is your child, too, that you shouldn't feel that way—that taking care of this child is something you should *want* to do!'"

Years later, when Francine looked back at this moment in her life, she realized she could have survived without Mickey's support. At the time she didn't see how. "I probably could have got some kind of welfare help, but it didn't occur to me. I would have been afraid to live alone. It never crossed my mind to put the baby in a foster home. I'd been carrying this baby, feeling it move, thinking about it all these months. It was *my* baby. I wouldn't have let anyone else have it for the world."

Another element in Francine's desire to resume life with Mickey was that she loved him. "I think there are different forms of love. My love for Mickey grew out of being with him, depending on him, being pregnant with his child. During the good times together we were very close. When he left me I realized I loved him more than I had known."

Flossie agreed that the coming child was Mickey's responsibility and urged him not to desert his family. Mickey's attitude softened and soon he and Francine were talking to each other on the phone every day, admitting that they missed each other. From that it was a short step to deciding to go back together. Francine packed her clothes and Mickey came to fetch her. Since their own apartment was gone he brought her back to the Hughes house in Dansville.

"For Mickey, Flossie's house was always a port in a storm. For me, having to throw ourselves on her generosity again and again was a humiliating drag."

As was usual for him at a critical moment, Mickey had quit his job, but luck was with him. He got a better job at a Lansing factory that made airplane parts.

"Mickey was really pleased and proud. It was more money than he'd ever earned and he liked the work. It made him feel more important than previous jobs. We got an apartment in Lansing for twenty dollars a week. It wasn't the greatest place in the world, but I fixed it up to look nice. Mickey was kind and considerate and caring, those last couple of months before the baby was born. He was trying very hard. He'd come home in the evening and we'd be together and watch TV. He even came home during his breaks from work. He stuck around the house a lot because he knew I might go to the hospital any time."

Though Francine was huge and uncomfortable, she continued to do heavy work, trying to keep house perfectly. Toward the end of her pregnancy she developed toxemia.

"One day I had a fever, pain, and nausea. Mickey was at work. I lay on the bed, hot and aching, thinking, 'I've got to do those dishes before he comes home.' So I got up and did them. When Mickey came home I was very sick. Mickey said, 'What's the matter?' I told him I felt awful. He touched me and I was burning hot. I started crying and said, 'I got up and did the dishes.' He said, 'You shouldn't have done that.' I thought, 'Why shouldn't I?' I had always done it before. I always had to have everything done. I felt like I had to get up and do those dishes before he came home, even if I was sick, pregnant, it just didn't matter."

Mickey took Francine to the doctor, who gave her medication and instructed Mickey on how to care for her. Mickey took her home and did his best. During the early hours of the next morning Francine went into labor. Mickey called his mother and then drove Francine to Mason General Hospital.

Francine labored for ten hours. "After about five hours I thought I was dying. I had never felt such excruciating pain. I watched the clock, thinking, 'How long is this going to go on? I can't take any more.' I kept asking the nurse, 'When? Isn't it time yet?' and she would say, 'Just be patient,' and go away. Mickey was with me, and Flossie was waiting outside. Mickey was very worried. He wanted to hold my hand. I didn't want to be touched. I was in too much pain. I said, 'Mickey, you can't do anything, so just leave me alone.'"

Mickey left the labor room and was sick in the hall. Flossie took his place beside Francine. "She sat by me trying to be nice and make me feel better, but she talked endlessly and I wasn't listening to anything she was saying. I knew they wanted to help, she and Mickey, but all I could think of was, 'Will this agony ever be over?' and try not to scream, only groan."

At last, through the fog of pain, Francine heard nurses bustling about, the doctor being paged, and wondered why. She no longer believed that it could have anything to do with her, that her ordeal could have an end. Then she was on the delivery table. A nurse was giving her gas to ease each contraction, but it seemed to have no effect. There was a last excruciating pain and she felt the baby come. "They cut the cord and laid her on my stomach. I tried to raise my arms to touch her, but I couldn't. They had my arms strapped down. All I could do was look. I was overwhelmed with

love and a sort of awe. Tears came streaming out and at the same
time I began to smile. I had never been so happy in my life."

Francine's baby was born five days before Christmas. A wreath
with a big red ribbon hung on the glass of the nursery where the
new babies slept in rows of cribs. Mickey, jaunty and proud, came
to the hospital and he and Francine looked at their daughter
through the window. They discussed what to name her. Francine
thought of Christmas and of a girl named Christy she had admired
in school—a girl who was neat and pretty, smiling, got good grades,
and was friends with everyone. "To me that girl was perfection.
We named the baby Christy, for her, and Marie, my mother's middle name—Christy Marie.

"From the moment she was laid in my arms for the first time I
loved her. I wanted to take perfect care of her. I looked down at
her sleeping and she was beautiful. I thought, 'My God, I'm her
mother! This is a life I've created. This is *my* child. I'm responsible
for everything that happens to her. Everything—values to instill,
things to be taught. I have to care for her and protect her until she
is grown.' When Mickey and I stood together looking at her I was
secretly wondering if all this responsibility would be mine alone."

Three days after the baby's birth Mickey came to bring them
home. It was evening. The baby was wrapped up and stuffed into a
red Christmas stocking. "I carried her out in my arms to where
Mickey was waiting in our old Chevy. The snow was falling. I got
into the car and nearly keeled over. Mickey had the heat going full
blast. We started off and I looked down at Christy and saw beads
of sweat on her face. I said, 'My God, Mickey, what are you trying
to do, cook us?' He said, 'I didn't want you guys to get cold.'"

Francine began a happy period of taking care of her baby. She
enjoyed bathing her, dressing her, cradling her while she drank her
milk. Francine did not nurse the baby because of a modest fear that
she might be forced to do it in public. As a child she had seen a
woman openly nursing a baby and had been shocked. Mickey remained pleased with the baby, though he didn't like holding her.
"Maybe he was scared because she was so little. He would hold her
and she would start to cry and he'd say, 'Take her! Take her!'

"For a while after Christy was born, Mickey was really nice. The
first time I remember a bad scene was when she was about three

months old. I was in a chair, holding her, when Mickey got mad and threw milk all over me and all over the wall." Quietly, without tears, Francine mopped it up. She had accepted the fact that she had to take pains to keep Mickey calm. "I always lived with the knowledge that there were things to be done to keep the peace. That fact was always there. He expected a clean house—neat, orderly, the wash done and put away, the floors mopped every day. He had to go to work very early. I got up before he did, prepared his breakfast, packed his lunch, made coffee, and then woke him. I had to practically drag him out of bed. I would lay his clothes out, sometimes even put his socks on his feet to get him to get up and go to work. He expected me to do everything his mother had done. I don't suppose she'd dressed him since he grew up, but she did everything else."

Nevertheless, when Mickey wasn't upset about something, Francine felt they were at last leading a normal married life. His jealousy had subsided. She was beginning to forget that Mickey had ever beaten her when suddenly his violence began again.

Mickey enjoyed weekend parties with friends, drinking beer and listening to music. One Saturday a group gathered in the Hughes apartment.

"They were playing records and guitars and smoking and drinking beer. The party went on from early afternoon into the evening. I was the only one with a baby, with responsibilities and work to do. I wished everybody would leave. I was sick of the noise and the smoke and the bodies sitting around with nothing better to do. Mickey told me to fetch somebody a beer. I'd been getting beers and emptying ashtrays all day. I blurted out my feelings. I said, 'Get it yourself. I'm sick of all this! I'm going to bed!' Mickey's hand shot out and he slapped me with full force across the face. Everybody shut up while I sat there, my face stinging. I wanted to die of humiliation. I got up and ran into the bedroom, trying not to cry till I got there. The party was quiet for a couple of minutes. Then I heard Mickey say, 'Put a record on, somebody,' and they all went on having a good time."

The moratorium on beating Francine was over. If Mickey felt like hitting her, he hit her, regardless of who might be watching. Bystanders either ignored a scene or, if that was impossible, beat a hasty retreat. No one wanted to mix in a "family affair." After a beating Francine instinctively tried to hide the fact. She wore sunglasses and makeup to cover a black eye or stayed out of sight while a split lip healed, and, in fact, no one seemed to notice. Friends and neighbors, Mickey's brothers and their wives, studiously ignored any marks on her. Francine felt as though she had an unmentionable affliction from which everyone turned away.

In spite of the beatings, after Christy was born the thought of leaving Mickey hardly crossed Francine's mind. They were a family at last and she was convinced that she could not possibly raise a child alone. She accepted that being beaten was the price she had to pay for Mickey's support. Usually, after a fight there was a period of calm and lovemaking. "In times when things would be good between us I'd have great hope and be happy. I wanted so much to be a good wife and mother and have my marriage succeed. I was so proud of my baby. I just didn't dream of trying to do anything but go on and make the best home for her that I could."

When Christy was about six months old Mickey began to spend less time at home. It was some time before Francine discovered that he and some friends from the factory had rented an apartment as a hangout, a place to bring girls.

On Fridays Mickey would bring home his paycheck, give Francine the share he had allotted to her for groceries and the rent, change his clothes, and dash out again. Francine became increasingly puzzled:

"One night we were in bed, and that's when I knew something was going on. He got up and said he was going for a drive. I said, 'Where are you going?' He said, 'Just for a drive. I can't sleep.' I said, 'Why do you want to get up this late? Can I go with you?' He said, 'No. I just want to go by myself. I want to be alone.'" Mickey went out and didn't come back that night.

The following day was Friday and Francine waited with rising apprehension for him to return. He breezed in, and, fending off her questions, began to wash up and change his clothes.

"Where are you going?" Francine asked. "Out," Mickey replied.

Francine was scared. She thought, "If he goes out he'll spend the rent money and the grocery money."

"Did you cash your check?"

"No," Mickey said. "I'm going to cash it now."

"Well . . . can I have some money for groceries?"

"No. I'll give it to you tomorrow."

"I need it now. Go to the bank and give it to me. Then you can go out. Where are you going? You're running around with women, aren't you?"

"No," Mickey said. "Who told you that?"

"I'm not totally dumb," Francine said. "I know. What are you going to do? Take your whole check and waste it? How are we going to eat and pay the rent?"

Francine tried to pull the paycheck out of Mickey's pocket, but he held her off with one hand and went on shaving with the other. "I was furious. Here was this guy, my husband, who had a wife and a baby, going to gallivant all weekend, and leave us sitting there. I remember thinking, 'We're supposed to come first, not anyone else.'"

For once Mickey was imperturbable. He hurried into his windbreaker, ran a comb through his thick black hair, gave a last glance at the mirror, and turned to go. Francine picked up an ashtray and hurled it at him. Laughing, Mickey ducked, and reached out to field the missile. It shattered; he looked at his bloody hand in anger and surprise; he picked up a vase and threw it at Francine. Turning quickly, he made for the door. Francine threw a coffee cup. It hit him in the back of the neck and broke, but Mickey kept going. Francine saw blood on the back of his neck where the jagged cup had cut him.

Instead of going to his rendezvous, Mickey went to his mother. Flossie took him to the hospital emergency room, where his wounds were stitched, and then brought him home with her to Dansville.

After he had gone, Francine, alone with Christy, waited for the phone to ring. She was jealous, indignant, and scared. Their margin was so slight that even one lost paycheck meant trouble: rent in arrears, bill collectors at the door, and not enough to eat. The weekend passed without any word from Dansville, where she felt sure Mickey had gone. She was too proud to telephone. She used her remaining dollars for groceries and wondered what she would do if Mickey abandoned her and Christy.

Finally a call came. It was Lillian, Wimpy's wife. She told Francine that Mickey was at his mother's and that Flossie was burning with indignation because Francine had injured him. Lillian warned

Francine that she could expect a visit from Mickey's parents. Francine's own anger rose anew. "Fine," she said. "Let them come."

Flossie and Berlin came to the apartment. Flossie berated Francine for her violence. "You could have hurt him very bad! You could have killed him!" Francine stood her ground. "What about me?" she cried. "What do you think could happen to me when he's hitting me? How do you think he's treating me and this child he's responsible for?"

The visit allowed both sides to vent their feelings. A few days later, to Francine's relief, Mickey came back, and their life together resumed.

For a time Mickey's mind seemed to be diverted from women by his enthusiasm for a project he and Bill Hensley undertook—building a stock car. The two young men put all their spare time into working on the car and most of their cash into buying parts. "It was like pulling teeth to get the rent money because they always needed something for the stock car—big slicks, special engine parts—it seemed endless."

In October 1965, when Christy was nine months old, Francine found she was pregnant again. A foam contraceptive recommended at the hospital had failed. At first she felt desperate at the prospect of another baby, but after a few months, as the child became a reality that she could feel inside her, love and protectiveness overwhelmed her qualms. Mickey, as before, was delighted. He was proud to have a pregnant wife.

Summer came and Mickey and Bill were still busy with their stock car. On weekends Mickey took Francine and Christy to visit Sharon in Jackson; then he and Bill returned to Lansing to work on the stock car. "Somehow Sharon and I found out that they were having girls up in my apartment while Sharon and I were back there on the porch in Jackson on those hot summer nights—both of us pregnant." Francine first suspected it when she went back to the apartment one Sunday night and noticed someone had remade the bed. She could tell because the bedspread had a small rip in it and she always made the bed in a certain way so the rip didn't show.

"Who's been here?" Francine asked. "You've had a girl here, haven't you?"

Mickey denied it and stormed out of the house, but Bill confessed to Sharon, who told Francine that their husbands had been amusing themselves not only with the stock car, but with extracurricular sex. Francine was jealous and bitter. "It made such a mockery of what Mickey had made me believe when I married him only two years before." She kept her tears and anger to herself, afraid that if she made a scene Mickey would walk out as he had before. She was in the last month of pregnancy. She needed Mickey's support to get through the weeks ahead. Their finances were at a low ebb. Mickey had put so much money into the stock car that the rent was in arrears. Their landlady dunned them constantly and Mickey always left it to Francine to placate her and put her off.

One day when Mickey was at work a policeman appeared at Francine's door. The landlady had called him to evict them. "When I saw the policeman I got a lump in my throat. I thought, 'My God, what am I going to do? How can I get the money? Will they put me out on the street or take me to jail or what?' The policeman saw how pregnant I was and tried to handle the situation with kid gloves. He calmed the landlady down for the moment. But I knew I had to do something fast."

Francine discovered that a house nearby—one she'd often noticed because it was so pretty—was vacant. She found the owner and, miraculously, he agreed to rent it to her. It was a Friday and when Mickey came home with his paycheck he gave Francine money for a deposit and she closed the deal. The new house had a nice yard, a garage where Mickey could work on his car, a big window in the dining room. "I pictured how I would fix it up; how nice it would be in the dining room in the morning having coffee, looking out the sunny window into the yard. I persuaded our landlady to let us take our things out of the old apartment. I promised we would pay the back rent later. We moved in, or rather, I moved us into the new house. Mickey was at work and left it all to me. Vicky, his adopted sister, helped me. I was absolutely huge but somehow I packed up, even though I could hardly bend over."

"Vicky and I carried everything down the stairs and into the new house. There was a lot of heavy stuff—dishes, clothes, Christy's things, a TV, and a record player, that I shouldn't have carried but I had become so programmed that I felt I had to do all that whether or not I was nine months pregnant."

Two days later Francine went into labor. The second birth was faster and easier. Knowing what to expect, she was less frightened. She was happy that she had a son: a healthy, pretty baby whom they named James.

Good luck came with the new baby. Mickey got a job with better pay at the Oldsmobile factory in Lansing, thus restoring their credit. The new house was unfurnished. Mickey got a loan at the credit union and bought a refrigerator, a couch, and a chair. Francine's mother contributed a dinette set, curtains, and plants. This was the first time that Francine had had furniture of her own and she was delighted with each new piece. She felt that in collecting their own things they were putting together a home that wouldn't be blown apart by a sudden storm of anger, as their previous households had been.

Mickey felt so flush that he got a second loan and bought a '64 Malibu: a showy car, metallic silver with air conditioning, a black interior, and bucket seats. He also began joining his new friends at the Oldsmobile factory for beers after work, something he had never done before. When he came home late he told Francine he was delayed "at the office." Francine was puzzled. "I couldn't figure out what he meant by 'the office.' Mickey laughed because I was so dumb. He told me it was a bar. I didn't worry at first. Mickey got drunk sometimes, but he wasn't a regular drinker. I thought: 'He has to get along with the guys and go where they go in order to fit in.'"

Now that she had two babies, Francine's time was totally taken up with caring for them and they became the center of her life, justifying everything she had forfeited by her marriage.

"I loved Christy so much. I was proud of how nice I kept her—bathed every day, and dressed in clean clothes. She always smelled sweet. She was so responsive and bright, a happy child. I gave her vitamins and was careful to poach her eggs, not fry them, so she wouldn't get any grease. I talked to her and sang her songs. I wanted her world to be perfect. When Jimmy came along it was the same thing over again. It seemed as though I must have wanted him all along to balance my love for Christy and make the family complete. I thought I was lucky to have two such great kids."

Three months after Jimmy's birth Mickey was assigned to the late shift. He went to work at eleven in the evening and was gone until seven the next morning. Francine was frightened at being left alone.

"We lived in a tough part of town. Night after night I would have these horrible thoughts that somebody might break in and harm me and the kids. I would take Christy and Jimmy into my bedroom and lie there awake, listening. There were noises late at night. Mice rustled in the waste basket and I would stiffen all over. I would lock the bedroom door and stick knives in it to hold it tight. One night the wind blew and made a sudden humming noise and I flew out of bed. I stood in the middle of the floor shaking. Then I realized it was just the wind, but my heart kept on pounding. I was so relieved when morning light came. I'd lain awake all night waiting."

Although Francine didn't recognize her anxiety as a symptom, two years of emotional buffeting, of violence, erratic cruelty, insecurity, and constant change, had taken a psychic toll, sapping her confidence in herself and increasing her dependence on Mickey. At the same time her commitment to her children, especially Christy, became more and more intense.

"Christy and I spent so many nights alone when he would be gone—working, running around, or whatever. Christy was my strength. She talked at an early age, walked early. I talked to her all the time. I wanted her to grow up to do all the things I couldn't do. I read aloud to her. I'd get fairy stories at the supermarket and also books with information in them. I taught her everything I could. I loved her beyond anything. I used to sing her a song, 'You are my sunshine, my only sunshine, you make me happy when skies are gray.' I meant every word."

Francine's life in the house in Jackson ended abruptly. Mickey's brother Dexter had moved to Kansas. He wrote Mickey telling him that there were great opportunities there. Mickey, tired of the night shift, telephoned him. Dexter said, "Come on down. I'll get you a job." Mickey instantly decided to go. Francine was dubious. She knew Dexter was inclined to exaggerate success. He loved to sport flashy clothes and cars that, likely as not, would never be paid for. She was also reluctant to tear apart the home she had worked so hard to put together: the nice house, the furniture and belongings that represented building for the future. She was overruled and Mickey left for Kansas.

He returned shortly, full of enthusiasm for the construction job he had found. They emptied the house, dispersing their furniture. Flossie took the new refrigerator. Other things were given here and there. In a car packed with clothes and baby things, Mickey drove Francine and the two babies to Overland Park, a suburb of Kansas City.

There Francine found a surprise. Mickey had rented the most beautiful apartment she had ever seen. It was in a new building and had two bedrooms, two baths, a big living room with glass sliding doors opening on a terrace, draw drapes, a dishwasher, wall-to-wall carpeting, and new furniture. The rent was in keeping with such luxury. Dexter, who was living in equal splendor, could afford it because he was earning high pay as a bricklayer and his wife, Cleo, was working. Mickey was only an apprentice and Francine saw his pay wouldn't be enough. "I remember loving it so, but thinking, 'My God, we'll never be able to make it.'"

Francine was right. After a few weeks Mickey's employer went bankrupt. Mickey and Dexter were out of a job. The two men went scouting for work, leaving their wives behind. Francine spent an anxious week until Mickey returned with the news that he'd found a construction job in Camden, Missouri, seventy miles away.

In Camden, Francine and Mickey rented a modest house, one of a cluster of summer cottages. Francine was relieved to be living in something they could afford. This time, Mickey assured her, the job would be a steady one with good money coming in. The house was unfurnished, but on the strength of Mickey's job a furniture store gave them credit and they bought what they needed.

Once again Francine did her best to settle down. She found the area desolate. There was wind and blowing sand, ticks and chiggers, and violent, frightening thunderstorms. The house had tile floors. It seemed that she had no sooner finished sweeping than they were gritty again. On the other hand, there were good neighbors. An old man and woman in a house across from hers were kind to her and the children. All the children in the settlement called the couple "Grandma" and "Grandpa." Francine could wander from her yard over to theirs for company. Mickey was happy because he was training as a brick mason and saw better earnings ahead. He took considerable pride in his increasing skill.

Suddenly Mickey's work ran out, and he found there was no chance of another job in the area. Since Mickey and Francine lived from paycheck to paycheck, they were virtually penniless. Mickey invested their remaining funds in gasoline. Francine packed up their personal belongings. The new furniture was still unpaid for and they left it behind. Francine said goodbye to the elderly couple and closed the door on the little frame house with the gritty tile floors. Mickey had wrecked his flashy silver Malibu in a drag race and replaced it with an old station wagon. In it they returned to Michigan, where, as always, Flossie took them in.

Mickey found a job in a factory on the outskirts of Lansing. No sooner were they settled than he decided to go back to Missouri, where Dexter had found work in the town of Richmond. Mickey drove out, got a job, and returned for Francine. They packed the children and a few belongings into the elderly station wagon and were off again.

In Richmond, Francine and Mickey rented a small house that pleased Francine. It was a cute house, up on a hill. Best of all, the rent was low. They were soon joined by Mickey's brother, Donovan, then sixteen, who had in tow a girl who had two little boys. Mickey, Dexter, and Donovan were working together on a construction job. After work they went to bars and before long had a feud going with some men in town.

"I didn't know anything about it until one night when Mickey and Donovan were out bombing around in Mickey's car. They drove up to our door and told me to be careful because they were going to have a fight with these local guys. They said the locals had sawed-off shotguns. Donovan and Mickey had also gotten a gun. They took off, leaving me in the house with the kids. I was scared, wondering if the local guys would shoot at the house. It got dark. A car with a loud muffler came by, full of guys yelling out the window. I turned out the lights and the kids and I lay on the floor. The car went away but it kept coming back so I didn't dare get up. After a while the car pulled up at the house and the guys banged on the door and yelled for Mickey. I yelled back, 'Only me and the kids are here.' They went away, but I still didn't dare get up. The kids and I lay on the floor in the dark for two hours."

Francine learned later that there had been a wild chase through the countryside culminating in a fight in town. Mickey was thrown in jail. Francine went to see him. "It was a little jail; you'd go down a little dirt alley and there was a shack with bars. He was mad as hell."

Mickey was released in a few days. He came home to collect some clothes and tell Francine that he and his brothers were leaving for Florida. When they found work, he said, he would send for her. Francine asked for money to feed herself and the children. Mickey refused. He said he needed every cent for gas to get to Florida. The argument became a fight, in the course of which Francine took refuge behind the refrigerator. Mickey tipped it over on her. As it crashed to the floor, Francine ducked away. Mickey slammed out and was gone.

"He left us there, without a cent. I didn't know what to do, even for that day. Then I decided the logical thing was to get a job. I had no car, so I walked everywhere, looking for work. After two days I got a job in a nursing home about a mile and a half from where we lived. The girl with two kids who had come with Donovan was stranded too. She moved in with me and got a job in the same nursing home. She worked the night shift and I worked days so there was always one of us with the kids."

Until the two women collected their first week's pay, they and the four children had to live on what food was in the house. They managed to get the refrigerator upright, but it wouldn't work and the contents spoiled. For a week the household lived on pancakes and canned milk.

Several weeks went by with no word from Mickey. Francine wondered if he had deserted her for good. Then a postcard came. He had found no work in Florida and was in Dansville with his parents. He was setting out in the station wagon to bring her home.

When Mickey arrived, Francine had no strength to waste on recriminations. They piled what things they could into the station wagon, abandoned the rest, and Francine, with a sense of having survived yet another shipwreck, wearily allowed Mickey to drive her and the children back to Dansville, where Flossie and Berlin took them in.

Mickey's luck turned. He landed a job with a construction firm in Jackson at what seemed an enormous wage—eight dollars an hour—

twice what he had ever earned before. Francine rented an apartment on Trail Street in Jackson. It was small and dingy, but with Mickey's poor credit, the best she could do. It seemed that with Mickey's high earnings, life would become easier, but Mickey spent his money as fast as it came in, and the savings account Francine hoped to build up never materialized.

They had been in the Trail Street apartment only a few weeks when Francine discovered she was pregnant again.

The prospect overwhelmed her. After Jimmy's birth two years before, she had asked the obstretrician for birth-control pills. He was Catholic and refused. Francine lacked the money to visit another doctor, but in Kansas her sister-in-law, Cleo, shared her prescription. When Francine came back to Michigan she intended to see a doctor and get her own prescription, but, always short of cash, she put it off until too late. Now she felt desperate. "I had heard that hot and cold baths could cause a miscarriage. I got in the tub and nearly scalded myself. Then I ran icy cold water and sat in that. I didn't do anything extreme, like taking a drug. I kept hoping against hope the bath routine would work. It didn't."

To make matters worse, Mickey was laid off from his high-paying job. Even though Mickey had had enough money, he had let the rent fall in arrears and once again they lost their apartment. While Mickey was out of work, his parents housed and fed the family. After they'd been in Dansville several weeks Mickey was called back to his job, but made no move toward finding another place to live.

"Mickey would have liked to stay at his mother's indefinitely, but he didn't want to pay his share. Berlin and Flossie kept track of every dime and when Mickey went back to work they began to gripe at him: 'You're earning good money,' they'd say. 'If you're gonna stay here, you're gonna have to help.' I knew they were right. I'd say, 'Mickey, it's only fair.' What I wanted most was a place of our own, and finally Mickey said okay, if I could find one he'd move."

Francine found a trailer for rent in the Sunset Trailer Park near Mason, and Mickey agreed to move in. Francine loved the trailer. It was clean and new. There was carpeting in the living room and the kitchen was sunny. Best of all were the close neighbors. Francine enjoyed having people to visit with during the day. She had spent so many days confined with small children that companionship was a tremendous treat.

A family with four young girls, the oldest about fourteen, lived in a trailer across from hers. The girls often came over after school and helped Francine with Christy and Jimmy. Francine also made friends with a young wife in a neighboring trailer.

"The trailer park was out in the country. It was spring when we moved in. I was a couple of months pregnant, but I didn't let the landlord know it or he wouldn't have rented to us. The weather got warm and the grass turned green. The girls and I took the kids for long walks and we'd pick flowers. Christy and Jimmy were just big enough to keep up. Sometimes I rode the girls' bike. Afterward we'd sit together in the sun and listen to the radio. The ladies in the trailer park and I gave recipes back and forth. A woman from West Virginia taught me to bake bread. My kids loved it when I baked bread. They'd be outside playing and Jimmy would put his nose to the screen and ask, 'Is the bread done yet, Mommie?' When it came out of the oven we'd slice off big hunks and eat them, still warm, with butter and jam."

Mickey was working steadily. He was proud of his increasing skill as a brick mason and of his high earnings. For the first time Francine felt stability. She and Mickey talked about buying land and building a house. In spite of all that had occurred between them, Francine took it for granted that she loved Mickey and that he, in his fashion, loved her and the children. There were moments of tenderness and pleasure between them that helped erase the episodes Francine wanted so much to forget. But whenever she became unwary Mickey would see to it that her fear of him was revived.

"One night he didn't come home until late. I had gone across to my girl friend's trailer and we were there playing records. There was an older lady there and the fourteen-year-old girl and her little sister. A couple of teenage boys dropped in. I had Christy and Jimmy with me. When Mickey came home and found I wasn't there he came to get me. I saw him at the door and the look on his face made my heart sink right down into my shoes. I knew I was in trouble. I thought, 'I haven't done anything wrong, but I'm going to be punished. I'm going to be punished because I don't like being alone.' Sure enough I was."

Grimly Mickey escorted her and the children back to their trailer.
He shoved Christy and Jimmy into their room and then turned on
Francine.

"Who were those guys over there?"

"They weren't guys. They were just boys, friends of Cathy's. We
were just sitting there."

Mickey hit her in the face. "Why weren't you home? The kids
should of been in bed!"

"It's not that late!"

Mickey's face took on what Francine had come to know as his
"crazy" look. He went on to beat her while she tried not to cry out,
hoping the sounds of her humiliation would not reach the group
she had just left. After that Francine was afraid to visit her friends.
If she did risk it she made sure she was home by the time Mickey
returned.

Francine's third child, a boy, was born in August 1969. She went
into labor early one morning. She and Mickey drove Christy and
Jimmy to Flossie's and then Mickey took her to the hospital in
Mason. It was an easy birth, and once the baby was in her arms she
knew that she would love this child as she did the others. Mickey
chose the baby's name—Dana.

Soon after Dana's birth the period of comparative happiness in
the trailer park drew to a close. In spite of Mickey's good earnings,
bills had piled up. They had no medical insurance and the total of
hospital bills, obstetrical bills, and pediatric bills came to a large
sum. The credit bureau was dunning Mickey for payments on a
new car, and there were other bills as well. Mickey arranged to file
for bankruptcy. For a while he kept up with the weekly payment
he had agreed to. Then he began to skip payments. His creditors
garnisheed his pay and made phone calls to his employer's office. As
a result Mickey was fired. He was furious and aggrieved. He signed
up for unemployment payments and made little effort to find another job. His mood became sullen and Francine realized that
being fired had badly damaged his self-esteem.

It was autumn. The leaves were turning and the nights were
cold. Mickey had failed to pay the fuel bill and Francine used the
electric oven to heat the trailer. When the rent was unpaid at the
end of the month, the landlord told Francine they would have to
move. Mickey, meanwhile, was spending his unemployment checks

in bars and bringing home six-packs of beer to drink in front of the television set.

As she prepared to leave the cozy little trailer Francine felt lower than she ever had: "We would just get settled in a house; I'd clean it up and fix it up. It would start to feel like home and then I would have to leave it all. Even furniture was left behind. We were kicked out of place after place for not paying the rent. Mickey always sent me out to rent a new place and I was the one the landlord always complained to. I tried to do too much to keep the family going. Mickey saw this and the more I did the less he'd do."

From the Sunset Trailer Park, Francine and Mickey moved to a shabby duplex on the outskirts of Mason. The driveway was a sea of mud. Cold air sifted through the cracks in the window frames. Again they had no furniture. Francine bought a cheap couch and some beds at a second-hand store. They couldn't afford a phone. The place seemed beyond anyone's powers to fix up and Francine didn't try. The care of three children under five took all her strength.

Mickey continued to collect unemployment compensation. Francine suspected he wasn't looking for work, but was spending his time drinking and running around with women. "He would take off and leave us there all day long. After the rent was paid and a few groceries, he'd take the rest and disappear. One time he left to get his check and didn't come back for three days. The only food I had in the house was popcorn and a jar of jelly. Dana was still on the bottle. To stop him crying I dissolved jelly in water and gave him that. Christy and Jimmy and I ate popcorn. Another time we ran out of fuel oil. The fuel company refused to come. While there was no heat the kids and I sat in one little room with an electric heater. I didn't have enough money for the laundromat. Diapers and baby clothes piled up in mountains. A couple of times I took laundry to Flossie's house, but mostly I washed by hand. When Mickey came home he was drunk and broke. Things were really grim."

Francine's greatest anxieties centered on the children. The more she loved them, the more she rationalized the hurts and deprivations of her life with Mickey. It never occurred to her to leave him. She thought, "He's having a hard time supporting us, how could I ever do it alone." She held the firm belief that the children needed

a father as well as a mother, and felt unequal to the responsibility
of raising them alone. "I loved the kids so much I thought I could
take any amount of hardship and abuse to keep their home intact. I
kept hoping that if I stuck it out Mickey might change and our life
get better. As for myself, I believed that if Mickey and I separated
my married life would be over forever. It wasn't within my thinking
to imagine I might have a life with any other man."

The Hughes family's tenancy of the duplex ended, as usual, when
Mickey ceased to pay the rent. "I had been putting the landlady off
for weeks. The place was only fifteen or twenty dollars a week, but
I didn't have even that. One Saturday morning she came to the
door and when I told her I couldn't pay her she began yelling and
screaming at me. Mickey was in bed. He heard, but he didn't get
up."

Once again they were evicted. Francine found an apartment on
First Street in Jackson. It was better than the one they were leaving
—sunny and with a fireplace. Francine wanted it very much, but
she feared that if the landlord discovered Mickey's record of unpaid bills he would refuse to rent it. She gave the name of Mickey's
brother, Marlin, who was solvent, and got the apartment. They
moved in with the remnants of their possessions, now reduced to
the barest essentials.

In May 1970, when Dana was nine months old, Francine discovered she was pregnant for the fourth time in six years. After Dana's
birth she had gotten a prescription for birth-control pills and filled
it at a drugstore in Mason. When her supply of pills ran out, Francine, by then living in Jackson, had no way to get to the drugstore
in Mason. "I asked Mickey and he agreed to get the pills when he
picked up his unemployment check. He didn't come home all weekend. When he came home he had no money and no pills. I tried to
avoid sex. I kept saying, 'Please, Mickey, don't. I'll get pregnant.'
He'd say, 'Come on. I'll be careful.' The result was I got pregnant. I
was totally crushed."

Mickey's unemployment pay ended but he made only feeble
efforts to find another job. Dexter and Marlin had begun working
independently on construction jobs, hoping to become contractors.
Mickey began to work with them. The business did not prosper.
Dexter got few contracts and kept the lion's share of what little
earnings there were.

Day after day Mickey was gone from five o'clock in the morning until dark. When he came home he'd drink a six-pack and go to bed. Francine never knew whether or not he and Dexter had had a day's work, but Mickey brought almost nothing home. The rent went unpaid. As always it was Francine, not Mickey, who stalled the landlord, pleading for another week of grace.

"Things got really bad. I didn't even have soap to wash the dishes. One day a salesman left a sample of soap at the door. I was ecstatic because I could wash some clothes."

It didn't occur to Francine to ask anyone for help. Her father had died four years before. Her mother worked, cleaning houses, to support her younger children, David and Kathy, and had little to spare. Joanne was divorced. She and her six children were on welfare. Francine knew that Flossie and Berlin would take her and Mickey in, but starvation seemed preferable. Day after day she eked out sustenance from whatever trickle of cash Mickey produced.

"Sometimes the only thing to eat in the house was mustard, or something like that. The kids were hungry. They'd ask for milk. They cried a lot. We all had hunger pains. I wouldn't come right out and tell her, but Mom suspected I was in bad trouble. I would help her shop and she would give me a few dollars' worth of groceries. It would have to last us a week."

Francine begged Mickey to apply for welfare. Some quirk of pride caused him to refuse. Francine herself had been to the welfare office several times and each time had been told that the rules required that the "head of the household" make the application.

"Mickey wouldn't give any reason; he'd just flatly say, 'No.' He'd say, 'You go.' I'd say, 'You know they won't help unless you come with me.' He acted as though he didn't care."

Somehow Mickey himself remained sufficiently nourished. He continued to smoke and bring home beer. Francine smoked the butts Mickey left in ashtrays. Mickey often promised that things would get better soon. Once, when there was nothing in the house to eat, he promised to bring back some money that evening. All day Francine looked forward to his return. When he came home he put seven dollars on the kitchen table. Dexter's cement mixer had broken down and he had taken most of Mickey's share of their earnings to fix it. Francine wept with disappointment. She felt sorry for

Mickey too. "Sometimes when he saw how we were suffering I'd see a look in his eyes that told me he felt bad about it. I'd feel that he wanted to be responsible, wanted to do what was right for his family, but couldn't. For a few seconds it would be plain on his face. Then he'd shrug it off and leave."

Francine doesn't remember how long this period lasted—only that at last she reached a point of desperation.

"I sat at the kitchen table and thought about my life. I can still feel it—the way my heart ached. So many times I'd climbed the mountain only to be pushed down to the bottom again. I was completely miserable. I felt overwhelmed by my situation. I was pregnant, with no money for a doctor. I thought of my kids and how they were suffering. My beautiful Christy. At six she was old enough to know I was worried and scared. Jimmy was so little and thin. I couldn't stand them having to do without proper food. Even Dana, the baby, wasn't getting what he needed. The last time I had been to the welfare office I had told them, 'We're starving but my husband absolutely will not come.' The social worker told me again, 'Unless you are divorced or get separate maintenance from him we can't help you.' Her words kept echoing in my head. I thought, 'If Mickey won't do anything then it is up to me. These kids have to have food and they have to have a roof.' I got up from the table and went out and phoned Joanne. I said, 'Would you come and get me and take me to welfare?' She said, 'Why?' I started crying. I said, 'The kids and I are starving to death. We're dirty. We can't even wash our faces. There's nothing in the house. If you don't believe me, come and look.' Joanne said, 'I'll get my girl friend, Joyce, who has a car, and we'll be right over.' She and Joyce came within an hour. They looked at the empty cupboards and shook their heads. Then Joanne said, 'Come on, let's go.'"

At the welfare office Francine again went through her list of woes. "The rent is overdue. The landlord wants us out. I'm pregnant. I don't have a doctor. We're hungry and dirty." The case worker listened and then said, "Well, what are you going to do?"

Francine answered, "Whatever I have to do, I'll do. Just tell me how."

The case worker advised her to ask the Legal Aid office to prepare separate-maintenance papers; as soon as she signed them she would be eligible for a food order. When she found a new apartment, welfare would pay the rent.

At the Legal Aid office Francine talked to an elderly, dignified man named Baker. "What seems to be the problem?" he asked. When Francine had finished describing her situation Mr. Baker looked appalled. He asked if Mickey had ever hit her. Francine admitted that he had. Mr. Baker got up. "Wait here," he told Francine. He spoke to his secretary in the outer office. Then he called Francine. "Mrs. Hughes, we've got the papers you need. Have you got seven dollars for the fee?"

Francine said, "If I had seven dollars I probably wouldn't be here." Baker reached in his pocket and put seven dollars on the desk. His secretary spread out papers for Francine to sign.

"I saw the words 'Decree of Divorce.' It floored me. I thought I was applying for separate maintenance. I looked at Mr. Baker and said, 'A *divorce* decree? Is that what I'm getting?' Mr. Baker gave me a stern look. 'You *do* want a divorce, don't you?' he asked, as though I must be crazy if I didn't. As the idea sank in, it scared me to death, but I thought, 'I've got to do it. I've got no choice. I have to feed the kids.' I signed the papers. Mr. Baker told me that in six months I would have to go to court to get a final decree. I thanked him and left. I was shaking. My heart was pounding. I felt terrifically excited. I realized I was elated. I was thinking, 'It's over! This long, useless struggle is over. I'm going to start a new life; I'm going to be free!'"

That evening, when Mickey came home, Francine did not tell him what she had done. From Mr. Baker's office she had returned to welfare and had been given an order for groceries. She was cooking hamburgers when Mickey came in. He asked no questions. Francine supposed he thought her mother had given her the money and had no desire to be told so. Francine was intensely nervous, afraid that her betrayal must be visible on her face. To her relief Mickey ate quietly, drank a few beers, and went to bed.

The next day as soon as Mickey left, Joanne and Joyce came for Francine and took her apartment-hunting. It was a disheartening quest. Time after time she was turned down when the landlord discovered she was single, on welfare, and had three children. Fortunately, her pregnancy was not yet apparent. At last she found a small apartment—two rooms on the second floor of an old frame building—whose owner seemed sympathetic. Francine told him that she had looked everywhere, that her situation was desperate, and promised to move as soon as she could find something else. He reluctantly agreed.

Francine's plan was to pack and move her belongings before Mickey returned—and hope he wouldn't find her new address, on the far side of Jackson. Joanne rented a trailer to tow behind the car. The three women worked all afternoon, carrying cribs and diaper pails and kitchen things. The trailer was small and they had to make several trips. It was late afternoon when they returned to the old apartment for a final load. As their car entered the block Francine saw Mickey standing in front of the building talking to a man in a business suit. She saw the man hand Mickey an envelope and it flashed across her mind that he was a process server and the envelope contained a notice that she had filed for divorce. As she watched, Mickey glanced angrily at the envelope and threw it, unopened, on the pavement. Then he looked up and saw Francine in Joyce's car with Joanne and the children. The trailer made their errand clear.

Joyce picked up speed and they pulled away. Mickey jumped into his own car and followed them. It soon became a dangerous game as Mickey pulled alongside, trying to force them to the curb. There was a police station a few blocks away and Francine told Joyce to go there. Joyce pulled up in front of the police station with Mickey close behind. Francine dashed inside and asked for help. Two officers came with her to the car, where Mickey was cursing and threatening Joanne. Francine hastily sketched the situation for the police. They told her to leave while they detained Mickey. As Joyce pulled away Francine looked back and saw the police holding Mickey, who was yelling and struggling. She heard him shout, "My kids are in that car!" Then Joyce turned the corner and he was out of sight.

At the new apartment the trailer was unpacked and Francine's bits of furniture were carried upstairs. They looked shabbier than ever in the cold light from the uncurtained windows. Joyce and Joanne sat down for a cigarette with Francine. When they rose to go she felt like crying out, "Don't go! Please don't leave me here alone! I'm so scared!" When the door closed Francine pulled Christy to her and hugged her in silence. She was thinking: "Here we are, me and the kids, in this dingy little place. All alone. Now what? What do I do now?"

The next day Francine pulled herself together, straightening things up, cleaning, trying to make the place feel like home, but her depression did not lift. Though she reminded herself that at last she had food and shelter, her anxiety didn't go away. Each day her loneliness increased. She had no phone and depended on Joanne to take her to the welfare office to get her check and to the market for weekly shopping. These were her only contacts with the outside world. Most of her hours were spent alone with the children, reading, preparing meals, cleaning up, reading again, or playing games until their bedtime. Then, when evening came, she felt totally forlorn.

Night after night she lay awake wondering what Mickey was doing. Did he miss her? Was he searching for her? Would he lie in wait outside Joanne's house and follow her to the apartment? Francine pictured him beating her horribly, and shivered with fear. In another mood, she would begin to wonder if she had really done the right thing. Loneliness would overwhelm her and she would long to see him. "Is he really so bad?" she asked herself. Did he deserve this? She couldn't forget the look on his face as he struggled with the police—a look of unbelief that said, "I never dreamed she'd do a thing like this." Francine would cry with pity for them both: for Mickey because she'd deserted him and taken his children away, for herself because she felt so desolate. "My thoughts seemed to go around and around until I'd be exhausted and then I'd cry myself to sleep."

Francine didn't know then that her state of mind had a clinical name. In fact, she was in the grip of a depression in the medical sense of the term. Leaving Mickey after years of dependence, she felt as though she had stepped into a loveless void. She was flooded by a sense of loss, as she had been in her childhood when her grandmother died. Depression clouded her thinking and made her future seem more hopeless than before.

After a few weeks of despondency Francine could bear it no longer. She used the landlord's telephone to call Flossie. Flossie told her how relieved she was to hear from her and asked to see the children. Francine gave her the address. Flossie and Berlin came to the apartment. Flossie was distressed by the separation. "These children need their father," she said. "I wish you two would straighten up and get together and be a family, like you should be."

Francine tearfully told Flossie that she had left out of desperation, because she and the children had to have money for food and shelter; that though she still wanted a family, life with Mickey was impossible unless he would do his share. Flossie replied that Mickey wanted another chance, and assured Francine that she needn't be afraid to see him. He wasn't angry and wouldn't hurt her. Francine agreed to see him.

Mickey came to the apartment the next day. He was calm while Francine poured out her grievances. "We talked. Really talked. We talked about our life together. He listened, but the look on his face told me he didn't want to change. I could see I would be putting my head in the noose if I went back—that even though I was sad I was better off single. At least the kids and I had food and a roof over our heads."

Finally Mickey said, "So you don't want to go back together and try again?"

Francine said, "No. We just can't make it."

Mickey got up. He had been serious; now he became jaunty. He told Francine that since she had left him he'd been living with a girl named Carol. If Francine didn't want him back, he and Carol planned to go up north to a town where Carol had friends.

Francine bit her lip and said, "Well, go ahead. Lots of luck!" But as Mickey left, she thought, "It still isn't over between us. Not yet. I know it and so does he."

Francine went on trying to find some meaning in her single life. Sometimes her spirits would rise and she would almost convince herself that better times lay ahead, but it was hard to imagine what they would be. She knew she wanted to love and be loved, but saw no possibility of it happening. "All my life I had heard that guys don't want other men's leavings. I felt I had already been used. I saw no way a decent man would want me and all my kids."

Sometimes, for the sake of change, Francine and the children walked up and down her block. To her surprise she encountered a woman she knew, the ex-wife of one of Mickey's friends. She was about Francine's age—twenty-three—and though she, too, had children, she seemed to be enjoying her freedom. She and a girl friend came over to Francine's apartment a few times. They told Francine about the evenings they spent at bars picking up men and invited Francine to come with them. At first she refused, afraid that Mickey would somehow find out and be angry. "I never felt sure he wouldn't suddenly show up. I still didn't feel free of him in any way."

Finally Francine decided to take a chance. She left the children with her new friend's baby-sitter and joined the expedition to the bar.

"Nothing much happened except that I drank. I wasn't used to liquor and it was a bad experience. We didn't get picked up in a way that amounted to anything. A couple of seedy guys bought a round of drinks and that was it. I couldn't see how it was such a big deal. We were out late, until they closed the bar. I got the kids and went home and was deathly sick. The next day my head hurt and I was miserable. I realized that even if I had met a guy I wouldn't have dared start a relationship of any kind. I couldn't until there was real finality between me and Mickey, and there wasn't, even though he was living with somebody else."

One day, as Francine had known he would, Mickey arrived at the apartment. He explained that he had just dropped in to see the children; his girl friend was waiting in the car. Francine's heart was pounding but she kept a cool manner. She told him the children were at Sunday school. Micky was cool, too. He asked if he could come back later. "Sure," Francine said. "If you want to. Come back this afternoon."

Mickey left, leaving Francine to deal with emotions that she knew were irrational—a longing to rush into his arms. Within half an hour Mickey returned. He'd dropped the girl somewhere. He shut the door behind him and they faced each other. He said, "How about it, Fran? Do you want to try again?"

Francine struggled to keep her voice level. She said, "Mickey, the kids and I are on welfare. If we live together I have to give it up. Will you get a job? Will you take care of us? That's all I'm asking."

Mickey bounded over and took her in his arms. "Sure I will, Fran," he said, kissing her. "Sure I will. I promise. This time I really mean it."

"I was real emotional and so was he. He'd missed the kids so much. I told him how miserable I'd been. Everything just came out: how afraid I'd been, how lonely, how I'd missed him. We made love and he held me and said, 'Everything will be okay.' He said that this time it would be a new start. We'd make a good life together."

Mickey moved his things into the apartment and found a job on a construction project. The morning he was to start work Francine got up early to pack his lunch. His work clothes were laid out, clean and ready. Mickey left, but returned quite soon. He said he had changed his mind about the job; he'd decided not to take it, but to look for something better.

After the first ardent days of their reunion, Mickey resumed the routine he'd followed before Francine filed for divorce. He was gone most of the day, presumably looking for work, but found nothing. The difference was that now it was Francine who received a weekly check and was able to pay the rent and buy groceries. She prudently postponed notifying the welfare office that Mickey had come back to live with his family, putting it off until he found a job as he'd promised.

Before long Mickey's absences stretched from all day to overnight and then to two, three, or four days at a time. He would come home to eat, pick up clean clothes, get a good night's sleep in Francine's bed, and then be gone again. Francine, swelling with pregnancy, was not currently to his sexual taste. Francine wondered where he was spending his nights. He told her that he was working on some vaguely defined project with his brother Donovan, who lived not far away with his wife, Alice.

"I walked down to her house one morning. She went to make coffee and I sat down at the table. There were dirty dishes. I looked into a cup and there was green stuff in it. I said, 'What's this?' She sort of laughed and said, 'Don't you know what that is?' Then it dawned on me. I had heard people talking about it, but I'd never seen any. It was marijuana. Alice told me that Donovan and Mickey and some other guys had been smoking it. I guess that's all they'd been doing these past weeks—just bombing around, smoking pot and drinking. I wondered why he'd come back to me if that was what he wanted to do. I remember thinking, 'Thank God, I didn't give up welfare. If he'd taken that job I'd have given it up and we'd be starving again.'"

Francine, now large and uncomfortable with pregnancy, realized all her hopes had been foolish. Another depression came on. "I remember day after day alone with the kids in that dreary apartment; being pregnant; getting up and walking from one room to the other; looking outside at the snow. I didn't dare take the trash out because the steps were covered with ice and I was afraid I would fall. The trash was piling up on the back porch. Mickey wouldn't touch it. Looking at it I felt helpless. I didn't want the baby I was carrying. I dreaded it. I felt awful for not wanting it. There was nothing to take my mind off it. This was the dead of winter. Days were gray and it got dark early. Sometimes Bill and Sharon would come over and that helped, but after they had gone I'd cry. Bill and Sharon had a good relationship. They were saving money to buy a house. They were working together. I'd think, 'Why couldn't my marriage be like that? What have I done so wrong that I don't deserve the same?'"

The landlord, who lived in the apartment below Francine, didn't like the situation. Mickey's coming and going, sometimes in company with Donovan, who was also unemployed, was not what he wanted on his premises. He told Francine he had taken her in because she had told him she was single, and that she would have to move. Francine looked vainly for another place. No one wanted to rent to a welfare mother seven months pregnant. At the end of the month the landlord became insistent. In desperation she decided to move in with Joanne. Mickey had been absent for days and the landlord himself transported her belongings and piled them on Joanne's porch. Francine and Joanne's combined households made a total of eight children under one small roof.

Christy had begun school. It was a half mile away. Francine walked with her and returned to pick her up. Francine had a winter coat, but no boots or mittens. Her hands and feet froze on every trip. "It was hell to be poor and have to do stuff like that. One day, on the way to get Christy, I noticed an empty house on Detroit Street. It was a little brown house and there was something very inviting about it. I stopped in and found the owner lived next door. His wife said he'd be home later. That evening I walked back to the house. I remember shuffling through the snow—it was really quiet and snow was falling. I kept thinking, 'Gee, I wonder if we could get that house?' I went in and talked to the owner. While we talked I was thinking, 'He's not going to rent it to me because I look too dowdy. I look poor, pregnant. I'm living with my sister. I'm on welfare. He's not going to give it to me.' We talked and he showed me the house. It was so nice! It had hardwood floors in the living room and dining room; there were two bedrooms upstairs and one bedroom downstairs, a dining room, a kitchen; everything was newly painted. I told him I would love to have it. He looked at me and hesitated. I waited. He smiled and said, 'Okay!' I couldn't believe it. I was so happy."

Mickey's whereabouts just then were unknown to Francine. He had come to Joanne's only once and not stayed long. Francine called Bill and Sharon. They moved Francine's belongings from Joanne's porch into the new house. Social services gave her an order for a stove and refrigerator, which Francine bought from a used-furniture store. Flossie and Berlin gave a bed they no longer needed and an old wringer washing machine, in exchange for which Francine gave Flossie a haircut, as she had often done in earlier days. Francine's mother also provided a few furnishings.

At last Francine had a tolerable place to live. When Mickey came to the house, her first thought was, "Here it goes again. I'm going to get kicked out." She told him he couldn't stay. Mickey retorted that he had a right to be with his children. Francine said that he could see the children whenever he chose, but that he couldn't live with them while she was on welfare. Mickey refused to leave and Francine lacked the courage to provoke a fight. He stayed that day and overnight. In the morning he seemed to feel he had sufficiently asserted his claim on his family, and left.

Francine was alone with the children when she went into labor. It was about noon and she was lying on her bed when the pains started. To her consternation, she found she couldn't get up. She hadn't expected the contractions to be so sudden and so severe. "I called Christy into the bedroom, and told her to go next door to the landlady and ask her to call a taxi. Christy ran. I lay there wondering would she find the landlady, would the landlady understand the message? Christy came back and I asked her, 'Did you call a cab?' Christy said, 'Yeah.' She looked so scared. I told her to get coats for Jimmy and Dana, that we were going out. Then I told her to take my hands and pull. Somehow that little six-year-old kid pulled me up off the bed. I got everybody dressed. It was February and icy cold. We were at the curb when the taxi came. The driver looked at me and his mouth dropped open. He said, 'What's the matter?' I said, 'I'm in labor.' He said, 'Oh no!' For a minute I thought he was going to drive off and leave us. I said, 'Look, you only have to take me down to my sister's; it's only a few blocks away.' He said, 'Okay,' and we all got in."

Before she left, Francine had put a note on her mailbox: "Got sick and went to Joanne's." By coincidence Flossie and Berlin came by shortly after she left and followed her to Joanne's house. They took Francine to the hospital while Joanne stayed at home with the children. By the time Francine got to the hospital, the baby was well on the way. For the first time Francine was drugged for childbirth. When it was over she remembered little about it, and for the first time felt no joy.

"When I woke up I didn't want to see the baby. All those months I had worried, cried, felt ugly, depressed, and thought, 'Oh my God, another baby; how can I do it?' Now that she was born I still couldn't face it. I was weak, beaten, hopeless. I just didn't want her, but I couldn't tell anyone that. When they brought her in she had a pink ribbon in her hair. The nurse said she had the longest hair; my baby was the only one they could put a ribbon on. The nurse went out and left me holding the baby. I started to cry. Nobody was there but me and her. I was crying because she was so tiny, so little and pretty. I thought, 'How could I not want her?' I started checking her fingers, and made sure she had all of her limbs and that she was okay. I started with her hands and then I ended up undressing her to look her all over, as though I were thinking, 'My goodness, maybe she doesn't have a toe!' I fed her and fell asleep with her. So that was over. I knew I wanted my kid."

Flossie told Mickey that the baby had been born. He came to the hospital, drunk, in the middle of the night, demanding to see his wife and child. The nurses wouldn't let him see Francine, but allowed him to look at the baby through the nursery window. He returned, sober, the following day. Francine told him she was too tired to talk and turned her face away.

"I had postpartum blues but I didn't tell anybody. I didn't know there was a name for how I felt. I didn't want to see anyone or talk to anyone. Mickey kept coming. I said, 'Why are you coming every day?' He said, 'Don't you want me to?' I said, 'No. I don't want to see you.' I really meant it. There had been a radical change deep inside me as though whatever it was that held me to Mickey had finally snapped. Perhaps I had lost my last illusions about him. I saw that instead of helping me he would always drain me. I didn't have the strength to take it anymore. I was terribly weak. I would try to get up and couldn't make it. I drew the curtains. I wanted to hide and cry in peace. I didn't want to go home. I felt safer in the hospital. I was so exhausted, so tired of everything. I couldn't bear to look at Mickey. All I could think was, 'I don't want to see you anymore. I don't want you in my life anymore.'

"The doctor came in on Friday and said, 'Do you want to go home on Saturday or Sunday?' I said, 'Sunday.' I didn't want to go home at all, but I had to.

"Mickey came to get me and the baby. He was cleaned up and sober. We went to his mom's to pick up the kids. I knew that by that time Flossie and Berlin were probably pretty hairy with the kids. They had taken them over from Joanne. Mickey brought us all back to the house on Detroit Street. Then I found that he'd moved in while I was in the hospital. We talked and I said I didn't want to try anymore. I asked him please to go away and leave us alone. He said he would get a job. He said, 'Couldn't we try again?' I put my head down and cried. I said, 'No. Not anymore!'

"I knew for sure I didn't want to! I didn't want to! I didn't want to! He went away, but he didn't stay away."

Francine brought the new baby, named Nicole, home to Detroit Street, determined to start life anew—without Mickey. Her love for him had vanished during the dark days preceding Nicole's birth, when she had recognized that Mickey would never be a husband, no matter how she tried to make him into one. Her despondency had been a time of mourning at the death of what she had for so long tried to believe was a marriage. Now it was over at last. Her depression lifted. Her loneliness and anxiety were gone. She rejoiced that she could lead an orderly life and that she and the children were no longer at the mercy of Mickey's whims.

Mickey and his brother Donovan, who was separated from Alice, were shacked up in a trailer with two women, but Mickey refused to leave Francine alone. He was out of work and drinking heavily. He came to Detroit Street whenever he chose, demanding to see his children, and Francine was powerless to keep him out. He told her she could get a thousand divorces, but she would still be his wife and the children his children. When Francine told him not to come any more he beat her, threw dishes around, and smashed the kitchen chairs. Francine was frightened, not only of Mickey, but of losing her lease if the landlord, who lived next door, saw violent scenes. She did her best, whenever Mickey came, to avoid a fight.

"Mickey saw that he could come in anytime he wanted and that there was nothing I could do about it. He made the divorce a farce. He called it nothing but a piece of paper, and that's what it was. He was at my house the day I was supposed to go to court to get the final decree. I left him to baby-sit while I went downtown. After I got the divorce things were no different than before. Mickey came and went as he pleased."

The divorce became final in April. In July, Flossie's adopted daughter, Vicky, came to stay with Francine. She had recently graduated from school and was looking for work. Francine had always loved Vicky and was glad to have her company. When Vicky had been with Francine several weeks, Vicky received a check. On the same day Mickey had driven her on a round of job interviews and she had been hired as a waitress. Francine, at that moment, was broke. She asked Vicky to give her ten dollars toward the household expenses. Vicky refused. She had bought a new uniform and had paid Mickey five dollars for driving her. She said she had very little money left over.

Francine lost her temper. "I said, 'Vicky, you're staying here and I'm paying your rent and feeding you with money that is meant for me and the four children. I need milk for the kids. I need soap to wash the dishes. I think you ought to contribute if you can!'

"Mickey was in the kitchen not saying a word. He had his head down on the table. He knew the kids didn't have any milk. I stood over him and said, 'What about you? They're your kids, too!' He said, 'Don't put me in the middle of this.' I said, 'Why not. You *belong* in the middle of it. You're their father. Don't you feel any responsibility at all?' Mickey got mad. He got up and left."

Vicky had a change of heart and gave Francine ten dollars. Francine went out to buy the things she needed. As she walked down the street, Mickey's car roared by.

The Accident

When Francine got back from shopping she found a message to call Sharon immediately. Sharon told her that Mickey had had a car accident and was in the hospital. No one yet knew how badly he was hurt.

"I began to tremble. I put the phone down and told Vicky, 'Mickey's hurt. He's in the hospital. I'm going there to see how bad he is.' Vicky was upset, too. She offered to stay with the kids. I grabbed my purse. 'Don't forget I have to work tonight,' Vicky said. I said, 'I won't forget,' and ran out the door. It was three blocks to the hospital. I ran all the way. I kept wondering, 'How bad is it?'

"I went to the desk in the emergency room and asked if they had a Mickey Hughes. The receptionist said, 'Yes.' In a minute a doctor came out and asked if I was Mrs. Hughes. He said, 'Mickey Hughes was brought in, but we couldn't do anything for him here, so we've sent him to the Ann Arbor Hospital.' I said, 'What do you mean you couldn't do anything for him? Is he that bad?' The doctor said, 'He's in very bad condition, but we don't know the whole story. You'll have to speak to the doctors at Ann Arbor.'

"I ran back to my house and told Vicky. I was shaking all over. Nothing like this had ever happened to me; the possibility of Mickey dying terrified me. I remembered that the girl at the hospital had said something about a collision at an intersection; that Mickey had run through a stop sign and hit another car. I thought, 'Maybe he was thinking about me screaming at him. Maybe he was thinking about the kids. Maybe all our troubles were bothering him.' I knew he wasn't drunk; he hadn't drunk anything at the house and it was still early. Deep down I felt responsible for the accident. I had got him mad and upset; he must have been thinking about all the things he was doing wrong—that I had told him he was doing wrong.

"I called Bill and Sharon. They came for me and we drove to the Ann Arbor Hospital thirty miles from Jackson. The whole Hughes family was in the lobby. Flossie was sobbing. Berlin was pale as a ghost. The boys had tears in their eyes. They were smoking and pacing. They said Mickey was in bad shape, but they didn't know any details yet. I couldn't stop shaking. I was afraid I might have hysterics, but I held on.

"A doctor came out and told us what was wrong with Mickey. It was a list as long as his arm. He said, he's got this broken bone and that broken bone. His diaphragm is ruptured. He's had a heart attack. And he listed a lot more. They were waiting for a surgeon to fly in from Chicago to do a kind of surgery that was very difficult. He said Mickey would go into surgery the moment the specialist arrived. Half an hour later we were told that the operation had begun. Mickey was in surgery for hours—three or four—while the family and I sat in the waiting room. When it was over a doctor came out and said Mickey had survived, but was in very critical condition. He was in a coma and might die anytime. The doctor said that one of us should be at the hospital all the time. Flossie and Berlin and Mickey's brothers were completely distraught. I put myself in their place. Suppose I lost a son? I felt terrible beyond words. Their suffering; Mickey's suffering; it hurt me like a physical pain."

Francine didn't go back to Jackson that night. Wimpy and Lillian offered to pick up the children at Francine's house so that Vicky could go to work. The rest of the family stayed at the hospital. "Everyone was together. There was a feeling of closeness, of doing the best we could for each other. There was no question but that I was part of it. It never occurred to me to turn my back and desert the family when they needed me.

"Around midnight Mickey regained consciousness. I was the first one he called for. A nurse came to us and said, 'He's awake now and he's calling for "Fran" . . . which one of you is Fran?' I followed her. It was awesome . . . dim lights, long corridors, silence. We went into a room where Mickey lay in a crib surrounded by machines and tubes and bottles. A heart machine was hooked to his chest. The needle on the dial was flickering as though his life was flickering. There was a tube in his throat and a machine that went in and out, in and out, like a bellows to make him breathe. One leg was uncovered. It looked swollen and awful. There was dried blood behind his ear and in his hair. I thought, 'My God, he's never going to make it.' He opened his eyes and looked at me. He couldn't talk because of the tube in his throat. He moved his hand out to me, like saying, 'Hold my hand.' When I took his hand he began to cry and I did, too. I stood there thinking how awful it was; that nobody deserved this. Was he really that bad? Was this his punishment? He was still so young. I prayed he would have another chance. I thought, 'If we hadn't argued maybe it wouldn't have happened.'"

Francine never went back to her house on Detroit Street. She stayed at the hospital for the next forty-eight hours while Mickey's life hung in the balance. By then Flossie had gone back to Dansville and taken the children to her house, where Vicky helped to care for them. When Flossie returned to the hospital she told Francine that there was an apartment vacant in a duplex next to her house on Adams Street. She urged Francine to move there so that the family could be together, and it would be easier to arrange for them to take turns going back and forth from the hospital. Francine agreed.

The fact that Mickey had survived thus far was encouraging, but he was not out of danger. He had had abdominal surgery and his spleen had been removed. His legs were broken and in casts. He had a head injury that was described to Francine as a "swelling on the brain." The doctors said they still wanted a family member present at all times. That Francine would share in the vigil was taken for granted by everyone, and she made no objections. She felt obliged to consent to whatever was asked of her, anything that would lessen the family's worry and grief. "I didn't even go home to move my things out of the Detroit Street house. His brothers packed them and took them to the apartment in Dansville. I gave Flossie the rent money and she made the arrangements with the landlord. Two days later I walked into my new apartment for the first time. It was a dingy, broken-down place. Whoever had moved my things had left them sitting in a heap in the middle of the floor. Then I realized what I'd done. I'd given up my home and had to start all over again."

The family arranged a routine of bedside vigils. They decided that Francine should be at the hospital every other day, going there at ten o'clock in the morning and staying until someone came to relieve her at ten the following morning. Flossie, Berlin, and the brothers divided their twenty-four-hour shifts among them, but Francine's time on duty was unrelieved. Day after day she sat by Mickey, ready to hold his hand if he should open his eyes. During the long nights she catnapped curled up in a chair. She was always exhausted. Her days at home were spent in a frenzy of hard work, putting things away, cleaning the apartment, and looking after the children. She could barely catch up with the housework and get a little sleep before it was time to go back to Ann Arbor to take up her post at Mickey's bedside. Since she had no car, Berlin or one of Mickey's brothers drove her there. Too hard-pressed to take stock of the conflicting emotions building up within her, she pushed aside thoughts of what the outcome might be.

Mickey slowly improved. He was moved from intensive care to a private room, but he continued to need drugs to relieve his pain. He was disoriented and had a fixation on Francine. He wanted her beside him day and night. Whenever he woke he would call her name. His voice, urgent and panicky, calling, "Fran! Fran! Come here, Fran! Where is Fran?" made her heart swell with pity. "Here I am, Mickey, right here," she'd say, and come to hold his hand.

Francine came to believe that it was her love that was pulling Mickey through: "The more I would promise him and assure him that I loved him, that I would be there, the better he got." A dozen times a day Mickey would reach out with his good arm and pull her to him to ask if she loved him. Always she answered, "Yes," and felt a stab of guilt because she knew that the love she had once felt was gone. Now it was his pathetic dependency that she couldn't turn her back on. "Even though he got better, he clung to me. They decreased the medication, but he still acted confused. Every time I went home he'd raise a ruckus. He'd say to whoever was there, Flossie or Berlin, 'Go call Fran. She hasn't been here since I've been sick. Why doesn't Fran come to see me? She's my wife!' In order to calm him down they would pretend to go to the telephone and call me. Then they'd tell him that I'd be there in a little while. One night I was sitting in his room and he dozed off. He woke up and said, 'Who are you?' He was looking right at me. It scared me. I said, 'I'm Fran.'

" 'No, you're not. You're not my wife. I want Fran.'

" 'Mickey, I *am* Fran. Look at me! What are you talking about? C'mon.'

" 'You're not Fran. Go call my mom and dad. You call them and tell them to come up here. They'll tell you you're not Fran. I know you're not Fran. Fran don't look like you!' "

Francine got up and took his hand. As she put her cheek next to his, petting him until he relaxed, she felt icy with a new kind of fear.

After a month Mickey was well enough to sit in a chair. He was moved to a ward and the doctors promised that in another week or so he could go home. His head had cleared, but he still had moments of acting in a way Francine could only describe as "weird." He knew where he was, but his memory was cloudy and his attention span short. Francine talked to the psychiatrist who had examined him. The doctor refused to predict the outcome. "Is he going to stay like this?" Francine asked. "Probably not," the doctor said, "but we don't know. He could be that way for six months or six years." Francine thought, "God! What am I in for now?" When thoughts of her divorce and her freedom went through her mind she pushed them aside.

"I couldn't have walked out on him. It would have been as hard for me to walk out on him as to walk away from one of my own children. It would have been like saying goodbye to my kids, telling them, 'So long, I'm not going to be your mother any more.' "

Forty days after the accident Mickey was ready to go home. He would need a hospital bed for a few more weeks. Francine's apartment was too small to hold one, so one was set up in Flossie's living room. No one in the Hughes family asked Francine if she was willing to continue caring for Mickey. From the moment she agreed to move next door to Flossie and Berlin in Dansville, her compliance had been taken for granted, and Francine could not bring herself to protest.

Flossie and Francine discussed Mickey's home care with his doctors, who told them that Mickey's physical recovery had been miraculous. He was still pitifully thin—down to 110 pounds from a normal weight of 185—and had casts on his legs and a pin through one elbow, but they predicted he would regain almost normal use of his limbs. They were more guarded about his psychological state. "Don't baby him," the psychiatrist told the two women. "He'll be dependent as long as you let him! To a great extent the outcome depends on how you handle him at home."

Francine didn't go to Ann Arbor when Flossie and Berlin went to bring Mickey home. She was sitting in the yard, waiting with the children, when they returned. Berlin parked the car. Flossie pulled out a folding wheelchair and Mickey slowly swung into it. The children gathered around, gazing with interest at his casts. Berlin pushed the chair up the cement walk to the front door. "No! No!" Mickey protested, irritably. "I want to sit out here, out in the yard with Fran." Berlin wheeled Mickey's chair beside Francine's.

Flossie and Berlin and the children gathered around, talking. Mickey wanted to know where his brothers were. Would they be over soon? Flossie discussed the dinner she was fixing for Mickey. Francine was silent. "I was thinking, 'My God, am I supposed to take care of him the rest of my life? Everybody expects me to—his brothers, my sisters-in-law, Flossie, Berlin, Mickey himself. I'm in prison. Can I leave? How could I? What would the kids think of me if I walked away and left their father? Could Mickey take it? Would he get sick again? Die? Look at him; he's so thin, so pathetic. If I said I was leaving now he'd go to pieces; his parents, his brothers would just go up in smoke. They'd think I was horrible, with no feelings.'"

Francine got up. It was time to pick up the baby from her nap. "Fran," Mickey called, "come back. Stay here with me."

"Okay, Mickey. I'll be right back." She walked across the yard to her own apartment, thinking, "Why do I have to go back? Why do I have to do everything I'm told?" She picked up the baby and returned to sit beside Mickey. "Inside I was crying. A voice was saying, 'Leave! You know you want to leave! You've done what you had to do. You don't owe any more! Get out now!'"

Mickey said, "Fran, I'm thirsty. Get me a Coke." Obediently, Francine got up and went to do as he asked.

In the days that followed, the doctor's orders not to baby Mickey were ignored. His mother and father, and his brothers, when they came to see him, hung on his slightest demand. But it was Francine's attention that Mickey wanted every moment, and if she didn't respond rapidly enough Flossie or Berlin reproached her. Francine wanted to hire a nurse—whose time she would pay for—to take some of the work load, but Mickey wouldn't hear of it. Francine nursed him: baths, changes of dressings, bedpans, and meals, and at the same time took care of her own household of four.

Francine's apartment was separated from the Hughes house only by a grassy yard. She wore a path between the two. "I had to run back and forth all day, cooking and feeding the kids in my house; dragging laundry over to Flossie's and back again; watching the clock for Nicky's naps and bottles, for Mickey's bath and meals. It was September and there was a late heat spell. I was wet with sweat all day. I had no time to sit down and my feet swelled. I was bone weary, harried and hassled and hot. I'd never really got over the physical exhaustion of the pregnancy, and then the siege of forty days at Mickey's bedside. Sometimes when daylight came and I opened my eyes I'd think I couldn't get up."

After several weeks the cast was taken off Mickey's leg. He began to move around, shakily, learning to walk again. His head had cleared, but his personality still showed the effects of his accident. He was nervous, fretful, unable to concentrate. Reading or watching TV quickly bored him. He wanted people around him constantly, most of all Francine.

"I'd leave him for a few minutes, and he'd start to holler, 'Fran! Fran!' He'd just keep yelling 'Fran' until I came back to see what he wanted. Flossie or Berlin were always calling me, or sending one of the kids over to my house with the message 'Mickey wants you!' It didn't matter if it was something they could take care of themselves. I was supposed to drop whatever I was doing and come running."

The day came when Francine rebelled. She hadn't planned it, but suddenly, when she had been summoned over and over within a few hours, she stood in Flossie's living room where Mickey and Flossie sat before the babbling TV, and announced, "I'm going home and I'm going to stay home! I can't take it anymore!"

She turned and went out the door. The screen door slammed

behind her. She heard Mickey shouting after her to come back, but she didn't turn her head. The screen door slammed again. Mickey, supporting himself on one crutch, was following her. Flossie was screaming that he might fall, ordering Francine to turn around, to help him before he got hurt.

"I just kept walking. I walked right past Berlin, who was in the yard. His jaw dropped and then he was yelling, 'You can't do that!' I said, 'Yes, I can!' Mickey was following and calling, 'Fran!' All I could think of was, 'I'm going home and I'm staying there. I'm not running back and forth any more. I'm not going to kill myself any more. None of them are killing themselves. Why should it be only me?'"

A moment after Francine reached her house Mickey opened the door and hobbled inside. He stood, leaning on his crutch and scowling angrily as he looked around the cramped kitchen that served as a living room as well.

"What a *dump*!" he said.

Francine glared back. "Well, Mickey, it may be a dump, but as of this minute it is my home. We've been living here, me and the kids. I've been paying rent here and I don't have any other home."

"It's a stinking little shack!"

"If you're living in a shack, by God, it's your home," Francine shouted. "What else do you call it? Do you call it 'the shack I frequent once in a while'? No! It's your home!"

"It's still a dump!" Mickey said. "I can't live in a place like this."

"Okay, fine! Go on home and stay up there with your mother."

"Yeah," Mickey snarled, as he eased himself into a chair. "I'll do that."

He remained in Francine's kitchen until Flossie came over to see what had happened. It wasn't much of a place, he told her, but since Fran refused to go back and forth between the two houses anymore, he'd decided to move in. Flossie and Berlin promptly brought over the things he would need. Francine didn't protest. "At least it would be easier taking care of him there than running back and forth. That night he went to bed in the double bed. I got in beside him and lay awake for the longest time, just rigid. He still had a cast on his arm and wires in his stomach. I was afraid I'd roll over on him or bump him or hurt him. I was afraid to move."

Dansville

Mickey spent his convalescence sitting in the comfortable chair he'd chosen, watching Francine do her work. His left arm was still in a cast. The enormous scar across his upper abdomen healed slowly. He hated the inactivity. Nothing pleased or amused him for long. He read the papers, dropping them in sheaves on the floor, watched television, and sometimes played with Nicky, who loved to climb into his lap. When she irritated him he called Francine to take her away. Two or three times a day he walked across the yard to his parents' house, giving Francine an hour or so of peace.

Flossie continued to fuss over Mickey. He wasn't eating well and she worried that he wasn't gaining weight fast enough. She came over daily to check on what Francine was cooking and to make suggestions on his care. Although it was easier for Francine to have Mickey and the children under the same roof, she still had to work to the limit of her strength. "I had two babies under two, plus Jimmy who was five, and Christy, seven. I had always done all the work—cooking, shopping, cleaning, laundry—but now that Mickey was sitting there all day, watching me and wanting my attention, too, it seemed twice as hard. I never had a minute to myself. I was exhausted all the time."

As Mickey grew stronger Francine tried to wean him from his dependence on her. He resisted every step. "He was like a kid who doesn't want to grow up. One morning he was in the bathroom while I was very busy in the kitchen. He yelled, 'Fran! Come here!

Brush my teeth!' I went to the door and said, 'Mickey, I can't drop
what I'm doing. You can do it yourself!' He said, 'I can't!' I said,
'For God's sake, Mickey, squirt the toothpaste on the brush and
stick it in your mouth!' He said, 'I've only got one hand!' I said,
'You've got fingers sticking out of the end of your cast. Hold the
toothbrush with those fingers. With the other hand put toothpaste
on it. Lay the toothpaste down. Pick up the toothbrush with your
good hand and put it in your mouth!' His mom and dad didn't like
it when I told him to do something for himself. His brother Wimpy
heard me yell, 'Mickey! Do it yourself!' and bawled me out: 'Francine, you shouldn't talk to Mickey like that after all he's been
through!'"

Gradually Mickey improved physically, but Francine and the
children remained his single interest.

"He was constantly on my back about something. All day long,
he watched every move I made, saying, get this or get that; do this
or do that; get that child; that kid is crying, shut her up! People
came to see him, but it was hard for anyone to talk to him. He'd
suddenly break in on whoever was talking to holler at me or the
kids. Visitors took me aside and said, 'My God, Fran, how do you
stand it!' People stopped coming. Sharon and Bill hardly ever came
anymore. Then it was just me and Mickey and the kids and the
Hughes family, closed into this little corner of Dansville. My family
didn't come. Mickey didn't like having them around."

Francine looked forward to the day when Mickey would go back
to work. His frustration at being housebound and idle was under-
standable. He was only twenty-six years old. He had been strong,
vigorous, quick in his movements. It hurt Francine to see him walking painfully, using a cane and holding his broken arm at an awkward angle. Francine was trying to revive her love, but her feelings
failed to respond. All she could feel was pity. Mickey was eager to
resume their sex life. Though Francine complied, she found she had
become strangely numb. In their better days—though less and less
toward the end of their marriage—she had enjoyed sex. Now she
rarely did. Mickey took it for granted that Francine loved him as
before. Wishing it were so, she told him that she did.

A turning point in their relationship came when Mickey asked
Francine to marry him again. "When he asked me to do that something inside me just rebelled. I'd given up everything else, but I

couldn't give up that last little shred of independence. At first I tried to put him off. I'd say, 'Mickey, it's too soon. Let's not talk about it.' He kept at me about it and I kept saying no. Finally he realized I wasn't going to do it. He got mad. He hit me for the first time since the accident. After that his gratitude dried up and disappeared."

Two months after his discharge from the hospital the cast was taken off Mickey's left arm. The doctors at the Ann Arbor Hospital congratulated him on the success of their repair job and told him that in time he would regain full use of his arm. Now that he was almost well Mickey was increasingly bored at home. As soon as he could walk easily he began to spend afternoons at a saloon called the Wooden Nickel near the Dansville crossroads a few blocks away. It was a man's hangout, where he could always find someone willing to have a glass of beer and a game of pool. At first Francine was so glad Mickey had found something to take him out of the house that she didn't worry about his drinking, but before long he started to come home not only drunk, but angry and mean. Francine had a foreboding that he would start beating her again. She thought, "He's going to take revenge on *me* for all the pain he's been through and show me he's still boss."

A few weeks after Mickey started drinking the outbreak came. It was near supper time and Francine was cooking when Mickey came home from the Wooden Nickel. Francine glanced up as the door opened. The look on his face told her trouble was coming. He came over to where she was working at the kitchen counter.

"What the fuck are you doing?"

"I'm fixing some pork chops. They've been thawing."

"How're you gonna fix 'em?"

"I thought I'd just fry them." Francine kept her voice soft. She knew she was in danger.

"I don't want any greasy pork chops! All you know how to fix is greasy food."

"I thought you liked pork chops, Mickey. You always ate them before."

"That was before. All you do is fix garbage anyhow."

Mickey pushed Francine aside and opened the freezer section of the refrigerator where he kept his beer stein. He liked beer very cold. He took a can out of the lower compartment, opened it and took a drink, filled the stein and put it back in the freezer. He turned to Francine. She saw the danger signs she knew so well: eyes glittering, the muscles in his jaw twitching as he clenched his teeth. She felt her pulse begin to race, her stomach contract, her head pound. For nearly a year she had been free from fear of Mickey. "Please God, no," she thought. "I can't stand to have it start again." Desperately, she tried to divert him.

"The kids are hungry, Mickey. I'll give the pork chops to the kids. I'll fix you something else."

"Goddamn right you will," Mickey said. "You're my wife. Go get ten divorces. It won't do you any fucking good."

"I'm acting like your wife, Mickey," Francine said. "I don't know what more you want." She moved to the cupboard and began to look among the cans. "How about some tuna fish? I could fix that real quick."

Mickey followed her. He was breathing hard.

"I wouldn't marry a fat ass, fuckin' bitch like you. Not for a million bucks. How do you like that, whore?"

Francine turned, saw the blow coming and ducked, but his fist hit her on the side of the head. She put up her arms, crying, "Please, Mickey, please!" and dodged around the kitchen as he followed, pummeling her whenever he caught her. Francine saw Christy standing, crying, in the doorway. "Get Grandma," Francine panted, and Christy ran out.

A moment later Berlin arrived, followed by Flossie. They tried to pull Mickey away from Francine. Mickey lunged at Berlin and threw him against the wall. Flossie flew at Mickey and he struck her across the face.

Francine ran out into the yard and stood uncertainly. Where could she hide? It was early twilight. Lights were on in the houses across the street—the Johnsons' and the Quembys'. She thought of running to one of them. What would she say? I'm just dropping in? It would be absurd. The battle in the kitchen was still going on. She could hear Mickey cursing, dishes crashing, and Flossie screaming at him to stop. Francine decided to run to the Hughes house and call the police.

She was in Flossie's kitchen, telephoning, when she heard Mickey at the side door. She started for the back door, but he caught her and dragged her outside into the yard. Francine fought back, twisting, trying to hit and kick. Flossie and Berlin tried, ineffectually, to intervene. Mickey knocked Francine down and was pummeling her when a squad car drew up. As the deputies approached, Mickey got up and swung on them. It took them several minutes to bring him down. He continued to struggle, biting and kicking as they held him pinned to the ground. He seemed to have gone out of his mind with rage. One of the officers put in a radio call for an ambulance. Now Flossie, hysterical, shrieked that the officers were hurting Mickey, that he was a sick man, and tried to loosen their grip. Then the ambulance came and Mickey, still fighting, was strapped to a stretcher and carried away.

Francine led the frightened children into the house and told them to wash up for supper. They asked no questions. Francine's hands were shaking as she prepared their food. Her head ached, but her mind was empty with shock.

Flossie and Berlin came over. Berlin kept a somber silence while Flossie, still near hysteria, questioned Francine about how the "racket" had started. What had Francine done to get Mickey so riled? Had he been hurt fighting the police? Francine called the Sheriff Department in Mason, which had sent the police car, and learned that Mickey had been taken to the hospital. She called the hospital and was told he was unhurt. He had been given a sedative and was sleeping. Unless charges were brought against him, he would be released in the morning. Reassured, Flossie and Berlin went home.

Adams Street is normally a quiet street and Mickey's outbreak did not go unnoticed. Mrs. Alice Quemby, a cheerful, friendly woman in her fifties who lived directly across from Mickey and Francine, first became aware of trouble when she glanced out the window and saw a little girl standing in the street crying. The child had no coat or shoes. Mrs. Quemby recognized her as Christy Hughes and felt surprise. She knew Francine took good care of her children. From her chair by the window Mrs. Quemby had a good view into Francine's uncurtained kitchen and watched as Mickey beat Francine. When Flossie and Berlin arrived Mrs. Quemby saw Mickey throw his father against the wall and slap his mother across the face. Shocked by the scene, Mrs. Quemby hurried next door to her neighbor, Donna Johnson. She found Donna at her own window from which she, too, could see into the kitchen. The two women were fascinated spectators as the drama ran its course.

They saw Francine run across the yard to the Hughes house and Mickey drag her outside and beat her; they watched the police arrive and the struggle that ended when Mickey was strapped down and taken away. Mrs. Quemby and Mrs. Johnson both liked Francine. They liked Mickey, too, but they were appalled by the violence they had seen.

In the morning Berlin went to the hospital and fetched Mickey. He pulled up at Francine's door and helped him out of the car. Mickey shook his father off and limped into the house. He looked pale and sick. Briefly, he was contrite. He hugged Francine in silent apology. Francine pushed him away and told him that if he beat her again she would leave.

Mickey's eyes hardened. "Where do you think you're gonna go?" he asked contemptuously. Francine had no answer. Mickey took a shower and changed his rumpled clothes. Within an hour he was feeling well enough to walk to the Wooden Nickel for a game of pool.

During the next few months Mickey beat Francine several times. Sometimes he stopped after one or two blows; sometimes he went on until she ran over to his parents' house. Mickey would follow and, while Francine hid, Flossie and Berlin would calm him down. In the morning he would have nothing to say about what had happened and Francine knew it would be unwise to remind him. Flossie and Berlin also wanted to forget each episode as quickly as possible. Flossie told Francine she should make allowances for Mickey and not get him mad.

After a beating Francine found it hard to think straight. All day aching bruises would remind her of the nightmare scene of the day before. She felt spent, unable to pull her mind together. She would think, "I've got to leave. I can't let it happen again," but then, as she went a step further and tried to think of a place to go, the obstacles would seem insurmountable and she would give up the struggle.

One day in March, while Mickey was at the Wooden Nickel, Francine decided to go across the street to visit a neighbor, Laura Eifert, who lived opposite Flossie and Berlin. Laura was about

Francine's age—twenty-five—and also had young children. She was a slim, blue-eyed woman with a perpetually harried look. Her husband, Chris, a burly blond factory worker, was a friend of the Hughes boys and shared their pleasure in drinking, women, and fast cars. Francine had no time for anything more than brief visits with Laura and never confided in her. She guessed that Chris probably thought that beating his wife was something Mickey had a right to do.

Francine had timed her visit in midafternoon, so she would be able to get home before Mickey returned.

Mickey came home early and found the house empty. Francine, sitting with Laura, heard his voice, cursing and shouting her name. She looked out the window and saw him in the street. Gathering up the children, she ran out. Mickey seized her. "What were you doing over there?" he demanded. "You've got no business going out. You don't go to nobody's house unless I tell you." Francine ran into her house and Mickey followed. "He was so mad he was crazy. More crazy than drunk. He started hitting me and I ran into the bedroom and locked the door. He was wearing big boots. He kicked the door open and came after me. He knocked me down on the floor and started kicking me. He kicked and kicked and kicked. The kids were shrieking. I was screaming with pain. I thought those big boots would break my bones. Finally he quit long enough for me to get up and run out of the house. I ran to Flossie's house and she hid me in a closet. I waited in there, my heart pounding, my body aching all over, wondering if he would find me and start in again."

Mickey, confused as to where Francine had gone, pushed his way into Alice Quemby's house. Donna Johnson was sitting with Alice. They had been watching the drama through Alice's picture window. As Mickey burst in, Donna got up in fright and ran out the back door, while Alice's husband, Leonard, angrily shoved Mickey out the front door. Mickey ran next door to Donna's house. He burst in on Donna and her husband, demanding to know where Francine was hiding. Donna's husband put him out and called the police.

Just then Wimpy pulled up in his car, summoned by Flossie, and intercepted Mickey in the street. As Wimpy talked to him, Mickey calmed down. When, a few minutes later, a police car pulled up, the officers found the brothers leaning against Wimpy's car. One of the police, a burly deputy with a Syrian name, Mohammad Abdo, remembered Mickey as the man he had strapped to a stretcher a few months before. "What's the trouble?" he asked Mickey.

"There isn't any trouble," Mickey said. "But if I find my wife there will be. If I find her I'll break her fucking neck."

Wimpy took over the task of explaining. He told Abdo that when Mickey got drunk he went crazy, but that he was calm now, and promised that he, Wimpy, would take charge of him. Abdo noted that Mickey seemed in complete control of himself. He watched as Mickey got into Wimpy's car and the two brothers drove away.

Abdo went to the home of the elder Hughes, where his partner was questioning Francine, and told her she could bring charges against Mickey by going to the office of the prosecutor in Lansing and swearing out a complaint. Francine asked what would happen then. Abdo said that Mickey would be charged with a misdemeanor. He might be put on probation or be sentenced to thirty days.

Mickey spent the night at his brother's house. When Wimpy brought him home, Mickey apologized to Alice Quemby and Donna Johnson, but not to Francine. Everyone—Flossie, Berlin, Wimpy, and Mickey—ignored Francine's swollen face and the purple bruises on her arms and legs. There were worse bruises hidden by her clothes. Christy saw them and said, "Oh my God, Mom." Then she, too, said no more. Dana, three years old, was fascinated. He came to her several times and asked, "Can I see your bruises, Mommy?" Francine raised her skirt and the little boy stared for a long time. "Daddy kicked you?" he asked, and Francine answered, "Yes." "I knew it was terrible for a little child to see a thing like that, but I couldn't hide it and I couldn't explain."

From then on, fear of Mickey was always at the back of Francine's mind, whispering caution, shaping the smallest decision. Only once in that particular period of her life did a stronger emotion take over.

"One morning Mickey was sitting in his chair watching a TV show. Nicky was very tiny, wearing diapers, and toddling around. I gave her some soda pop in a plastic cup. She took it and walked toward Mickey's chair. Just as I looked to see what she was doing, Mickey yelled, 'What are you letting her come over here with that for?' He raised his foot and kicked her over. She fell back and the pop went all over her face and up her nose. Without even knowing what I was doing I began to pound on Mickey with my fists. I was yelling like crazy, 'Why did you do that? How can you do that to a little kid?' I completely blew up. I felt like pounding him to a pulp! Mickey didn't hit back. He just put up his arms and took it."

For the first time in her life Francine had shown that she, too, could be seized by ungovernable rage.

A few weeks before this last outbreak of Mickey's, Francine had made arrangements to buy a house. The apartment was dingy and cramped. When Francine heard of a government program that helped low-income families buy homes, she applied for a loan. It was granted and she began to look for something suitable. She wanted to put some distance between herself and her in-laws and hoped to buy a house in Jackson. Mickey and Flossie preferred that she stay in Dansville.

Flossie discovered that the house at 1079 Grove Street, next door to her own, was for sale and urged Francine to buy it. The house fitted Francine's needs. The price was $16,000. It had two bedrooms upstairs, a bedroom and bath downstairs, a living room, dining room, and kitchen. There were two enclosed porches and a detached garage. Mickey liked the house. The garage would be convenient as a place to keep his tools.

"It's better for you to be close so we can help you with the kids," Flossie urged. "Suppose something happened to Mickey? Suppose he had to go to the hospital? It would be better if you were near."

Francine let herself be persuaded. "I look back and I still don't understand why I did whatever they told me to. The family would sit around discussing what would be best for the kids, best for Flossie, best for Mickey. Nobody said anything about what would be best for me. What I wanted didn't matter to anybody, and I would put my feelings aside as though they didn't deserve to be considered."

When, only a few weeks before they were to move into the new house, Mickey beat her, Francine's misgivings about tying herself to Hughes territory in Dansville intensified, but it was too late to turn back. She signed the final papers for the loan. Berlin and Flossie helped move her things. Mickey put his favorite chair and the television set in the position that suited him best in the living room. He took over the garage, filling it with his tools, and locked it with a combination lock. He complained that their double bed was sagging and told Francine to buy a new one. Francine objected that she couldn't afford a new bed. "You better do it, and do it soon," Mickey ordered, "or I'll take the goddamn mattress off and burn it. Do you want to sleep on the floor?"

Flossie solved the problem. She offered to sell Francine a pair of twin beds she wanted to get rid of. Francine paid thirty dollars for them and Flossie, in a burst of generosity, threw some bed linen into the bargain. The twin beds were moved into the downstairs bedroom of the new house and for the first time in their life together Francine and Mickey slept in separate beds.

It was spring when Francine and Mickey moved into the Grove Street house. Dansville's backyards were bright with forsythia and daffodils. Grove Street is on the edge of town. From her front door Francine looked into an open lot filled with shrubbery and trees breaking into green leaf. There was also open space to the right of her house. Except for Flossie and Berlin to her left, Francine now had no close neighbors. It gave her a feeling of freedom. The children could play outdoors without complaints from the landlord. If there were fights with Mickey she would be spared the humiliation of having them in public.

The new house gave a lift to Francine's spirits. She made flower beds and the children helped her plant her first vegetable garden. As she worked to make the house livable, painting cupboards, making curtains, sanding the floors, she was able to feel for the first time in nearly ten years of marriage that her labor was going into something that was really her own. Above all, the house was a decent home for the children. Francine had given up a great many dreams, but never her determination to give her children the best she could and the hope that their lives would be happier than hers had been. Francine felt that she could not have asked for better children. At eight, Christy was an intelligent, loving child, whose high marks in school filled Francine with pride. Six-year-old Jimmy looked like his father: a thin boy with narrow blue eyes. He was sensitive, and Francine felt especially protective of him as the child most affected by ugly scenes. When Mickey cursed, Jimmy watched silently, his expression stricken. Three-year-old Dana was sturdy and handsome, with his mother's heart-shaped face and tilted nose. His father had been absent or ill during so much of his babyhood that he had never formed the attachment to Mickey that Jimmy had. Nicky was an adorable two-year-old, and Mickey's favorite.

By summer, the first anniversary of his accident, Mickey seemed normal physically. However, because of his internal injuries he could not do the heavy construction work he had done before the accident, and the Social Security doctors classified him as totally disabled, assuring him a pension for life. Francine had assumed that when he was well enough to work he would find another trade. He was already a good auto mechanic and she thought he might work in a garage. Mickey toyed with the idea but did nothing about it, and his idle days stretched on. When Francine began to push him, he told her that he would be damned if he would do any rotten menial work for low pay. As a bricklayer he had earned eight dollars an hour, and he vowed he wouldn't work for anything less.

During Mickey's illness Francine had run the house and paid all the bills with stipends from Welfare and Aid to Dependent Children. Mickey's pension was an almost equal sum, but week after week Mickey's money disappeared into his pocket while Francine paid all the bills, feeding and housing six people on an allowance that was barely enough for five.

If Francine asked Mickey to contribute to the household expenses, he laughed. "If you need more money go to welfare. I'm not your husband. You divorced me. Don't come to me!"

On a hot summer afternoon in August, Mickey had another attack of fury. Francine ran to Flossie's to call the police. Berlin stood at the kitchen door to block Mickey from coming after Francine. While she was at the phone she heard Mickey shouting and banging on the door. "I heard Berlin say, 'Give me that knife!' and my knees shook. Mickey got the door open and I could see him and his dad struggling in the doorway. Berlin was small, but he was tough. He got the knife and sailed it into the weeds. Mickey got past him and lunged at me. He grabbed me by the hair and pulled me out to the yard. I was screaming and fighting. He got me down and was punching me. Oh God, it hurt!"

While Mickey punched and kicked Francine, Flossie and Berlin watched helplessly. Chris Eifert, in the house opposite theirs, heard Francine's screams and came to help. He knocked Mickey down and held him while Francine got to her feet. A police car pulled up and Eifert let Mickey get up. Still raving mad, he fought the deputies and they arrested him.

One of the deputies questioned Francine about what had happened and she told them that Mickey had chased her with a knife in his hand. The deputy turned to Berlin and warned him: "If I ever come out here and see your son with a knife, trying to stab somebody, I'd have to shoot him." With a murderous look Berlin replied, "I'll kill any son of a bitch that kills a son of mine."

As before, Mickey had been arrested not because he beat Francine, but because he had fought with the deputies. When they had taken him away, Francine went to her house and took stock of her injuries. Her mouth was bloody and her eyes beginning to puff up. She was trembling with shock. She thought, "I can't stand it anymore. I've got to get away. But how? Where can I go? If his parents can't protect me, who can?" Inflicting her troubles on her mother or sisters was out of the question. Suppose she brought charges against Mickey; what would happen then? The answer was discouraging. Flossie and Berlin would regard it as gross treachery. Mickey would serve a short term, if any, and when he came out his vengeance would be terrible. Francine put the thought of appealing to the courts out of her mind.

Flossie, still highly upset, came over to talk to Francine. She talked on and on, saying she didn't know what got into Mickey to carry on so, but she thought it must have something to do with his accident and the injury to his head. Francine said yes, ever since his accident he seemed crazy when he was in a rage. In fact Mickey's rages since the accident were not different, only more frequent than before, and they had intensified until he seemed totally out of his mind. A few times since the accident Mickey had been willing to talk about what had happened between them, and Francine had asked, "Why, Mickey? Why do you do this to me?" He always answered that it was because she had gotten him mad; if she would mend her ways it wouldn't happen again. Francine begged him to see a doctor, a psychiatrist. The suggestion infuriated him. "See one yourself. You're the one who's crazy. You're the one needs help!"

Mickey would never voluntarily go to a psychiatrist, but Francine thought he could be committed if Flossie and Berlin would agree. As Flossie talked about something wrong with Mickey's head, Francine felt a surge of hope. She began to talk about getting help for Mickey. Flossie agreed, but when Francine spoke of committing him, she drew back in anger. Mickey wasn't *crazy*, she said, he was still sick from the concussion of the accident and the aggravation of not being able to work. Yes, Flossie said indignantly, she wanted Mickey to see a doctor, but not a doctor for crazy people, and she didn't want Mickey locked up in a hospital. Her voice trembled with hysteria.

"I see what you're after," she cried. "You just want to put him away—out of sight!" Weeping, she went out, slamming the door behind her.

The next day, without saying anything to Francine, Flossie and Berlin got Mickey at the jail and took him to the hospital in Ann Arbor, where he was examined by the doctors who had treated him the year before. When Mickey came back late that afternoon he looked pleased with himself. He grinned as he told Francine how the doctors had examined him thoroughly. "They said there wasn't a goddamn thing wrong with me," he told her. Smiling in triumph, he opened the refrigerator and poured himself a beer.

In the months that followed, the idea that Mickey should be committed to a mental hospital often recurred to Francine, but she saw no way to bring it about without his parents' help. Since she was no longer Mickey's legal wife, it seemed impossible for her to do it against their wishes, but Francine knew that Flossie and Berlin felt that "craziness" was shameful—something to hide.

Even to have Mickey arrested wasn't easy. "I'd call the police in the middle of the night. I'd do it when there was a lull in his hitting me; usually while he was getting another beer. Sometimes Christy would call them. When Mickey realized the cops were coming he'd simmer down. He'd sit in a chair and tell me what he was going to do to me as soon as they left. The cops would come and find me standing there crying, everything in the house smashed up, the kids out of bed and scared to death, and Mickey sitting with a smirk on his face. I'd have a bloody nose and a smashed lip. I'd be hysterical after being tormented for an hour or so. I'd say, 'Officer, I need protection. He's going to kill me. Can't you take him away?' The officer would say, 'We're sorry, ma'am, but we didn't see him do anything, so we're not allowed to arrest him. Go down to the prosecutor's office in the morning and swear out a complaint.' The officers would tell Mickey to behave himself. Then they would leave. If Mickey was tired enough he'd go to bed. If he wasn't he'd have another beer and hit me some more."

At the beginning of December, four months after he had chased her with a knife, Mickey was arrested again. He had been goading Francine since early in the evening. As he drank beer after beer his fury worked up until he was "crazy mad." He hit Francine and knocked her to the floor. When she lay there he prodded her with his foot until she got up; then he knocked her down again. Francine had been sobbing. Now she screamed. Twisting on the floor she caught a glimpse of Christy, ashen-faced on the stairs. Mickey yelled to Christy to get back in her room and Christy disappeared. Francine got up and tried to get to the telephone. Mickey held her off and yanked the cord from the wall. Then he lunged and caught her. Francine fought and pleaded. Mickey's eyes were wild. He was gritting his teeth. "I'm gonna keep it up," he said, "until you're sorry you were born." Francine twisted loose. Dodging around the table she reached the front door and escaped into the dark. Barefoot, wearing only a nightgown, she ran across the yard praying that Flossie's door would be unlocked. It was. Francine locked it behind her.

Berlin was alone. Flossie was at work on the night shift at a nursing home. Mickey did not immediately follow, but Francine knew he would come. "Call the police," she sobbed, "I think he's going to kill me." Berlin went to the telephone. Francine hid in a closet in the bedroom. "It was dark. I could hear my heart beating. I was shaking and gasping for breath. I heard Berlin on the telephone and then I heard Mickey's voice—heard scuffling and banging at the front door. I prayed that the police would come in time. I knew Berlin couldn't stop him from killing me. Mickey was too strong. I heard Berlin say, 'She ain't here,' and Mickey cursing and saying, 'I know she is.' I heard something break and Mickey running through the house, shouting, 'Where the fuck is she . . . where is that goddamn whore?' My teeth were chattering. I buried my face in my hands. Then I heard Mickey go away; somehow Berlin had gotten him out of the house."

Francine stayed in the closet until she heard the voices of policemen in the kitchen. Berlin gave her Flossie's housecoat to cover her nightgown and she sat down on a kitchen chair. A deputy told her Mickey had been arrested and was in the police car outside. He asked her to tell what had happened. Francine tried to answer, but nausea swept over her. She got up and vomited in the sink. She sat down and, feeling herself begin to faint, put her head down on her knees. The deputy asked if she wanted to go to the hospital. Thinking of the children, terrified and alone, Francine said no. Her head pulsed with pain; nausea convulsed her stomach. She vomited again. The deputy called for an ambulance and Francine agreed to leave. She thought she might have an internal injury.

Francine was taken to the emergency room. An intern examined her without comment. He told her he could find nothing seriously wrong and gave her a sedative. She was free to go home, but had no car. She telephoned Wimpy. He came to the hospital and took her to his house. He telephoned his mother, who by then had returned, and told her Francine was in no condition to go home. Flossie agreed to baby-sit. Francine's sister-in-law, Lillian, gave Francine some hot milk and helped her to bed.

When Francine opened her eyes in the morning her first thought was, "Now they've got to admit he's crazy—that he's dangerous—that he's going to kill me. Now is the time to get him committed. It has to be done quick, before he gets out of jail." At breakfast she tried to talk to Wimpy about it. Wimpy was shocked. "You can't do that to Mick! He's no more crazy than I am; he just got a little drunk, that's all!" Wimpy had recently stopped drinking and joined the church. He drove Francine to Dansville. On the way he insisted that the solution to her problem was simple. She had only to persuade Mickey to go to church and God would straighten him out.

At home Francine saw the children off to school. As always after a night of hell, she felt sick and numb. She longed to lie down and let her mind go blank, but there was no telling when Mickey would be released and then it would be too late to carry out her plan.

Francine found Flossie, Berlin, and Wimpy at the kitchen table having coffee. Wimpy had evidently told his parents that Francine wanted Mickey committed. They were discussing it when Francine came in. Berlin sat silently, listening while Flossie talked. Flossie said she knew there was something wrong with Mickey, something that the doctors in Ann Arbor had failed to find . . . something to do with the injury to his head, and that they should try to find out what it was, even if it meant going to a psychiatric doctor. Wimpy didn't agree. "Just because the poor guy has some problems doesn't mean he's crazy," he said.

Francine began to cry. "That's great for you to say," she said bitterly. "You don't know what it's like! You're his family! You've got to do something. *I* can't take it anymore!"

"She's right," Flossie said. "I'd rather have him in the hospital than in jail. When he's mad he don't know what he's doing. He ought to see a doctor and get help before he hurts somebody real bad."

Wimpy protested that Mickey would never voluntarily go to a hospital. "I know that," Flossie said, "and I think he ought to be committed, like Francine says."

Suddenly Berlin pushed back his chair and got up, his face an angry mask. "If you was ever to have Mickey committed," he said harshly, addressing Flossie, "I'm leaving. I ain't gonna stand for such a thing."

Flossie glared back with determination. "I know what's right!" she snapped.

Berlin turned away without a word. He took his coat from the peg and went out the door. It slammed behind him. There was silence in the kitchen. Outside there was the sound of Berlin's car as he started it and drove away. Flossie looked stunned.

Mickey returned later that day, but Berlin stayed away for three weeks. During that time Flossie crumbled. She announced that she was ill and took to her bed, where she remained until, on a Sunday morning, Berlin took his place in the household once more. Francine saw his car parked at the curb and shortly afterward saw Flossie and Berlin leave, dressed for church. After church Berlin came to Francine's house and tucked an envelope in the mail slot. Francine opened it and found a bill for fifty dollars' damage to the door that Mickey had broken during his pursuit of her. Francine tore it into little pieces. The possibility of committing Mickey was never discussed again.

Soon after Berlin returned, Mickey beat Francine again. She called the police and Mickey incautiously hit a deputy. For this Mickey spent thirty-six hours in jail. During that time Francine brooded, groping for a solution. Her ideas were incoherent. She was ashamed of living with a man who was not her husband. She feared Mickey—she often hated him—but he could still arouse her pity, and she thought that if he would stop drinking their lives might still be salvaged. She seldom felt love, or tenderness, or sexual desire, but Mickey remained a part of her. He gave her nothing, and very little to the children, yet he had rights to his family that she felt powerless to take away. Living with Mickey meant unceasing fear, but the thought of life without him also filled her with fear; she needed a husband, the children needed a father. At the thought of casting Mickey out the earth tilted beneath her feet.

In the two years since his accident Mickey had abused her more horribly than ever before. His parents knew it. His brothers and their wives knew it. All of Dansville knew it. Her own mother knew it. No one, not even the police or the intern who treated her at the hospital, expressed indignation on her behalf. Each episode was buried as quickly as possible, as though to mention it would be obscene. Were they implying she was guilty, too? He shouted at the children, but he didn't beat them. What had she done that made him hate her so?

Beyond the emotional conflicts were practical dilemmas. Suppose she tried to leave? The house in Dansville was hers; she was committed to monthly payments. If she stopped paying she would lose everything she had put into it. She couldn't pay the mortgage and also pay rent somewhere else. Where could she go? Her brother, Bob, lived out of the state with his wife and children and couldn't take her in. Joanne's house was already crowded. Her mother, widowed, in poor health, easily upset, was a weak reed. Her family might help her briefly; then she would have to find a home of her own. Wherever she went Mickey would move in and she would be worse off than ever; she would have lost her house and find herself once more living with Mickey in a rented slum.

When the children were asleep and the last dish washed, she threw herself into bed in the strangely quiet house and surrendered. There was nowhere she could go, nothing she could do. Before she went to sleep she said a prayer. "Dear God, please give me some hope." In the morning Mickey came home and their life together resumed.

Mickey's brief stay in jail left him unchastened and angry. He blamed Francine for having called the police. He didn't beat her immediately but Francine knew he was brooding, and she tried to

avoid anything that would set him off. It was the Christmas season.
There was excitement and tension in the air. The children were
home from school. When the TV was turned on the sound of
carols and jingling bells leaped out. Mickey yelled at the children
to turn the damn thing off. The yard was heaped with snow and
there was no place outdoors for them to play. Mickey stayed longer
and longer at the Wooden Nickel. At home he kept a case of beer
on the back porch and his stein was always in his hand. In the evening, when Francine had washed the dishes and put the food away,
Mickey would order his supper. He wanted no leftovers; it had to
be something newly cooked.

On Christmas Day, Francine put up a plastic tree. She and the
children trimmed it. She had presents for them and cooked a tur-
key. The saloons were closed and Mickey stayed home. It was a
peaceful day. Later on they joined his brothers at Flossie and Berlin's house. Mickey was sober. Relaxed and festive, he ate mince
pie, joked with his brothers, and held Nicky on his knee. Francine
thought, "Why can't he be like this at home?"

On the day after Christmas, Mickey went to the Wooden Nickel
early in the day and returned quite drunk. The cheer of the evening before had vanished. He fumed for a while and then began to
beat her. "I'll teach you to call the cops on me," he snarled. "Don't
you dare call the cops ever again." For several hours, with intermis-
sions while he filled his beer stein or rested in a chair, glaring at her
and calling her names, he tormented Francine. "Don't you ever
dare put me in jail again! I'll break your fucking neck."

When at last he let her go to bed, she cried herself to sleep. Thus
ended the year 1973. It was only three years since she had filed for
divorce, but her independent life in the house on Detroit Street
seemed eons ago.

Of the next year, her tenth since she married Mickey, Francine
remembers that as life with Mickey grew harder to bear she returned to the religion that had comforted her as a child.

"I had a little cross that Jimmy got in Sunday school. It was yellow and had black writing on it, 'God is my refuge and strength.' I
hung it over the sink; every day I looked at it and said the words in
a whisper. I joined the church that Flossie and Berlin attended and
went with them every Sunday. I taught Sunday school. I loved

teaching. Those couple of hours were the happiest of my week. I prayed every day, asking God for help. 'Dear God, You know what is going on. I believe that somehow, in some way, You are going to change things.' I believed if I prayed hard enough He would. Church, and my faith that God's help would come, kept me going for months. But Sunday after Sunday I came home from church with the kids and found Mickey sitting there, drinking, waiting to harass me, with words if not with hitting. I had prayed so hard, believed so deeply that God would help me, that when He didn't my faith began to slip away. Even going to church didn't make me feel better. After a while I gave up. I didn't have the heart to go anymore."

Francine wanted to go to work. She thought that it was wrong for a family to be on welfare indefinitely. If Mickey wouldn't work she thought she should. When she asked Mickey's permission to look for a job he angrily said no. He said the children needed her at home and she would spend all she earned on baby-sitters. It was summer and Francine's sister Kathy, now seventeen, was out of school. Mickey despised Francine's older sisters—Joanne because she had given Francine asylum; Diana Lynn because she was feisty and had told him off when he yelled at Francine—but Kathy was demure and gentle, with large brown eyes and a soft voice. Mickey liked her; she was the only one of Francine's family he would allow in the house. Francine sounded out Kathy and Kathy agreed to come to Dansville for the summer and take care of the kids if Francine found a job.

Francine and Mickey had no car. Without a wage earner in the family and with Mickey's accident record, it was difficult to get credit. Mickey decided to allow Francine to work if she would not confess to welfare that she was employed, but use her earnings to buy a car. Francine agreed. She found a job in a plastics factory in a neighboring town. Kathy came to stay. Within a few weeks Francine had bought a car on credit, a Ford Maverick only two years old.

Francine found that going to work was like fresh air. She hadn't realized how deep and chronic her depression had become until it lifted and she could remember how she used to feel on days when it was good to be alive.

For the first weeks of Kathy's visit Mickey was on his good behavior. Then his internal weather changed. He found fault with everything Francine did, cursing her, pounding the table until plates and glasses rattled, throwing things across the room. Francine had never described to Kathy—or anyone else in her family—the full violence of Mickey's temper. Kathy watched, wide-eyed and miserable. As Francine knew was inevitable, Mickey came home drunk one afternoon. A fight started. When he began to hit Francine, Kathy tried to intervene. Mickey yelled at Kathy to mind her own business. Kathy picked up the telephone and told Mickey if he didn't stop she would call the police. Mickey snatched the telephone away and pulled back his fist. "You'll get it too if you don't get out of my way," he threatened. Kathy stared back, her soft eyes resolute. Francine, watching, held her breath. Mickey dropped his hands and turned away. Kathy put down the phone. She went upstairs and packed. Francine drove her home to Jackson. "I'm terribly sorry, Fran," Kathy said, crying, "but there's nothing I can do to help you and I can't stand watching, so I have to leave."

Francine did not go back to work. Mickey decided to take over the payments on the car, and it became his. He used it to go farther afield than the Wooden Nickel, finding other hangouts and now and then staying overnight with women. Francine no longer felt any jealousy, but Mickey's infidelity gave an ironic twist to his refusal to leave her. Then Joanne reported to Francine Mickey's boast —relayed through mutual friends—that stung Francine even more. Mickey had bragged that Francine supported him. "I'll never leave her," he'd said. "She pays for everything. I've really got it made!"

Now that the car was his, Mickey allowed Francine to use it only with his permission. If she wanted to go somewhere she had to describe her itinerary and her reasons. If Mickey was feeling mean he might decide she couldn't go. If she was late coming back, especially from a visit to any of her family, it was the pretext for a fight.

In the spring, Francine's sister Diana Lynn was to graduate from high school. She had dropped out and gone back. It was an important family occasion and Mickey knew how much Francine wanted to be there. He agreed to let her have the car, and Francine made plans to pick up her mother and take her to the ceremony. While she was dressing to go, Mickey began to glower and call her sisters names. Francine gave no answer. She dressed quickly, hoping to get away before he changed his mind about the car, and hurried out with little time to spare. The car wouldn't start. She went inside and appealed to Mickey for help. He smiled a strange smile.

"Try it again," he suggested. "Give it more gas."

Francine went out and tried again. She pictured her mother waiting for her. Still the car wouldn't start. Francine's hands began to shake and her lips trembled.

Twice more she asked Mickey to help her start the car. "Just keep trying," he advised. Finally, Francine, watching the clock, saw that it was too late to go. She telephoned her mother and explained the disappointment. When she hung up Mickey got up and reached in his pocket. He held a plastic cap in the palm of his hand.

"What's that?" Francine asked.

"The distributor cap," Mickey said. "It's pretty hard to start a car without it. It's in my pocket and that's where it stays. I want you to remember that's *my* goddamn car."

Day after day, month after month, Mickey's drinking increased and with it his compulsion to dominate his family by cruelty.

At first Francine had been the prime target of his anger. Now the children were included, and this was an added torture for Francine. When the children's presence bothered Mickey, he locked them out of the house or sent them up to their rooms. If he was particularly angry he wouldn't let them come down even to use the bathroom. If they crept down the stairs he yelled at them to get back up and they would scamper back like mice. At ten, Christy was overweight, and it annoyed Mickey to see her eat. He nagged her until she left the table in tears. Jimmy or even Dana might be suddenly slapped across the face. He ordered them all about, snapping his fingers for attention and pointing at the door with a scowl. The children became wary and stayed out of his way. It was not so easy for Francine to escape.

"Mickey would sit around drinking and watching me and getting lustful feelings. Sex was one of the duties I had to carry out. I'd get up in the morning and think, 'I've got to do this and I've got to do that, and Mickey is going to want sex. After I clean the house, mow the lawn, and do the laundry, Mickey will want sex; then I can do something else.' There was no caring; no love. Sometimes after six weeks or more I'd get sexual release, but instead of feeling good, I felt dirty. I'd hate myself for letting it happen. He would even want sex after he'd been doing awful things to me all day—been drunk, cursing me, calling me names, hitting me, making the kids cry. Afterward I'd go in the bathroom. I'd want to scream, but I'd put a washcloth over my face and sob without a sound. I didn't want the kids to know their mother was in the bathroom wishing she was dead.

"For a while I'd feel despair. Then I'd think, 'You can't spend your whole damn life in this bathroom with a washcloth in your mouth. You've got kids out there depending on you.' I'd wonder if God was testing my strength and my faith in Him. I'd say a prayer and feel better for a while."

Sometimes, instead of going to the bar, Mickey stayed home all day drinking. As the day wore on and Mickey became restless and ugly, Francine would know that there was a terrible night ahead.

She remembers a night that set the pattern. It began with Mickey talking about everything that angered him: politics, blacks, busing, jobs. As he got drunker his tirade became more personal; Francine was a rotten wife, rotten in bed, and stupid. "You're so fucking dumb!" he said over and over. He was glad he wasn't married to her. They were in the kitchen and he pounded the table. When Francine tried to leave, he ordered her to sit down. Mickey had a comfortable chair. Francine sat on a straight chair. When she shifted position he yelled at her to sit still. Francine froze, praying that talking wouldn't turn to hitting. From time to time Mickey got up to walk about, to get a beer, or to lean menacingly over her and glare into her eyes. He turned off the light. Now she could see him only in the dim light from the living room and it made the scene even more nightmarish. Hour after hour her captivity went on.

"He talked on and on, bragging he was a male chauvinist pig and daring me to say anything about women's rights. I kept quiet. He'd get up and lean over me and I'd shrink up inside, not knowing if he was going to hit me. If I tried to get up he'd say, 'Where do you think you're going? I told you to sit still.' I said, 'Mickey, please let me go to the bathroom.' He said, 'Make it quick!' When I came back he stood over me. 'Now sit there, bitch, like I told you.' So I sat there for another couple of hours. My body ached all over. I was so tired I'd think, 'How long can this go on? Am I such a bad person that I deserve this?'"

There were other nights when Mickey not only talked but hit.

"He'd hit me until I ran out the door and then he'd come after me, chasing me. I felt like a hunted animal; stumbling in the dark in the yard, mud squishing under my feet, my heart pounding, just scared to death. I know what an animal feels when it is hunted. I'd try to hide. He'd find me. One night I hid in Mickey's old car that was parked out in back. I huddled down in the bottom, praying. He came right to it. I heard him coming—heard him opening the door. He dragged me out and back into the house. He threw me into a chair and said, 'You sit there until I tell you to move.' He sat down close to me and began to call me all sorts of names. He asked me to admit what he said was true.

"'You know you're a no-good fuckin' bitch, don't you? Why don't you answer me? Answer me or I'll knock your teeth down your throat.'

"I didn't say anything.

"'Fat-assed cunt! Why don't you say it?'

"I sat there crying and he hit me across the face. Then he asked me again. Finally I said, 'Yeah.'

"'Yeah what? What are you?'

"'Yes, I am one.'

"'A what? Say it!'

"'I'm a no-good fuckin' bitch.'"

As time went on and Mickey's rages grew more frequent, his parents were no longer willing to help her. Berlin intimated that Francine was as much at fault as Mickey, that she goaded him into beating her. "Don't come running over here no more," he told her. "You take care of your own goddamn problems. If you acted right maybe he would act right too!" Flossie agreed with Berlin that if Francine were a better wife Mickey "wouldn't get started up." Francine had never liked Berlin. She thought him mean and cruel. He had slapped her children for small misdeeds and his miserliness went to incredible lengths. She felt betrayed by Flossie, to whom she had once tried to be a good daughter. Now Flossie seemed blind to Francine's suffering, but offered Mickey aid and comfort whenever he wanted it.

In truth, Francine knew, Berlin and Flossie were almost as helpless as she was when Mickey was in a rage. Berlin, now in his fifties, had contracted emphysema and had to give up factory work. He stayed home, doing odd jobs. Once proud of his hardbitten toughness, he was bitter over his failing strength. Francine knew he hated to admit that he was no longer any match for his son. On bad nights Francine felt there was no help anywhere. Mickey kept the car keys in his pocket. If Francine reached for the telephone he snatched it out of her hand. The idea of knocking on a neighbor's door was unthinkable. She was at Mickey's mercy; for hour after hour she could only dodge, and plead and endure, praying for the ordeal to end.

Her thoughts would race. "In the morning I'm going to leave. Somehow I'm going to leave. I can't let him do this to me again. I'll run away."

Always Mickey read her mind.

"Don't think you can leave me, you bitch. Not ever! You ain't *ever* gonna get rid of me! I'll find you wherever you go and when I do it won't be pretty. I'll kill you inch by inch. I'll kill your fucking ass!"

Mickey repeated those words over and over until they were drummed into Francine's mind. They seemed to give him particular satisfaction. Sometimes he would add, "Don't think I *wouldn't* kill you. I don't give a shit what happens to me. I got nothing to lose."

As the months of torture went on, Francine became aware of strange physical symptoms. She felt nausea. Sometimes she could eat nothing; at other times she was ravenously hungry and ate until she was sick. She felt starved for air, suffocated, unable to take a breath deep enough to satisfy her. Her pulse raced and she was dizzy even lying down. It occurred to her that she might have cancer. "I'd imagine I was going to die an awful death and think, 'Oh God, then the kids will have no one but Mickey!'"

There were psychological changes, too. Francine, who had always loved being with people, became afraid of them. She, who had once thought herself pretty, felt ugly, unattractive, stupid. She avoided speaking to neighbors on the street. In the supermarket if she saw someone she knew she looked the other way. She thought everyone in Dansville must despise her for living a degrading life. Vague fears came over her. It frightened her to go out of the house or to drive a car. She felt inadequate, helpless in every way. Rather than borrow Mickey's car, she asked him to drive her wherever she had to go.

These fears engendered a greater fear—that she would break

down, go insane, and be sent to a mental institution. "As my strange feelings got worse I'd ask myself, 'How long can you stand this? What does it take to drive a person crazy?'" Francine had never known anyone who had a nervous breakdown. She went to the library and looked up the symptoms. She found descriptions that fitted her so perfectly that she was more afraid than ever: depression, crying for no reason, anxiety, nervousness, being afraid of people. She pictured herself locked up in an asylum with bars on the windows and thought, "I'd rather be dead!"

She had to fight suicidal impulses. "I'd feel so low that death seemed like a way to get peace. A voice inside my head would say, 'If you kill yourself it will be all over. You won't have to live like this day after day.'"

Francine found that she could talk herself out of the depths of a depression: "I'd shut myself in the bathroom and say, 'Fran, you've got so much to live for.' I'd think about the children, each one of them, Christy, Jimmy, Dana, Nicole; how much each one needed me and loved me and how I loved each one. I'd look out the window and say, 'Think of the things you have to be thankful for, even if they are just ordinary things. The sky is blue. It has white clouds in it today. Aren't they pretty? Isn't the world beautiful? God created these things: flowers, children, the sky, the clouds.' Little by little I'd get my mind off my troubles. I'd think about what I was going to plant in the garden or how I was going to make new curtains. I'd go about my work, cleaning the house or whatever, keeping these good thoughts in the forefront of my mind. Mickey would be in the living room, sitting in his chair drinking beer. When I went through the room I wouldn't look at him. It would be like he wasn't there."

In this way Francine was able to endure another day, another week, another month with Mickey but she knew she was losing ground. Every time Mickey attacked her, verbally or physically, she felt herself sink a little lower. Looking in the mirror she saw herself as an old hag. "I was twenty-seven, but I looked fifty. I'd wonder, 'How long can I take it? How long can I go on living like this?' One day I thought, 'Fran, you can go on like this until you crack up, or you can do something about it. Which are you going to do?'"

As she looked back, Francine's bitterest regret was that she had left school without a diploma. It was the turning point after which everything in her life went wrong. One day a newspaper ad announcing free adult-education courses for high-school dropouts caught her eye. After toying with the idea for days, she found the courage to telephone the number given in the ad. She was told that she was eligible and if she completed the course would be given a GED—a General Equivalency Diploma. Though Mickey had harped on her stupidity—it was one of his favorite taunts—until she almost believed him, Francine remembered that she had once trusted in her native wits. She had no specific plan as to how she might use a GED, but it seemed a glittering prize. The question, of course, was whether Mickey would let her enroll in the classes.

She broached the subject on a morning when he was sober and in a good mood. "You can do it if you want to," he said with a shrug, "but you won't ever finish. You're too dumb."

"Well, I'll try. The classes are only two hours in the morning. I'd be able to get the kids off to school and be back before Dana gets home."

"What are you gonna do with Nicky?"

"I could take her with me. They let mothers do that. They have a room for little kids to play in."

Mickey thought it over. Francine could see him hesitating.

"Please, Mickey. If I got my GED I might be able to get a job that paid well; I could go on to some kind of training school. You see ads for them all the time: 'High school graduates earn high pay!'"

Mickey gave a grudging assent. "Go ahead," he said, "but you ain't never gonna finish. I just bet you ain't." When he said that, a voice inside Francine answered silently: *"Oh yes I will!"*

Mickey allowed her to use his car to drive the seven miles to the classroom in Mason. It had been eleven years since Francine had sat behind a school desk. She was trembling as she walked in. The teacher was a woman, not much older than Francine. She looked friendly. Francine glanced around at her fellow students. They were a mixed group: long-haired, bearded young men, women older than herself, a couple of working men in their thirties. No one stared at her. No one seemed to notice her or think it odd that a housewife should aspire to a high-school diploma.

After a few days Francine's nervousness vanished. The work, preparation for examinations in English, mathematics, science, geography, and literature, was easier than she expected. She had always read rapidly and with enjoyment. The classroom, with its orderly atmosphere, seemed a haven of peace and sanity. She hated to leave when the two hours were up. The course lasted two and a half months. Long before that Mickey became restive with her absence from home. When she didn't drop out as he'd predicted, he began to harass her. "He'd bitch about the gas I was using. He'd say, 'You're not gonna use up all my gas on me.' I'd say, 'No, Mickey. I won't. I put two dollars' worth in your tank.'

"'Two dollars' worth! That ain't enough.'

"'It's all I've got right now. But I'll fill up your whole tank as soon as I can.'

"Then Mickey would think of something else. He'd say, 'You better be here by the time Dana gets out of school. I'm not gonna watch him. I'm just gonna take off.' I'd say, 'I'll be back.' I was so scared he'd say I couldn't keep on. He'd say, 'By God, you better keep this house clean, too. You ain't just gonna go to school and come home and sit down on your big fat ass!'"

As the term came to an end Francine knew that it was not a moment too soon; Mickey was on the verge of forcing her to quit. As she took her final exams Francine felt sure of herself in English and literature. She worried about her other courses. When she found that she had passed every course she felt a thrill of pride that lifted her off the ground.

Mickey received the news with a noncommittal grunt; then he asked, "Well, now that you've got it, what are you gonna do with it?"

"I'm not sure. I was thinking about nursing school."

Mickey hadn't forgotten Francine's promise of a well-paid job.

"You better do something," he said. "You ain't gonna do nothing after I let you go."

Francine had already made inquiries and been advised to take a job as a nurse's aide so that she would have references when she applied to nursing school. She found a part-time job on the weekend night shift at a nursing home that specialized in long-term care. After a full day's work at home she took a brief evening nap before starting to work at midnight Saturday and again on Sunday night. By Monday morning she was groggy, but it was the patients, not the grueling hours, that defeated her.

"It was a terribly sad place because nobody there would ever get better. I came to realize that if you're a nurse there is so little you can do. Some of the nurses were really tough. I didn't want to become like them. Every week I felt more depressed. The lift I had gotten out of my schoolwork was gone. I knew I could never be a nurse."

After several dreary months, Francine quit the nursing home. Her spells of dizzyness and suffocation had abated while she was at school. Now they became worse. Convinced that she was physically ill, she went to a general practitioner, Dr. Jon Desquin, in Mason, and described her frightening symptoms. Dr. Desquin examined her and told her that her heart and lungs seemed all right, and that her sensations sounded like anxiety symptoms. Francine insisted that there must be something deeply wrong, and Dr. Desquin ordered more extensive tests.

When Francine returned, Dr. Desquin told her the tests were negative and that her problems were of emotional origin. "What's going on in your life?" he asked. Francine sketched her life with Mickey. Dr. Desquin raised his eyebrows.

"Why don't you throw the guy out?" he asked. "Or take the children and leave?"

Francine began to cry as she described how Mickey had threatened to kill her if she tried to get away. As for throwing Mickey out, it was equally impossible. If she succeeded he would move next door to his mother's house and harass her from there.

Dr. Desquin shook his head in commiseration and wrote a prescription for a tranquilizer. Francine asked the doctor if he knew of any agency that might give her help in getting out of her predicament. He suggested she try the local mental-health clinic and made arrangements for her first appointment. When Francine left his office she felt better. Having at last told someone of her circumstances seemed to be a sort of progress.

A week later Francine kept her appointment at the mental-health clinic in Mason. In order to get there she had to ask Mickey to drive her. Mickey was suspicious of anything having to do with mental health, but grudgingly agreed to take her. At the clinic Francine talked to a psychologist. She described the horrors of her life and the circumstances that held her trapped.

The psychologist asked if she felt angry. Francine said no, that mostly she felt afraid. The psychologist said, "You've got a lot of rage bottled up inside you. Where do you think it's going? Out the window? It's all that terrible anger that makes you feel you can't breathe." This was a new idea to Francine. It was a relief to know what caused her smothering feeling even if it didn't cure it. When the interview ended Francine again had a feeling of minute but tangible progress. Mickey was waiting for her, his curiosity aroused.

"Did they find out what's wrong with your head?" he wanted to know as they drove home. "What did you do in there anyway?"

"Nothing much," she said. "We just talked."

"What about? About me?"

Francine said no, they had just talked about her shortness of breath and about her childhood; but Mickey remained suspicious.

A week later Mickey took Francine to her second appointment. During this interview the psychologist suggested that Francine take assertiveness classes. He told her that she was letting people walk all over her and that she would never be able to end the situation until she learned how to stand up for her own rights.

As before, Mickey was waiting outside the clinic. "All the way home he questioned me about what the psychologist said. I kept trying to make up stuff to put him off. At home he went on badgering me. Finally he wormed it out of me about the assertiveness classes. He blew up and said I couldn't go to the clinic any more; if I went again he'd beat the shit out of me. I canceled my appointment. Actually I didn't see how going to assertiveness classes would be any help. I didn't assert myself because I was afraid. How do you assert yourself with a maniac? Stamp your foot and say you won't take it? A minute later you're lying on the floor getting stomped to death."

No Exit

Escape was constantly in Francine's thoughts.

"I would try to think through each step that I would have to take. I would make a plan to take the kids and go someplace like San Francisco. Then I would examine every detail, looking for flaws. It was like doing a puzzle. I would see that one way wouldn't work and go back to the beginning and think it through again."

In every plan money was a central problem. She barely managed to live from one welfare check to the next. Saving money was impossible. If she left on the day her check arrived, she would have enough to buy airline tickets to California, but there would be little left over. How would she get to the airport? She might take Mickey's car, pick up the children at school (making up a story to tell the teachers), and get to the airport just in time to catch the plane. If she left as soon as Mickey went to the Wooden Nickel, he wouldn't discover she was gone until midafternoon. What would he do then? He would report his stolen car to the police. They would find it at the airport and Mickey would begin his pursuit. He would ask about her at each ticket counter and someone would surely remember a woman with four children and tell Mickey their destination. Francine scrapped this plan and began another fantasy in which she went by bus to Detroit, and flew from there. It would be harder to trace her in a big, busy airport, but no matter how or where she went, Francine knew the children would make her conspicuous; they would make it easy to follow her trail.

Then Francine would imagine her arrival in San Francisco. She knew nothing about it except that it was a large, beautiful city and the weather was warm. Weather was important because she would have to leave without luggage. What would she do when she got there? Go directly to Social Services and ask for help. Yes, but what if there were a waiting period before they would give her money? Suppose she didn't have enough money to buy meals or rent a room or take buses while she waited for her first welfare check? Francine would imagine herself standing on the street with four hungry, frightened children and no one to turn to for help.

Mickey was certain to follow her. Quite possibly the police would help him look for her. She might be charged with kidnapping and the police in every major city alerted to arrest her. What about the debts she would leave behind? The mortgage on the house—was leaving it behind a crime? Would the welfare authorities in San Francisco notify the office in Michigan of where she had gone? Would Mickey check with them? Of course he would. She was certain he would dig until he got just one little piece of information, perhaps no more than a card pulled out of a file with the word "San Francisco" and her name. Once he knew what city she had gone to, he would haunt the welfare offices and check all the schools until he found her.

Though the children were the biggest obstacle in any escape plan, Francine never seriously considered leaving them behind. Sometimes she thought of leaving them while she got established somewhere, but how would she get them back? Kidnapping would be impossible. She would be caught and sent to prison. A legal battle was beyond her means and if she had deserted her home, even for a little while, the courts might decide against her. Meanwhile, what would be happening to the children? Whenever she imagined them in Mickey's care—or in Berlin and Flossie's—she knew that leaving them behind was something she could not do. She would take the children with her or she wouldn't go at all.

Sometimes Francine was able to imagine that she had overcome all obstacles, reached San Francisco with the children, and set up a home. The fantasy always ended in a single scene:

"I'd picture myself in this strange place, lying in bed, scared to death, thinking, 'Right now Mickey is hunting for us. Right now he is on our trail. He's found out where we live. Any minute he's going to come in that door.' I'd hear his voice saying what he said so many times when he was beating me: 'If you ever leave I'll find you and kill you. I'll kill your fuckin' ass. I've got nothing to lose.'"

At this point in her imagining, Francine's terror would be so great that she would wipe the entire scheme out of her mind.

When Francine did flee from home, she went suddenly, without any plan at all. It was the spring of 1976, a few days before Easter. Mickey began to harass her in the morning. By afternoon he was beating her. Francine called the police and two deputies arrived. Mickey stormed around the living room, cursing and threatening to kill Francine as soon as the deputies left. Francine, bruised and trembling, exhausted by anger, pain, terror, and tears, watched helplessly, praying Mickey would swing at a deputy and be arrested, but he was in a crafty mood and kept to verbal abuse. At length the deputies tired of the game and told Francine she had better leave.

Francine telephoned her mother. Her sister Kathy answered. She offered to come for Francine and the children. The deputies stayed until Kathy arrived. As Francine and the children went out the door, Mickey shouted after them: "I'm gonna come after you. I'm gonna come after them kids!"

Francine's mother had been in an automobile accident and her leg was in a cast. She also had a bad heart. When Francine arrived and saw the anxiety on her mother's face, she knew she couldn't put her through a long ordeal. Francine called the Jackson police, told them her ex-husband had threatened to kill her, and asked for help. The officer who took the call seemed unimpressed. He said there would be a police car in the area and advised her to call back if Mickey actually threatened her.

Moments later Mickey was banging on her mother's locked front door. Francine called the police again; this time the officer agreed to send a car. Francine told Mickey, through the door, that the police were on the way. He shouted that he wanted the children. If Francine didn't surrender them he would break down the door and beat her to death. Minutes passed while Mickey beat on the door. "Mom was getting terribly upset. I had visions of him getting in and Mom having a heart attack. She wanted me to let him have the children. She said, 'Just for now. It will calm him down and you can get them later.' I gave in."

Francine told Mickey he could have the children if he would leave in peace. He agreed and she opened the door. Mickey had sobered considerably in the hours since Francine first called the police in Dansville. Now he was furious, but controlled. He told the children to get into the car. As he drove them away Francine knew she had made a terrible mistake.

Within an hour Mickey telephoned from Dansville, drunk again. He told Francine he was coming to get her; if she didn't come willingly he would break in and drag her out. Francine called the police for the third time. The officer promised to send a police car. Francine, her mother, and Kathy waited, counting the minutes, praying the police would come before Mickey did. Mickey was the first to arrive. Kathy saw his car roar down the street and lurch to a stop in front of the house. She ran to the closet, took out a shotgun her brother used for hunting, and pointed it at the door.

For the fourth time Francine called the police. She told the officer, "My sister has a gun and it's loaded. If he comes in that door she's going to shoot."

The officer's voice took on a new tone. "Hold it," he told her sharply. "We'll have a car there in two minutes." In two minutes a police car drove up. The officers leaped out and ran to the front door. Mickey turned, cursing, ready to swing. They grabbed him and snapped handcuffs on his wrists. Watching through a window, Francine saw them lead Mickey to their car and drive away.

Francine's first thought was the children—were they all right? Her second was, "I've gotten away. I'm never going back. I've got to get the kids." She went out to Mickey's car, parked at the curb. He had taken the key. The Moran family had no car. Kathy had borrowed a car from a neighbor to get Francine in Dansville. Now she tried to borrow it again, but the owners were out. Francine telephoned her home and Christy answered. She assured her mother everything was all right. Before he left, Mickey had called one of his girl friends and she was at the house. Francine talked to the girl, who offered to spend the night and get the children off to school in the morning. Francine thanked her. There seemed to be nothing more she could do that night. In the morning she would make plans.

Francine went to sleep in the bed she had slept in as a child. She was so tired she lost consciousness the moment she closed her eyes, and slept late. In the morning she got up and looked out the window. Mickey's car was gone. It meant that he had already been released and gotten it while she slept. As she knew he would, Mickey telephoned. Francine told him she had made up her mind; she intended to rent a place in Jackson for herself and the children; she had left him forever.

"Okay," Mickey said with quiet menace. "You can do what you want, but you're never going to get those kids!"

Bitterly torn, Francine tried to think what to do. Have Mickey jailed for beating her? What good would it do? He would be released on bail and might not be tried for weeks. In the meantime he would have the children. He would serve a short sentence, if any, and come out in a murderous mood. Once again she discarded the idea, but Francine had never put out of her mind the idea that Mickey needed psychiatric treatment. Several times the police had mentioned the possibility of having Mickey committed to a mental hospital for observation and advised her to go to the probate court for further information. Francine decided to try. She called Joanne and asked her to borrow a car and take her to the courthouse. Within an hour Joanne was there.

At probate court Francine found herself talking to a woman who appeared to be in charge of deciding who could see someone higher up. "We talked standing up, as though it were no more important than mailing a letter. I was shaking, thinking, 'My whole future depends on what this woman does.' "

Francine told the story of Mickey's increasingly murderous mania. "He's going to kill me," she said. "Something has to be done. He's sick and he needs help." The woman asked if Mickey drank. Francine admitted that he did.

"Like how much?"

"Every day," Francine said. "He's drunk every day."

"I'm sorry," the woman said. "We don't deal with alcoholics. You'll have to go through other programs for that."

"He won't go to an alcohol program," Francine cried desperately. "If I could get him to go to a program I wouldn't be here. He won't go to a doctor. He needs to be sent to a hospital where he can't get out!"

The woman gave a sympathetic sigh. "I'm really sorry," she said.

"You say you're divorced. Why don't you try talking to the judge who gave you the decree. Maybe he will help."

Francine consulted the directory in the lobby and found the judge's name. She and Joanne trudged the long corridors to his office. His secretary, a middle-aged woman, asked what Francine wanted to discuss. Her manner, busy and suspicious, made it difficult for Francine to answer. Nevertheless, she explained that her ex-husband had taken her children from her and that even though she owned the house in which they lived she didn't dare go home for fear of being killed.

"That's a police matter," the secretary told her. "What do you want the judge to do about it?"

"I want him to help me!" Francine cried. "Can't he help me get the kids? Can't he keep my ex-husband from following me wherever I go? Beating me? Doing anything he wants?"

The secretary shook her head. "It's a common problem," she said calmly, "but there's nothing the court can do unless your ex-husband is arrested or you bring a legal action for custody of the children."

"How could I do that?" Francine asked.

"You might consult a lawyer."

"I don't have any money," Francine insisted. "And I have to do something *now. Today.* Before he gets drunk again and beats me to death!"

"Well," the woman said, "I'm afraid there's nothing more I can tell you. I know that a lot of women have to pack up and leave the state in order to get away from their ex-husbands. Maybe that's what you'll have to do." The telephone on her desk rang. She picked it up and dismissed Francine with a nod.

"Every door had been slammed in my face. I was worse off than before. Now I knew I couldn't get any help from the court or the hospitals. I was up against a blank wall."

As Francine and Joanne walked back to Joanne's car, Francine began to cry. "I'm stuck," she said. "I don't have any rights. Nobody cares if I'm killed. Nobody! There's nothing I can do!"

"How about welfare?" Joanne suggested. "He's not supposed to be living with you while you get aid. Maybe they know how you can get him out."

When she got back to her mother's house, Francine called the welfare office. On her visits there she had found it a busy place where no one was interested in the details of her life. She was interviewed by a different social worker each time. Now she had no idea whom to consult. Her call was switched several times until she found herself talking to an investigator in the Welfare Fraud Division. Francine explained that she was receiving Aid to Dependent Children, but her ex-husband was living with her and refused to leave. The man sounded baffled. He explained that the only action he could take would be to cancel her aid. "I don't see how that would help you," he said, "but I'll do it if that's what you want."

"Can't you prosecute him for fraud?" Francine asked. "It *is* a fraud, isn't it?"

"It certainly is," the investigator replied, "but the person we'd prosecute is *you*, not your ex-husband. You're the one committing fraud."

"Can't you make him leave?"

"That's up to you, not us. Why don't you put his clothes on the sidewalk and lock your door?"

"Because he'd beat it down."

"You could get a peace bond," the man said, "but if a guy is really determined a bond doesn't do much good." Francine asked what a peace bond was, and he explained that Francine could ask the courts to serve notice on Mickey that if he beat Francine again he would automatically be sentenced to jail.

"Nothing happens to him until after he beats me?" Francine asked. "What good is that if I'm dead?"

The man laughed. "That's about it," he said, "but I'm afraid it's all I can suggest."

Francine thanked him and hung up. The phone rang instantly. It was Mickey. He was at home and drunk. "Get your ass back here," he said. "You know you're gonna do it sooner or later. If you don't you'll never see those kids again."

Francine hung up. She told herself, "Don't give in, no matter what he says. You'll get the kids somehow. Just don't give in." In spite of her anxiety about the children, her head was clear. "I felt like I was thinking straight for the first time in my life."

By night Mickey's mood had changed again. He telephoned and told Francine that he had nothing to live for; that he was going to kill himself.

"Fine!" Francine said. "Go ahead!" She hung up.

Mickey called again. "Fran," Mickey said. "I really mean it. I'm going to cut my throat." His voice broke. "I don't want the kids to see it."

"Send them to your mother's," Francine said. "Then go in the bathroom and lock the door."

The phone rang several more times. Francine took it off the hook. The house was filled with a sense of siege. Kathy urged Francine to hold her ground, but their mother's nerves were at the breaking point. Francine's resolve was gnawed away, not only by anxiety over what might be happening to the children, but by guilt every time she looked at her mother's anxious face.

In the morning Francine felt sick with indecision; she was determined not to go back to Mickey, but wild with worry over the children.

She dialed her home and Christy answered. "Don't worry about us, Mom," Christy said. "Dad's asleep. We'll be all right. I promise."

Francine told her that if there was any trouble to get Flossie. There was silence all that day. By evening Francine's anxiety had risen again. It was difficult to imagine why Mickey didn't telephone. She couldn't believe he would give up so easily. What was happening to the children? Was anyone with them? She tried to call Christy. There was no answer.

The next day a letter from Flossie arrived. She wrote that the children were with her. Mickey had given up drinking and joined Alcoholics Anonymous. "Mickey really means it this time," Flossie wrote. "You should see how hard he is trying. He is doing it for you and the children. They need you. Why don't you come back to your home and your children and be a *wife*." The last word was heavily underlined.

The following day was Easter Sunday. It was a day of soft sunshine and a gentle spring breeze. Francine heard the church bells chime as she had heard them from this house as a child. She went out in the yard and began to tidy her mother's flower beds, trying to keep her hands and her mind occupied. Now that the acute crisis was over she felt at sea—unable to decide on her next move. Should she look for a job? Rent an apartment? How long could she stay at her mother's? How long would Mickey's sobriety last? Was there any chance he would keep his resolve to go to AA? Would he let her have the children? If he didn't, how could she get them back? The questions seemed as unanswerable as ever.

Francine looked up at the sound of an approaching car and recognized it as Mickey's. The children were with him. So were Berlin and Flossie. He parked in front of the house and a moment later the children were swarming all over her. She hugged them all and each in turn. "For the first time in days I felt my heart lift as though a great weight had been taken off me. I can't describe the relief of having those kids in my arms."

A quick glance at Mickey told her that he was sober. Pale and freshly shaved, he looked shaky, but resolute. He said, "Hi, Fran, the kids wanted to see you. Don't worry. We won't stay long."

Berlin and Flossie, dressed in their church-going clothes, stood beside him. When she had greeted them, Francine awkwardly asked if anyone would like a cup of coffee. Berlin said he would appreciate a glass of water. Francine went into the house to get it. As she was fetching the glass, Mickey followed her into the kitchen.

"He said, 'Fran, you don't have to come back. I'm not even gonna try to make you come back. But I want you to know I have quit drinking. Forever. Period. That was the whole trouble between us. That was what made me do those things. I'm going to Alcoholics Anonymous. I'm going to go to church. You don't have to worry about my drinking any more.' I said, 'Fine, Mickey. That's fine. But I've made up my mind. I'm not coming back.' Then he began to tell me how much the kids missed me. That they wanted me to come home. There were tears in his eyes. I said I was going to get the kids. He said he would never let them go. He kept his voice low-keyed, but he was completely determined and so was I. He said they were his kids, he loved them and he wouldn't give them up. I said I would get a lawyer and bring suit. He said if I did he'd take them out of the state. I said, 'Okay, Mickey, we'll just have to fight it out if that's what you want.' I took the glass of water and went out."

Flossie and Berlin were sitting on a bench in the yard. Francine gave Berlin the water and sat down on a chair. Nicky and Dana sat on the grass at her feet. Christy told her mother how she had taken charge, made breakfast for Nicky and Dana, and taken their laundry to the laundromat. Francine knew she was trying to reassure her that it was all right for her to stay away. Flossie said meaningfully, "It's a lot of responsibility for a little child." Francine let the remark go by. She looked at Jimmy, who sat in silence, with a look of brooding anxiety, swinging his feet and sucking grass blades. He avoided looking at either her or Mickey, and Francine thought, "He's the one who is having the hardest time." The painful moment dragged on. No one had much to say. Flossie got up. "Well," she declared. "I guess you've got your reasons and you've made up your mind, but it's a crying shame when he's doing his best. Come on, you kids, it's time to go." She took Christy and Jimmy by the hand and swept to the car. As Francine jumped up, Mickey and Berlin plucked Dana and Nicky from the grass and carried them after Flossie. As they were deposited in the car, the children began to wail. Francine followed. Mickey stood at the curb. He faced her squarely. "Fran," he said, "I mean it. Things will be different. Come home. I love you. I want you home with me and the kids. I'll never take another drink. If I do, you can leave and I won't bother you. I promise. Give me one more chance. You've got nothing to lose."

Francine heard herself say, "Okay, Mickey. One more chance. I'll go home. Just wait a minute while I tell Mom."

Mickey was sober, but whatever demons possessed him continued to torment him. He was taut, filled with anxieties. He watched everything Francine and the children did as though his vigilance was needed to prevent disaster. "Don't do that," he yelled at the children, "you'll hurt yourself." If the phone rang he leaped across the room to answer it. He smoked constantly. He depended on Francine for small decisions. "Do you think I oughta have a cup of coffee or am I drinking too much?" "I didn't sleep well last night. Do you think I oughta take a nap?"

Francine threw herself into nursing him through his convalescence from drink. She tried to be patient and attentive, on her toes to avert any problem that might upset him. When he wanted sex she responded warmly. They both said, "I love you," words that hadn't passed between them in years. Francine knew she didn't mean it, but she was trying to. She thought, "I prayed to God to make things different and He has. Now I've got to do my part. Mickey isn't drunk. He isn't beating me. He's trying to start a new life. It's harder for him than it is for me."

It encouraged Francine to see Mickey make an effort to be nicer to the children. Jimmy, at nine, was old enough to do things with his father. Mickey tidied his long-neglected workshop in the garage and began rebuilding an old engine. He let Jimmy help and the little boy responded eagerly. For years the children had begged to have a dog, but Mickey had always refused to allow it. Now he relented. Francine had gotten in touch with Sharon and Bill. They had a bitch with puppies and offered to give her one. The puppy was a female named Lady, half Labrador, half collie, with a golden coat. The children adored her, and Francine fell in love with her, too. "It was spring when Lady came. She fitted in with things blooming outside and the world looking fresh and new. She was full of fun and play. For me and the kids she represented the new happy life we hoped to have."

Every Sunday Francine and Mickey went to church. Several evenings a week Mickey went to a meeting of Alcoholics Anonymous while Francine met with the families of other problem drinkers in a group called Alanon. She learned that Mickey's symptoms of nervousness and anxiety were common in alcoholics who stopped drinking. Adjustment to sobriety, she was told, can take a long time. At first Francine found it a relief to be among people who also had troubled lives, but as she listened to their stories she discovered a basic difference between her problem and theirs. Other alcoholic men threatened their own lives, but not those of their wives. Suicide attempts and reckless driving were often discussed. Not a single woman in the group confessed to having been beaten in the savage way Francine had been. None had been threatened with death. None had lived in daily fear for her life. The troubles of the other women were so pale in comparison to her own that Francine couldn't bring herself to describe what she had experienced with Mickey: the sexual degradation, the pain of being beaten, the psychological tyranny enforced by fear of punishment or death that reduced her to a helpless state of self-loathing and depression. Other women had wondered if they should leave their husbands. None had wondered if they *could* leave. Francine never told the group her real story, and for her Alanon was an empty exercise.

With Francine's encouragement, Mickey enrolled in a vocational rehabilitation course. She believed that if he could once more work, it would restore his pride. The course included classroom study, such as Francine had gone through for a high-school diploma, and workshops in mechanical skills. Before each class Mickey was tense and apprehensive, and Francine spent hours boosting his resolve to keep on. If he experienced any failure in class, he came home angry and told her the whole thing was a waste of time. Francine would try to soothe him and build up his confidence for the next session.

After a few weeks of sporadic attendance Mickey quietly dropped vocational rehabilitation. At the same time, his effort to maintain the new relationship with Francine was draining away. When his nerves tightened, he yelled at her just as he had in the old days. He became terribly agitated over small problems, and no matter how a crisis began, it always became Francine's fault.

"Like one day he couldn't find a particular paper he needed. He began emptying drawers and tearing up the place. He was cursing and saying, 'I can't find this goddamn thing I have to take to Social Security.' Then he said, 'You look for it! You're probably the one who lost it anyway.' I said, 'Mickey, I never saw it. What does it look like? Just tell me and I'll help you look.' I started hunting for it while Mickey paced the floor, drinking coffee and watching me. 'You better find it,' he said. 'You better find it *fast*.' My head began to pound. I was so scared if I didn't find it soon he'd begin to drink. Then he blamed the kids. He began to curse and rant about them getting into his things, and that was my fault, too. Before I found the paper in the pocket of his windbreaker where he'd left it, I was trembling all over, a nervous wreck."

The hopeful period of Mickey's new start was brief. By summer he had dropped both church and AA. There was no longer any talk of love between him and Francine. Tyranny was the dominant mood. With the children Mickey was indifferent or cruel in ways that Francine found sickening.

"He used Lady to make the kids cry. He wouldn't let her in the house anymore. She didn't understand and would sneak in. Mickey would kick her, or pick her up and throw her out the door, and the kids would get upset. When she stopped coming in the house he found other reasons to get mad at her. Maybe she barked or whined. Then Mickey would threaten he was going to get rid of her. That would make the kids cry and beg him to let her stay. A couple of times he told them, 'This is it! I'm taking that goddamn dog in the car and I'm going to throw her out on the road!' He'd put her in the car and drive away. After a couple of hours, with the kids heartbroken, he'd come back with Lady, and tell the kids he'd decided to give her one more chance."

When Mickey began to drink it was without warning. One hot afternoon in August he got in his car and drove off without explanation. He didn't come home at dinner time and Francine began to wonder where he had gone. Though he had been comparatively calm that day, she felt an eerie intuition of something impending, of disaster bearing down. She was asleep when Mickey came in about midnight and turned on the light in the bedroom. Face flushed, eyes bright, he looked down on her with a smile of triumph, as though he had pulled off a spectacularly clever trick.

"Mickey!" Francine said. "I thought you weren't drinking!"

"That's what you get for thinking," Mickey said. "You were getting too smart. No goddamn woman is going to tell me I can't take a drink!"

"He hit me across the face and when I got out of bed he chased me through the house. He hit me and kicked me and threw the furniture around. I was crying and begging. He cornered me in the kitchen and got me down on the floor. The next thing I knew he was holding a kitchen knife at my throat. His eyes were crazy, completely insane. Suddenly he got up and threw the knife down. He said, 'Get out of here before I cut your throat.' I ran out of the house in my nightgown. I was so scared I didn't even think of where I was going. I just ran."

When she reached the end of the block Francine realized Mickey wasn't following. She stood still wondering what to do. Flossie and Berlin would be in bed, their door locked. She decided to go to the home of Donovan, who lived three blocks away. As she walked down the dark street her head cleared and she hoped no one would look out a window and notice her wearing only a nightgown. She knocked on Donovan's door. He and his wife, Alice, got out of bed. Alice said, "Jesus Christ, Fran! What are you doing?" She said, "Mickey's drinking again." Donovan and Alice looked at each other. Neither had anything to say. Francine went to sleep on their sofa. In the morning Alice lent her a pair of pants and a shirt. Francine started for home to give the children their breakfast and get them off to school.

As she approached the house her heart began to race and her breath was short. She thought, "Last night was real. He almost killed me last night and it's going to happen again. I can't do anything about it. All I can do is go home and wait for it to happen. Go home and wait to be killed."

When Mickey began to drink again, Francine's depression and suicidal feelings returned full force. She was convinced it was impossible to run away unless she left the children behind; something she would never do. She had tried all the other remedies she could think of and they had all failed.

As it had before, the thought of further education, learning a skill, seemed a step toward independence and a way to raise her morale, but where could she get money for tuition? What school would accept her? What could she study? Would Mickey let her go? She put the idea aside until one day, at the public library with the children, she casually picked up a government leaflet in a rack on the counter. It was an application for a Basic Opportunity Grant for adult education. Francine took it home, filled it in, and sent it off. To her astonishment, there was a prompt reply informing her that her grant had been approved. If she enrolled in an accredited school the grant would cover her tuition and provide a small amount for books and transportation. Her excitement was tremendous. Without daring to hope that she could really bring it off, she read the ads in the *Lansing Star*. The school that attracted her most was Lansing Business College, which offered a general secretarial course. Reading and writing were her best subjects. She thought secretarial work would be a wonderful career. She called Lansing Business College and learned that she was eligible to enroll for the semester beginning the first week in September—two weeks away.

In the morning, when Mickey was sober, Francine tentatively unveiled her plan. He scowled. "School again? You were gonna be a nurse. You wasted away all that time and quit just like I said you would. Now you want to do it again."

"I can't be a nurse, Mickey. I'm not smart enough. I can't do chemistry and biology like you have to do in nursing school." Francine knew she was on thin ice—any success of hers would underline his failure.

"So what good is it to go to some other school. You won't be able to do that either."

"Maybe I can, Mickey. I'm good at spelling and writing and English. That's what you need to be a secretary."

"A secretary! You want to be a goddamn secretary? They don't make any money!"

"Sometimes they do," Francine said. "It depends on where you get a job."

"No," Mickey yelled. "You ain't gonna go! You ain't gonna go to school and waste all that time and be a fucking secretary!"

"Mickey! There's nothing wrong with being a secretary!"

"For you there is! You can't do it. That's all!"

Francine reminded Mickey of the tuition grant. Free government money was something he would find hard to pass up.

"If I don't enroll in school I lose the money, Mickey. I don't know any other school I could go to. What else could I try to do?"

Mickey considered the question and grudgingly agreed she should use the grant. Then he thought of a new obstacle. "How're you gonna get there? You're not driving my car!"

Francine was stymied. Lansing is twenty miles from Dansville. "Please, Mickey. I'd only need it in the morning. I'd be back every day at noon."

"No!" Mickey said. "You're a rotten driver. I'm not gonna have you screw up my car. Get your own goddamn car if you're so smart."

"Okay," Francine said. "I will."

Francine had no idea if she could buy a car without making a down payment, but she decided to try. Mickey agreed to take her on a round of used-car lots in Lansing. She asked to see their cheapest cars. "I looked at one rattletrap after another. I thought one of these heaps would be worse than nothing; strand me on the highway when I was supposed to be home or in school. And I wondered how I was going to pay for it anyway. I hardly had enough money to buy a tank of gas."

At a large Ford dealer a friendly salesman latched on to them and wouldn't let them go. He had no cheap cars but insisted Francine look at a blue 1975 Granada. The price was $2,700. "Just take it for a drive," he urged.

Francine thought, "There's no sense in it," but Mickey was willing, so she got behind the wheel and drove it around the block.

"Well, do you like it?" the salesman asked when they returned.

"Sure, I like it," Francine said. "It's a nice car."

"Well . . . how about it? Is it what you're looking for?"

Francine shrugged in embarrassment. "I like it," she said, starting to turn away, "but I can't afford it. I don't even have enough for a down payment."

"Wait a minute," the salesman said. "Do you have a trade-in?"

"No," Mickey said. "She's got nothing to trade."

The salesman glanced at the Maverick. "How about credit? Is that car paid for?"

"It's paid for," Mickey said, "but she ain't putting that car up."

The salesman gave up. "Sorry," he said, "but I don't see what I can do." Francine didn't either. She and Mickey got into the Maverick and he started the engine. Suddenly the salesman sprinted back to their car and leaned in the window to speak to Francine.

"Can you come up with twenty-eight dollars for taxes and registration?"

"Yes!" Francine said.

"And payments of one hundred dollars a month?"

"Yes, I can," Francine said recklessly.

The man took her telephone number. "I'll check into the Maverick," he said. "Maybe I can work a deal. I'll let you know."

As they drove away, Mickey said, "Even if he lets you have it, you'll never be able to keep up the payments."

Two days later the salesman called.

"Mrs. Hughes? I've checked into your credit. Since the Maverick is paid for you don't need a down payment. The Granada is all yours."

Mickey took Francine to pick up the car. As she drove it home she could hardly believe how her outlook had changed. "Suddenly I had a car. I had tuition money. I was going to enroll in business college. I felt as though I had climbed a mountain. Each higher step had looked impossible, but I had somehow got to the top. Me! Francine! The woman Mickey called dumb and worthless was going back to school!"

Francine entered Lansing Business College in September 1976. It was lodged in a large office building near the state capitol. Francine arrived for her first day breathless with excitement and amazed at her own audacity. As she took her seat she felt as dumb as Mickey said she was. The teacher, a pleasant-faced, middle-aged woman, distributed written tests in reading comprehension, spelling, and composition. Francine picked up a sharp pencil and, with her heart in her mouth, began. The pencil flew. The tests were easy. Francine relaxed in relief and thought, "If it's no harder than this I can make the grade."

At midmorning there was a coffee break. Francine followed the other students to a lounge where there were tables and chairs, a coffee machine, and snacks. Her classmates, mostly young women and a few men, were already beginning to talk and make friends as they sorted themselves out at the tables. Francine filled a coffee mug and stood uncertainly. A small, dark-haired girl spoke to her. "Hi! Would you like to sit with me?" Francine gratefully followed her to a table. Two other girls joined them. They introduced themselves and began to talk. The dark-haired girl was named Betty Cover. She had a strong foreign accent and explained that she came from Brazil; she was married to a graduate student at Michigan State. Betty was friendly and vivacious. Francine admired her dark-eyed good looks. The other girls, Sally and Joan, were younger than Francine, but they seemed to enjoy her company and she soon forgot the difference in age. When the coffee break ended Francine felt she had found friends.

For the first few weeks that Francine attended school Mickey left her alone. By working at top speed she was able to get everything done—get the children off to school, get to classes in Lansing, come home to do her shopping and clean the house, cook a meal, and do her homework. She had to be careful; the sound of her typewriter—she had borrowed an old one from her sister Diana Lynn—annoyed Mickey. He didn't like to see her reading or writing either. If he was drunk enough he fell asleep soon after he had eaten and she had the evening in which to work, but when he was wakeful she had to stay up until midnight or later, and then get up at five to start her morning chores.

Francine liked the schoolwork, but what meant most to her was being among people who accepted her.

"At the beginning I was afraid to open my mouth in class. Little by little I began to express myself and people listened. I stopped feeling like a freak. I didn't tell my new friends much about myself or Mickey; I liked to pretend that the other part of my life didn't exist. I'd sit with my friends in the lounge at coffee-break time and laugh and joke the way I had years ago in school. We talked about a lot of interesting things that I'd never had a chance to discuss with anyone before. Betty Cover and I became special friends. She told me about her life in Brazil. I'd never met a foreigner and I loved hearing about the wonderful places she had been. What thrilled me most was that she found me interesting too."

Within a month there were signs that Mickey was working up a dangerous mood. He taunted Francine about her studies and predicted she would fail. He yelled at the children and gave arbitrary commands. One cold autumn night there was an episode involving Lady, the dog, that tore at Francine's heart. Since Mickey had banished her from the house, Lady had been chained to a dog house out in the yard. When she came into heat for the first time, Francine, inexperienced with dogs, hadn't expected it so soon. Suddenly the yard was crowded with male dogs. Francine and Christy dashed out and brought Lady onto the porch, where she could be closed in. Mickey, quite drunk, became angry at the commotion and ordered her returned to the yard. Lady was cowering and terrified. The dogs in the yard were fighting and barking. "We begged Mickey. We told him she was going to be raped. Mickey didn't care. He said, 'I'll kill that fucking dog if you don't get it out of here. Right now!' The kids were crying. I cried. It didn't do any good. We put her outside and the males were all over her. She yelped and screamed. Mickey acted like he didn't hear."

Once or twice a week Mickey beat Francine. "First he'd play cat and mouse with me. For two or three hours he'd watch me as though he were daring me to do something wrong. I'd creep around, cold inside with fear. If I sat and watched TV and the chair squeaked I'd look up quickly thinking that might be the thing that would start him. Then I'd look back at the TV so he wouldn't know I was afraid. He might get mad just because I flinched.

"Sometimes when he hit me I'd try to defend myself. It made things worse. If I ran out of the house, Mickey would lock the door with a bolt so I couldn't get back in. I'd have to stay out there freezing, or sitting in my car, for an hour or so. When he calmed down he'd unlock the door. Then, if I was lucky, we could go quietly to bed. In the morning my face would be all puffy and purple. I'd put on makeup and go to school, hoping no one would notice."

On those mornings Francine would be quiet in class and avoid attracting attention. She tried to imagine what her schoolmates would think if they knew how she had spent most of the previous night: fighting, dodging, being hit, screaming with fear and hate while obscenities were poured on her head like filthy rain. She thought, "They'd think I'm crazy! They'd say, 'Why doesn't she just go away?'"

In October Mickey very nearly killed Francine. It began in the usual way, as a long harangue interspersed with blows. Francine, in her nightclothes, had been trying to calm him down. Mickey's eyes had the glare that always sent a chill through her heart as he stalked her around the dining-room table.

"I was on one side, dodging back and forth, pleading. He was on the other. He was drunk, but not so drunk he couldn't move fast. Mickey lunged around the table and grabbed me and knocked me down on the floor. He got on top of me with his knees on either side and his hands on my neck. He began to choke me. I tried to pull his hands away but I had no strength. My head was roaring, my chest was bursting. I couldn't speak. I heard the kids calling, 'Mommy, Mommy!' Their voices were far, far away. My last thought before I blacked out was, 'It's happening. Mickey is going to kill me after all.'"

Francine never knew why Mickey let go. A moment later would have been too late. She opened her eyes and gulped air. "I couldn't get the air in at first. It wouldn't go down deep enough."

Mickey got to his feet. "Now, you bitch, get out!" He went for some beer. Francine scrambled to her feet and, with shaking hands, pulled on slacks and a sweater. She slipped into her loafers. She didn't dare speak to the children, to tell them she was all right. Any wrong move might make Mickey change his mind. He seemed not to notice as she slipped out the door.

Francine had no idea where to go; all she could think of was how close she had come to death. She got in her car, and started down the road to Mason.

At the town limits, headlights flashed in her rearview mirror.

Glancing back, she recognized Mickey's car behind her. He passed her with a roar, slewed around, and stopped, blocking the road. Francine slammed on the brakes, barely avoiding a crash. He jumped out and came toward her. Francine thought, "He's decided to finish the job." She backed quickly, then drove up on the shoulder, got around his car, and pulled away. Looking in the mirror she could see Mickey after her again. He caught up and tried to force her off the road. For terrifying seconds they drove side by side. Francine rounded a curve, barely avoiding a telephone pole, and saw a police car parked in a shopping plaza just ahead. Tires squealing, she pulled in, with Mickey close behind.

Mickey leaped out of his car and the officer intercepted him. Francine watched as Mickey and the officer argued, then scuffled. She could hear Mickey yell that he wanted to get his hands around her throat. When a second police car arrived, two deputies helped the first handcuff Mickey and shove him into a police car. Francine told an officer what had happened—her husband had nearly strangled her and then tried to run her off the road. The officer asked if she needed any further help. She told him she felt able to drive home, thanked him, and left.

She found the children awake and very scared. She told Christy to get the younger ones dressed—that they were leaving.

"Where are we going?" Christy asked. "To Grandma Moran?"

"No. We're leaving for good. We're never coming back. We're going far away!" As she said it Francine had no plan, only determination. Remembering the previous flight to her mother's, how her mother's anxiety had eroded her resolution, she knew she would have to find some other place to go. She dared not wait until morning. She couldn't be sure the police would hold Mickey overnight. She counted her money. She had a little more than fifty dollars with which to start her escape.

As she drove away from home for the second time that night, Francine decided that in the morning she would go to the prosecutor in Lansing, lodge a complaint against Mickey, and ask for protection. She felt sure attempted murder must be a serious crime. If Mickey served a term it would give her time to get away. On the outskirts of Lansing she drove in to a low-priced motel. A room with double beds cost fifteen dollars. As she counted out the money she realized how quickly her funds would melt away. In the morning Francine bought breakfast for the children and herself. When she had paid the check another five dollars was gone.

It was a clear, cold, autumn day. As she drove into Lansing, following the route she normally took to school, the familiar landscape made last night's terror seem like a horror movie, meant to be forgotten in the morning light. She imagined herself saying to the prosecutor, "My husband is going to kill me." It had an unreal sound. But this time she had witnesses: the deputies who had seen their cars careening into the shopping mall and heard Mickey's threats. This time, Francine told herself, no one could shrug her off.

Francine found a parking place near the capitol building and asked a policeman how to find the Ingham County Prosecutor. She and the children set off. Christy and Jimmy were silent, but Dana and Nicky were balky, on the verge of tears, giving Francine a foretaste of how difficult it would be to manage four children during a long stay away from home. At the prosecutor's office a receptionist listened impassively as Francine explained her business, and waved her to a seat. The waiting stretched on and on. The children were restless. Nicky hadn't eaten her breakfast, and cried with hunger. Jimmy and Dana were squabbling while Christy tried to keep order. Francine's nerves tightened until she felt giddy and sick with strain.

At last Francine was led to an office where an assistant prosecutor, a young man in a well-pressed suit, sat behind a desk. He greeted her pleasantly. "What's your problem, Mrs. Hughes?"

Francine began her story. "Well, last night my husband . . . I mean my ex-husband . . . tried to kill me . . . he choked me until I blacked out . . . then he chased me in his car and tried to run me off the road. He nearly killed me. He keeps threatening me. . . ."

The young man showed no surprise; he seemed to find attempted murder an everyday affair. He sent for Mickey's criminal record. A secretary put a file on his desk and the prosecutor looked through it quickly. "I see he's on probation," he remarked. In September Mickey had driven his car into a ditch and had been arrested when he fought with an officer. He'd been given a suspended sentence and probation for six months. "Have you been in touch with his probation officer, Mrs. Hughes?"

Francine shook her head.

"Since he's on probation," the prosecutor said, "he'll be automatically picked up. That should be enough."

"When?" Francine cried. "I need protection now!"

The prosecutor looked a trifle impatient. "Mrs. Hughes, I've just explained. He's violated probation. He'll be picked up and serve time for that."

"Can't I make a complaint for attempted murder?" Francine asked. "Can't I get some protection? He's going to kill me. I don't know what to do. . . ."

"I'm going to let Probation handle it," the prosecutor said. "Come back and see us if you have more trouble." He got up and ushered her out of the office. The interview had lasted less than five minutes. As Francine walked down the hall to the waiting room she thought, "He doesn't understand. Nobody will believe it until after I'm dead."

When she and the children reached the lobby Francine went to a telephone booth and called the Probation Department in Mason. She was connected with a man named Mathews who had been assigned Mickey's case. Francine explained what had happened, and that she didn't know whether Mickey had yet been released. She pleaded with Mathews to act quickly. "The kids and I are in a phone booth in Lansing," she told him. "I haven't any money and I'm scared to go home."

Mathews told her he would check into it and asked her to call back in an hour. For an hour Francine walked the children around the block trying to answer their questions about what she was going to do and where they were going to go. When she called Mathews back he told her that unfortunately Mickey had already been released. He would be arrested for parole violation, Mathews said, as soon as he showed up.

"Shows up?" Francine asked. "What does that mean? Why can't you do it right away?"

"Because we don't know where he is," Mathews replied. Mathews said he had called Mickey's parents and that Flossie said Mickey wasn't home. Mathews promised Francine he'd check again in a day or so.

"You mean it could take days?" Francine asked. Mathews said that he was sorry; arrests for parole violation weren't a priority item, but he'd do the best he could.

There was one person whom Francine had not yet asked for asylum: Mickey's stepsister, Vicky, now married and living in a town called St. Johns, twenty miles north of Lansing. Francine called her and asked if she and the children could come there for a few days. After a slight hesitation, Vicky said yes.

When Francine reached St. Johns, Vicky welcomed her as best she could, but Francine saw that it would be difficult for her to stay long. Vicky had small children, and four more filled the house to bursting. Vicky was uneasy about provoking Mickey's anger, fearful that if he discovered where Francine was he would follow her there.

Francine prayed that Mickey would be arrested soon so that she and the children could go home. She had made up her mind to use the time while Mickey was in jail to do whatever was necessary to get custody of the children and get away. She telephoned Mr. Mathews every day. All he could tell her was that Mickey's arrest was "in the works." With each call Francine's confidence that it would ever happen ebbed. Meanwhile she and the children were wearing out their welcome in Vicky's home. Francine paid her share of the food bills, and her funds were running low. When, after a week, Mathews had still not arrested Mickey, Francine knew her escape had failed. She couldn't stay longer with Vicky. She had just enough money to buy gas to get home. Furthermore, as always after a crisis with Mickey, depression and anxiety were sapping her determination. She felt her will crumbling under the prolonged strain. Now it seemed that failure had been inevitable from the beginning. Going to see the prosecutor, running to Vicky, everything she had done had been another exercise in futility; no matter what she did, Mickey always won.

Francine telephoned Mickey. He was sober. "Come on home, Fran," he said. "I've quit drinking. You don't need to be afraid." Francine and the children drove back to Dansville. When she walked into the house the scene was just as she had left it a week before; overturned furniture, broken dishes, Mickey sitting in his armchair drinking. He said, "Welcome home, you dumb bitch. You've got a lot of housework to do."

Three weeks after Francine returned home, Mickey was arrested for parole violation and sentenced to forty-five days in the Ingham

County Jail. Francine drove him to court to surrender so that she could bring his car home. Mickey was sober and apprehensive. He asked her to promise to come on visiting days. Just before she left him at the entrance to the courthouse he hugged her and said, "Fran, I know this isn't your fault. Don't worry. I don't blame you for this." Looking into his eyes, Francine saw tears. "You'll be okay, Mickey," she said, and with a brief kiss turned away. Driving home, she thought, "If only this had happened at the right time, I'd have got away."

Flossie and Berlin thought it unfair that Mickey had to serve time, since no damage had been done. A few days after he went to jail, Flossie received a letter from Mickey.

Hi Mom and Dad,
Well, this place is for the birds. Just got your letter today and I got Fran's Saturday. Tell her to write me more often. This place is awfully boring. Tell her not to forget visiting Wednesday at 5:30. Please.
Boy, you don't know how much you love your kids, honey, and everybody else, Mom, Dad, brothers and all till something like this. I feel like crying. Tell everyone I love and miss them. Especially Fran, Chris, Jim, Dana, and Nicole. Kiss the kids for me and tell them I love and miss them very, very much. Tell Fran to send envelopes, stamps, and writing paper. Please. I love her so much. I wish I had a lot of things I could do over. Tell her that. I hope to see her tomorrow. I have it set up so she can visit. She had better!
Well, guess I'll close. Wish I could go to church with all of you. I sure miss it. Boy, I didn't realize how religious I was until I got here. Some of the language you hear! Be sure to watch over to Fran's and help her all you can. Man, I can't help worrying about them. Tell her to drive careful. I don't know what I'd do if something happened to her or the kids and me in here.

Mick

Instead of forty-five days, Mickey served eight. The jail was overcrowded and he was among those chosen for early release. Francine was notified and went to pick him up at seven in the morning. When Mickey saw her car he bounded across the parking lot and kissed her exuberantly. His eyes were clear, his color good—he looked better than he had since the accident, six years before. On the way home he talked excitedly about the details of prison life. Francine left him at home and went on to school. When she returned, about one o'clock, Mickey had a stein of beer in his hand. By night he was drunk.

During the next few days he made up for lost time, pouring down beer so that he was drunk by noon instead of late afternoon. Several times Francine tried to talk to him early in the morning. Whenever she worked around to the possibility that he needed help to pull his life together—in short, a psychiatrist—Mickey angrily dismissed it. "You're the one that's sick! Get your own head examined. There's nothing wrong with me!" He began to brood over his stay in jail and to blame Francine. He told her she had been getting away with murder and, by God, he was going to straighten her out. On Saturday, five days after his release, he kept her in the bedroom most of the day while he got drunker and drunker, and berated her for her sins. "Mickey talked on and on about what he would do if I ever again tried to leave. 'Don't get any ideas,' he said. 'I'll be coming to get you. When I find you, believe me, it ain't gonna be pretty.'"

Thereafter, week after week, Mickey grew worse: more drunken, more angry and brutal, and, it seemed to Francine, more insane.

"Anything anyone enjoyed annoyed him. He'd hit one of the kids just for laughing. He'd make them stay in their rooms. There was no bathroom up there and they'd have to use the waste cans. Mickey would hit me for no reason at all. When Jimmy would see me with a bruise or a cut lip he'd ask, 'Did Dad do that?' I'd say, 'Yeah, he did.' A couple of times Jimmy said, 'God, I hate him.' He told me, 'Dad isn't gonna do that when I grow up!' Jimmy's teacher called me in for a conference. She said that Jimmy had been given a psychological test. One of the questions was, 'What are you most afraid of?' Jimmy wrote, 'My Dad.' When the teacher told me she raised her eyebrows, sort of asking if it was true. There was nothing I could say. I know she was thinking, 'If this woman is any kind of a decent mother why doesn't she take the kids away?' There was no way I could explain how much I wanted to, but that I was too afraid.

"Christy would talk about how she wished she could grow up faster. Once when she found me crying she said, 'Mom, you could go away and send for us later.' I told her I couldn't do that; no matter how bad things were I wouldn't leave her and the others behind. I told her that maybe when I got my diploma in the spring things would be different; I'd be able to get a well-paying job and earn enough money so we could all go away.

"Poor little Nicky had loved her dad when she was a baby. Now she was very confused—especially after what Mickey did to the cat."

Nicole loved animals, but Mickey wouldn't allow any in the house. A stray cat came to the backyard and Nicole fed it on the sly. She liked to pet it and hold it in her arms. One cold day she brought the cat onto the enclosed porch, wrapped in coats to keep it warm. Francine, busy in the kitchen, was only dimly aware of the cat, but Mickey saw it and told Nicole to put it outdoors. As soon as Mickey's back was turned Nicole brought it back in. He quickly discovered it and Francine heard him yell, "Get that fucking cat off the porch!"

A moment later Francine heard Nicky scream. She ran out to the porch. Mickey had disappeared. "Nicky was crying so hard she couldn't talk. I'd never heard a child cry like that. I picked her up and carried her upstairs. I put her on her bed and held her in my arms until she calmed down enough to tell me what had happened. Mickey had warned her that if he found the cat on the porch he'd wring its neck. When he caught her with it the second time he took it out of her arms and just broke its neck in his two hands. Then he flipped it out into the weeds. Nicky kept sobbing, 'Why did he do it? I hate him. I hate him. I hate him. He's a bad man!' While I was upstairs Mickey went to the saloon. When he came back he was very drunk. I started to tell him what I thought of him, but the look on his face told me I better keep quiet—and I did, but I hated him beyond words."

At the same time Lady had become a terrible problem. She was swelling with pregnancy. The weather was cold, below freezing much of the time, but Mickey still wouldn't allow the dog in the house. "On cold days she'd shiver and shake. The kids would beg me, 'Can't we bring her up on the porch. Please, Mom, for a little while?' I'd go ask Mickey and he'd say, 'No! I don't want that damn dog in. If you bring it in, I'm gonna kill it.' I'd say to the kids, 'Guys, you can't bring her in now, but if Dad goes to sleep maybe we can. . . .' Every night it was a nerve-wracking hassle, waiting for Mickey to go to sleep and sneaking Lady up onto the porch.

"One day I came home from school and Mickey said, 'Somebody

better go check on that dog.' I said, 'Why?' He said, 'She's having her pups.'

"The kids and I went out. It was bitter cold. There were three puppies lying on the ground. Frozen. Dead. The kids began to cry. The worst part was that Lady had a pup hung up inside her, half-way born. She was crying in pain. Christy ran in the house and looked up a veterinarian in the Yellow Pages. She called him and he said to bring Lady to his office right away. Mickey was listening. He yelled that he wasn't going to waste money on a goddamn dog. The vet told Christy that if we couldn't bring Lady to his office the next best thing was to get her warm and comfortable and for me to pull out the pup. I got the puppy out. It was dead. The look in Lady's eyes was awful. She was bleeding, in pain, shivering with cold. We went to Mickey and all of us begged. I was crying, too. I said, 'Please, Mickey, just this once. She's suffering. She's freezing to death!' Mickey was drunk. All he said was, 'You ain't bringing that fucking dog in!' We put hay and blankets in her dog house and left her there. In the morning I went out and found her lying on the ground, frozen. I just walked away. I couldn't make myself go out there again for about three days. Finally I picked up her body and wrapped it in newspapers and put it in a trash can. Mickey had nothing to say. He acted like he didn't care."

At school Francine usually spent the half-hour coffee break in the lounge with Betty Cover and several other girls. One morning, early in the second term, she found Betty sitting at a table with a man in police uniform. Betty introduced him to Francine. "His name was George Walkup. His eyes were the deepest blue I'd ever seen. We began to talk. He showed an interest in me, kidding me a little, and before I knew it I was blushing like a fourteen-year-old kid. I got very nervous and clumsy, hunting through my purse for cigarettes and matches, and then dropping everything on the floor. I began to pick up the stuff I'd spilled. George was laughing at me. He got up to help and we both groped around on the floor picking up small change. I had turned bright red. I didn't know how to act around men, especially an attractive man. I felt like an awkward fool. I got my purse together and went to the coffee machine. When I came back I spilled the coffee. George mopped it up and was very much at ease. The three of us made small talk, but George kept looking at me. His smile was warm. I liked his soft voice and southern speech."

Francine learned that Walkup, a native of Georgia, was a member of the State Police Security Force assigned to the state capitol nearby. He had come to the lounge with a friend who knew one of the girls at the school. Now he made it a habit to spend his coffee break there two or three times a week, talking with various girls, who, like Francine, were attracted by his good looks and easy, softly sexy manner. Francine listened with covert interest as her classmates gossiped about Walkup. He had told several girls that he had been married and had children, but that he was getting a divorce and was no longer living at home. From the moment Francine saw Walkup she wanted him. She found herself having fantasies of sex, love, even marriage. She imagined George to be everything she longed for: passionate, tender, protective, and kind. But after their first meeting George made no special move in her direction, though Francine knew that he asked several girls out on dates. She didn't really expect George to ask her, a married woman, and yet couldn't help wondering what it would be like if he did.

When the second term began Francine had enrolled in a psychology course whose objective was self-awareness. Miss Johnson, the teacher, had selected Socrates' admonition, "Know thyself," as her theme. For Francine it was a new concept and, as the course progressed, its emotional impact was tremendous. Each week's assignment was a short paper describing "One thing I learned about myself this week; about another person; about people in general." Her first effort at self-analysis was difficult. Her paper entitled "What I Know About Myself" began:

"My name is Fran Hughes. I am a twenty-nine-year-old female. I really don't know too much about myself. But I will try to think real hard.

"One thing I know is that I let people walk all over me. I do as I'm told, not as I wish to do. I've been trying to stand up for my rights as a person. I think I am basically nice.

"I love school, but I have a fear of failing. I was so scared because school was something I wanted to do so bad. I have a hard time relaxing most of the time. I get so uptight I have to take hot baths, aspirin, and drink warm milk. Sometimes all I can do isn't enough. I have guilt feelings about the children and housework while I'm at school. I guess I'll keep striving until I feel right about myself."

Francine was startled by how much she learned about herself merely by putting her thoughts into written words. Each week new ideas came forth. "I learned that I like to overcome obstacles. I was anxious and scared to death first term, but I overcame my fears. After I do something I'm afraid of, it's not so bad next time!" Another week she wrote, "I learned that I am stronger in will than I thought. I learned that if I speak up and say what I really think I feel better about myself."

For Francine these discoveries—coupled with Miss Johnson's lectures and reading in her textbook—were important revelations. Halfway through the course she was able to write: "It suddenly dawned on me that I am happier with myself. I feel better about myself now than I ever did before. I've learned that most people are happy with their lives. If not, they try to change things. They try to face their problems. Most people make it, too! Some don't. I guess they are the ones who crack up!"

Miss Johnson had also asked her students to keep a daily journal of "thoughts and events that impressed me," and promised that it would be confidential, for her eyes alone. Francine dared write nothing about her life at home, not only because she was afraid Mickey might find her diary and read it, but because she could not confess to Miss Johnson the sort of things that happened almost every day. Instead she tried to invent "normal" items, but her imagination refused to cooperate; often the best she could do was something as meager as "I don't feel good," or "I don't feel like writing today." Every day the blank page underscored the increasing schizophrenia of a life divided between the sanity of her hours at school and the madness of her time as Mickey's prisoner. Once she wrote, "I realized today that I am a prisoner"; then she shredded the paper and hid it in the depths of the trash can.

Meanwhile, her infatuation with George Walkup grew. He had begun to notice her, and to flirt with her more than with any of the other girls. She told herself that it was silly, nothing could come of it, but she found it impossible not to respond. Each day at coffee-break time she went to the lounge flushed with excitement. Francine and George were never alone. Betty and one or two other girls usually shared their table, but George wooed Francine with glances and meaningful remarks until her tension built up to an unbearable pitch. At last he asked her to spend an evening with him and she unhesitatingly said yes.

When Francine went home she told Mickey she wanted to go to a birthday party that evening for one of the girls at school. He was in a good mood and agreed. As she got ready for the date she tried not to be carried away, but she couldn't suppress her hope that she might be falling in love at last. She was already divorced. If she found a strong, resolute man to protect her, a man armed with the power of the law . . . the implications were irresistible.

George had asked her to meet him at a bowling alley. He was still bowling when she got there, and she sat on a bench and watched. He was skilled and athletic. To Francine, his body in motion was a lovely thing to watch. George finished a shot, glanced at her with a proud smile, and came over to sit beside her, waiting for his final turn. Francine felt a secret understanding, an electric excitement between them. When the game ended he steered her into the bar. Francine did not normally drink. George ordered a whiskey sour for her. It tasted like ambrosia. While she sipped it George told her how much he was attracted to her. When the drinks were finished, he suggested they go out to his car. As soon as Francine had gotten in, George kissed her passionately and Francine responded. George started the car and for a while he talked about himself: how he needed love and hoped she might be the woman who would give it to him. Then he parked and they made love.

Afterward they talked. Francine asked questions about his marital problems, his children, and his divorce. George talked freely, and with every word Francine felt growing dismay. His story was rambling, filled with contradictory details, but Francine gathered that though a divorce was in progress it was far from certain. Furthermore, it became clear that he was still emotionally involved with his wife and living at home. Francine's image of George was shatteringly transformed from protective lover to philandering husband, out for a one-night stand, but she kept her disillusionment to herself. She couldn't bear to confess that she felt used and taken in. George drove her back to pick up her car. They kissed goodnight and Francine drove home. "I wasn't ashamed of what I'd done, but I felt like a fool for building up my dreams. I was glad I'd seen reality before any real damage was done."

The next day at school Francine waited for coffee-break time, wondering how she would behave when George appeared. He didn't come. Later, he telephoned her at home. Fortunately Mickey was out. George said he was crazy about her and that he hoped she felt the same about him.

"I'd like to," Francine said, "but I can't." "Why not?" George asked. "Because you're married," Francine said. "I didn't know you and your wife were still together. I'm not a home wrecker. I think a guy should stay with his wife and kids." George said she had misunderstood. Couldn't they meet so he could explain? Francine was resolute. She told him that only if he were divorced and no longer seeing his wife would she go out with him again. George said he was sorry she felt that way, and their conversation ended. Francine never saw Walkup again. He no longer came to the lounge at school. Francine had no idea whether it was because of their affair or because his schedule had changed. Briefly she mourned the lost fantasy, but in a sense found it a relief to have her fruitless yearning ended. She had no energy for anything but the grim struggle to get through each day.

Michigan winters are cold and bleak. Dark falls early. Mickey, Francine, and the children were confined together in the house on Grove Street for what seemed to Francine endless hours of darkness and violence while tension built up. Mickey was getting worse, more irrational and more abusive every day. A sense of impending catastrophe was always at the brink of Francine's consciousness. She felt she was living with a bomb, waiting for it to explode.

The house was full of reminders of recent violence. Mickey had broken all the dining-room chairs. He had picked them up and smashed them on the floor, one by one. He had thrown a can of beer at Francine that hit the china cabinet, breaking most of her china. He had ripped the telephone out of the wall four times. While she was without a telephone, her sister Joanne came to see if she was all right. During the visit one of Joanne's children swung on the storm door and the hinges had broken. Mickey noticed the damage after Joanne left. "He flew into a rage. He said Joanne would have to pay to fix it. He never fixed anything he broke, but he was furious about this. I said, 'Mickey, Joanne doesn't have the money. How can she fix it?' I was trying to cook dinner. I was just ready to put it on the table. Mickey grabbed me and said, 'You're gonna phone her right now!'"

Francine pointed out that they had no phone.

"You go call her from Mom's. If you don't get your ass over there and call her right now I'm gonna break up everything in this whole fucking house." He picked up a lamp and smashed it on the coffee table. He held another aloft and waited.

Francine said, "Okay, Mickey. I'll call her."

Mickey took her by the back of the neck and pushed her across the yard to his mother's house.

"Now, what's the matter?" Flossie asked.

Francine went to the telephone. Joanne had no phone either, so Francine phoned a neighbor and left a message. While they waited for Joanne to call back, Mickey sat in a chair cursing. From time to time his mother said, "Mickey, don't you talk like that!"

Joanne did not immediately return the call and Mickey, tired of waiting, ordered Francine and the children into the car. He was drunk and drove wildly, while Francine prayed they'd make it.

"When we get there," Mickey instructed Francine, "you're gonna tell that fucking bitch she's gotta fix that door! You gotta say *you* want it fixed."

Joanne, Francine later learned, had been prepared for the visit. While they were en route she had called back and Flossie advised her to "baby him and not pay any attention if he says bad things."

When they arrived, Francine followed Mickey's orders. She told Joanne she expected her to pay for the door. Mickey stood beside her and added a number of obscenities to the message. Joanne remained calm and promised to pay when she got the money. Then Mickey allowed Francine and the hungry, white-faced children to get back in the car. He drove them home to the supper that Francine had left on the stove several hours earlier. When Mickey had fallen asleep Francine picked up the wreckage of the lamp and the coffee table, thanking God that greater disaster had been averted for one more day. Then she sat up late into the night working on her school assignments. In her mind school had become the life raft by which she might escape her private Devil's Island.

Francine was always hard pressed for money. Since Mickey paid for nothing and fixed nothing, any extra expense became an enormous problem. Mickey noticed that the toilet in their single bath-

room was leaking around the base and that the floor of the bathroom was damp. He told Francine that, by God, she'd better get it
fixed.

"I said, 'Why don't you try to fix it, Mickey?' It probably only
needs a seal.' He said, 'I ain't gonna fix it. *You* are!' I said, 'Okay,
Mickey, okay. But it'll have to wait till I have the money.'"

The next time Mickey worked up a rage he returned to the subject of the leaking toilet.

"I thought you were gonna get that fixed?"

"I will, but I haven't had the time. I haven't had the money and I
don't even know how to find somebody to do it."

"I'll fucking well fix it for you," Mickey said. He went out to the
locked garage, now wholly "his," and returned with a sledgehammer, with which he smashed the toilet into small pieces.

Mickey was aware that welfare gave clients a home-repair allowance. Now he insisted that Francine ask welfare to pay for a new
toilet. Francine flinched at having to explain how her toilet had dis-
integrated. She told the welfare case worker only that the toilet was
"broken." Welfare agreed to provide money to buy another one,
second-hand. So that the cause of the breakage would not be dis-
closed, Francine asked Berlin to install it. He agreed to do so for a
price—twenty dollars. While they waited for the allocation to come
through, the family used a bucket. Finally the welfare money came.
Berlin drove Francine to a plumbing-supply house, where she
bought a new toilet, and he installed it.

Unfortunately, Berlin's plumbing work was less than perfect.
Mickey discovered that the new toilet was also leaking. "Okay, you
dumb bitch," he said, "you better get it fixed right, this time."

"How?" Francine demanded. "How can I call welfare again
when they just paid for this one?"

"You can do it," Mickey said. "And you better. I'll give you three
days to get it done!"

Francine called the welfare office and reported that the new toilet was leaking. They said they would have to send someone out to
look at it and it would take several days. When three days had
passed and the toilet had not been repaired, Mickey picked up the
sledgehammer and smashed it.

This time when Francine called the welfare office she told the
truth: that her ex-husband had smashed it with a sledgehammer.

The case worker sounded startled, but agreed to put through another repair allowance. When it arrived, Francine called a professional plumber and a new toilet was installed. Fortunately it did not leak.

By then the long winter was nearly over. The days were lengthening, the snow melting. By the first week of March, Francine was more than halfway through her second term and praying that her luck and stamina would take her through to the end, but every day the going seemed harder. She was beginning to fall behind in her work at home and at school. It was becoming harder to drive herself to stay up late at night to finish her homework, harder to face the daily insults and difficulties that Mickey devised to torment her. He was complaining more about her going to school and she had a growing fear that he would forbid her to go. She had a feeling of "everything building up."

Francine had worked especially hard on her term paper for Miss Johnson. The topic, "What I Know About Myself Now," had caused her to search deep into her memory, where old longings still lived. With a feeling of sudden insight into her failings and disillusionments, she ended the paper thus:

"It is hard for me to make changes in my life. It is easier for me to leave things as they are and not disturb anything. I know I should disturb things more.

"I know that I am too trusting of people. I will believe anything if there is the least bit of truth in it. I know I can change that. I should gather more facts and look before I leap!

"I wish I could share my life with someone and have an open relationship with love and trust. I don't believe I will ever have it.

"I know that I am capable of much more than I have been doing. Now I realize that I have to do things for myself. I was waiting for something good, or someone, to happen to me. Now I know that nothing ever happens from luck, and that you have to make things happen. I was always waiting for my ship to come in, but it never came!"

The Burning Bed

On Wednesday morning, March 9, Francine got up at 5 A.M. as usual. She drank a cup of coffee and read her term paper over before she put it in her book bag. As she had worked on it the night before she had thought that it expressed a great deal. Rereading it, she had a feeling of so much left unsaid.

"I left for school, anxious to get away from the house. Mickey was sober in the mornings and saw that the older kids got off to school okay. I took Nicky to a sitter. I got to school and that day, I remember, was unusually good for me. I had all my homework done! It was like spring outside and I get spring fever every year. I felt suddenly happy. Some girls and I took our coffee and sat by a sunny window and laughed and joked; it was a really nice day. As usual I didn't want to go home, but the kids would be waiting. As I was getting into my car one of my classmates, a girl who lived outside Dansville, asked if I could give her a ride. I said, 'Sure.'"

As a result of the detour to drop off her classmate, it was about 1:40, ten minutes later than usual, when Francine reached home. The minute she entered the house she knew she was in trouble. Mickey was already quite drunk, already in a glowering rage. He wanted to know where she had been. Francine told him she had taken a friend home.

"Shit! She's got you suckered so now you'll be taking her home all the time."

—

"No, Mickey. She's got a regular ride to school. But today the girl she rides with wasn't coming home until later."

Mickey was not convinced. "Oh yeah, sure! You do this for her a couple of times, she'll be wanting a ride with you back and forth every day."

"What's wrong with that? Suppose she did? She'd help with the gas."

"Well, why didn't you collect today?"

"Oh God, Mickey!" Francine exclaimed in disgust and went to the mailbox. In it, as she had expected, she found her check from the Aid to Dependent Children program. Nicky arrived, dropped off by her sitter, and Francine hugged her. Christy and Jimmy had had only a half a day of school that day and were playing in the backyard, where Mickey had told them to stay. He had, in fact, locked them out. Dana had gone to a hockey game with a friend.

As usual, on the last day before her check arrived, there was nothing in the refrigerator except Mickey's beer. Francine told Mickey she was going into town to get some groceries.

Mickey popped the top off a can of beer, poured some into a mug, and considered her statement with a frown. "Wait a minute!" he said. "Ain't you getting a little ahead of yourself?"

"What do you mean?" Francine sat down. She suddenly felt terribly weary. Her stomach was churning with hunger pangs.

"I mean," Mickey said, "that you ain't got a grocery list and you ain't going to the store unless you write a grocery list."

"Oh Christ, Mickey!" Francine exclaimed. "I don't feel like writing a grocery list. I'm tired! The kids are hungry. I'm just going to get a few things."

"You're gonna write a grocery list or you ain't going! And I want to see what's on it! And I don't want you buying none of your goddamn greasy food! It's your greasy food that makes me sick!" The glare of rage was coming into his eyes. Francine saw it and thought, "Oh God, here we go again!"

"Okay, Mickey," she said, tiredly. "Just tell me what you want for dinner."

Mickey didn't answer. In the past months he had been eating very little. Food, any food, often caused him to vomit, and then he would blame Francine's "greasy food."

"Mickey," Francine said, "can I please go and just get something for dinner—something I can fix quick. The kids are real hungry. It's late."

"You know who's fucking fault it is that it's late." Mickey took a draft of cold beer. "Yeah," he said, "you can go and you better be back on time. Don't be fucking around in that store all day."

Francine called the children from the yard and they piled into the car. Before they shopped she had to cash her check and get her food stamps. Finally they were in the market. Francine asked the children what they wanted. "Let's pick something easy," she said. The children voted for TV dinners. Francine seldom bought them and the children considered them a special treat. She gave in easily; she wanted to make up for the lateness and the bad time they'd had with Mickey earlier. She told the children to pick out what they wanted. She bought a chicken dinner for herself and decided on a Mexican plate for Mickey; he had liked it once or twice before. She bought milk and eggs and bread for breakfast, some paper towels, and a few other odds and ends from a bargain display near the cash register.

Driving home, Francine went over in her mind the things she had to do before bedtime: a typing assignment; speedwriting practice; a chapter in psychology to read; a lesson on data filing to study. The laundry had piled up and the kitchen floor needed doing. The joyful morning had clouded over. "I was weary and hassled. The rest of the day was like a mountain ahead."

It was nearly three by the time Francine got back to Grove Street. She and the children carried the grocery sacks into the kitchen and put them on the table. Mickey left his chair in front of the TV and pounced on the sacks.

"He began taking things out and looking at each one and saying, 'What'd you buy this for? What'd you buy that for?' I'd say, 'Because we were all out,' or 'Because it was cheap.' Then he said, 'What'd you get for dinner? There's nothing in here for dinner! No meat! Nothing!' I said, 'I got some TV dinners.' He started cursing and saying, 'You fucking, no-good, lazy-ass bitch, you know I don't like TV dinners.' I said, 'Well, I didn't think you were going to eat anyway!'"

"That's the trouble with you. You're always thinking." He paused and Francine felt a horrible foreboding. She knew the signs so well;

he was pausing to consider what strategy would force her to provoke him into beating her.

"If you ain't got no more sense than to bring that garbage home, you ain't gonna fix it. I don't even want to smell that shit cooking."

Nicky, standing in the doorway, let out a wail. Mickey turned on her. "You goddamn kids get out of here. Get out in the yard and stay out!" Christy took Nicky's hand and, with Jimmy following, went outside. Mickey locked the door behind them.

Francine stood silent.

"I was trying to keep calm, hang onto myself and not make him worse. I was thinking, 'Those poor kids, they're so hungry.' I was feeling sort of faint myself. I sat down and waited, not saying anything. Sometimes if I was very quiet he would calm down."

But a new thought crossed Mickey's mind: "And there's something else you ain't gonna do. You ain't gonna go to school no more. You're gonna stay home and do what a wife is supposed to do!" Mickey took a can of beer and left the kitchen.

Francine had feared this disaster for weeks. Even so, the impact was enormous. She was thinking, "No! I won't give it up! Not now! I've worked so hard. It's the only thing I've got." She turned on the oven and thrust in the TV dinners, without thinking of Mickey's anger over them. Sometimes he made a scene about something as trivial as a TV dinner and forgot it shortly after. This time he didn't forget. She was putting the groceries away when he returned, went to the stove, and turned off the oven. "I told you you weren't fixing TV dinners!"

"Mickey," Francine cried. "The kids have to eat! They've had nothing all day! Please let me heat them just for the kids. I'll fix you something else."

Without answering, Mickey went back to the living room. Francine turned the oven on. Within a few moments the tantalizing odors of warm food were in the air. Anxious and angry as she was, Francine felt suddenly ravenously hungry. She'd had nothing but coffee since breakfast. She was putting a kettle on the stove and thinking of going to the back door to unlock it and call the children in when Mickey returned. He bounded across the room, turned the oven off, and hit her across the face. Then he crowded her against the stove, cursing her. "No-good slut. I told you you weren't fixing TV dinners and you ain't gonna!"

Crying, trying to shield her face, Francine squirmed away from the stove. Mickey caught her and hit her again. He took her by the arm, dragged her into the living room, and shoved her down on the couch.

"Listen to me, you bitch, I've made up my mind. You're quitting school right now."

Francine jumped up and screamed with a fury she had seldom shown before. "I am not quitting school! You can't make me!"

"Oh yes I can. What makes you think I can't?"

"Nothing can make me quit!"

"I'll fix you so you won't ever go back!"

"I don't care what you do," Francine screamed. "I'll still go in. If I have black eyes I'll go in. If I have to limp in there, I'll go in. There's nothing you can do!"

Francine's resistance seemed to please Mickey. He sat down and took on a crafty look. His tone was quieter as he taunted her. "I can always fix your car so it won't go. It's a long walk to Lansing, whore!"

"If you bust it, I'll get it fixed."

"You won't have it fixed when I get through with it. I'm gonna do the job right. I'm gonna do it with a sledgehammer."

Francine thought, "Oh Jesus, he'll do it! I know he'll do it!" She said nothing.

Another thought struck Mickey. "You're gonna get rid of that car. Call the Ford place and tell them to come and get it. Tell 'em you want to turn it back in."

"Mickey! I can't do that! They won't cancel a deal just like that. I signed a contract!"

"Yes, you can do it!" He got up and came toward her, fully menacing again. "You got about three seconds to do it or I'm gonna get the sledgehammer. Is that what you want?"

Francine went to the telephone. While she looked through her address book and dialed, her mind worked frantically. She did not dial the final digit. After a pause she began to fake a conversation with the car dealer. "I want to turn in my car. . . . No, I don't want it anymore. . . . You won't take it back? Why not? . . . I see. . . . You'll do it next month? . . . I see. . . . Thank you very much."

She turned from the phone to Mickey. "They said they wouldn't come and get it unless I was behind in the payments, but I'm all paid up. If I don't pay next month they'll come and take it then."

Mickey said nothing. He was sitting in his chair again, a can of beer in his hand. Francine sensed that he was brooding over his next move. She went to the kitchen, hoping that if she were out of sight he might cool off. A moment later she heard the thump of books cascading to the floor. She ran back. Mickey had emptied her book bag in a heap. He picked up a textbook and his face contorted as he struggled to rip it apart. Her notebooks and papers were easier. He tore out pages and crumpled them. Francine watched with frozen fury as weeks of work was destroyed, but dared not utter a word. Mickey turned from her papers to her pocketbook. He took out her car keys, checkbook, and money and put them in his pocket. Then he ripped her wallet apart and threw it on top of the heap. He smiled at Francine in triumph. "Now, bitch! Betcha you don't go to school!"

Francine looked at the ruins on the floor and her self-control broke. "I'll get more books," she screamed. "You're not going to stop me. You can't tell me what to do anymore. You can't run my life anymore! I'll go to school without books. No matter what you do I'll go!"

Mickey leaped across the room and caught her by the neck. He delivered a stinging slap across her face. He was gritting his teeth.

"Pick up that stuff on the floor! Clean it up right now, or I'll break your fucking neck. Take it out to the burn barrel and burn the whole fucking lot. Do you understand? Got it?" His fingers were biting into her neck like steel clamps. "Are you gonna burn 'em? *Are you?*" He shook her, holding her so close that she could smell sour beer, feel spit on her face as the words exploded out of his mouth. His blue-green eyes were glaring and wild. "Do you want your neck broke right now?"

For a moment Francine didn't answer. Tears were sliding down her face; her stomach was knotted with fear, but she glared back. His fingers tightened. Pain and panic swept through her. She gasped.

Mickey's fingers relaxed. He shoved her away and went to the bedroom. Francine began to gather up the ruins. Tears and slime from her nose wet her hands and blurred the ink on notebook pages. Her head throbbed when she bent down and her lips were puffing up. She tasted the sickening taste of blood on her tongue. She picked up classroom notes on psychology and laid them on top of her data filing homework; she flattened out the pages of her term paper, "What I Know About Myself." Her speedwriting exercises had been ripped into shreds. Her mind recorded each detail, but her emotions had become quite still. She got a large trash can from the kitchen and carefully put the debris into it. She put on her coat and carried the trash can outside to the barrel in the yard in which the trash was burned. She tilted it and watched as her books and papers sank into the ashes of the winter's burning.

Francine cannot remember lighting the fire, but knows that she stayed until she saw flames working at the edges of the pages, saw them shrink and blacken. When a plume of smoke rose, she turned and went back into the kitchen.

Mickey called her from the living room. "Come here. I want to talk to you. Come in here and sit down." Mickey pointed to the love seat and Francine sat down.

Mickey said, "*Now* are you gonna go to school"

There was a pause while Francine thought the question over. With a sense of surprise she heard herself say, "Yeah, Mickey. I am. I'm going to keep on going to school."

Francine remembers the rest of that day:

"While we were fighting the kids were at the door, knocking, saying they were hungry. I said, 'Mickey, can't we talk about school later? Let me feed the kids, please!' He said, 'You ain't gonna cook that shit. I already told you that. You ain't gonna do *anything*. You're gonna sit right there, and you're gonna tell me that you're gonna quit school.'

"I was thinking, 'Maybe I should say it and get him quieted down and figure out later how to go back to school.' But I couldn't do it. Something rose up in me and said, No! Not this time. Don't ever say it. If you say it, it will be all over. Mickey will win, like he always has, and you'll never go back to school again. Mickey said, 'Hurry up and say it before I get really mad! Hurry up, you mother-fucking bitch.'

"His eyes were really dangerous, but I couldn't give in. I thought, 'I'm going to go to school if I have to walk all the way to Lansing; if I have to hobble in there on crutches; if I have to replace my books fifty thousand times.' School had given me a new look at life. I had gained strength, glimpsed how happy life could be. I wasn't going to go back to being afraid to walk down the street, afraid people were talking about me, being paranoid and loathsome to myself. I had fought so hard to climb out of that pit. I wasn't going to let him throw me back in it now.

"Mickey kept threatening me, but I wouldn't say those words, 'I'm not going to school anymore.' 'You ain't going,' Mickey kept repeating. 'You're gonna stay home and do things you're supposed to do. You're gonna clean and cook, not buy TV dinners.'

"I said, 'What difference does it make? You don't eat anyway. Why should you care what we have to eat? When you do eat you throw it up.'

"He got up and threw his beer all over me. I jumped up and he shoved me down and started punching. He was calling me every filthy name; saying I was *gonna* quit school and if I didn't say it he would break every bone in my body. I was crying and screaming that I hated him, that I would never say it.

"He stopped hitting me, I don't know why, and sat down. I got up and went to the bedroom and changed my clothes, all wet and sour with beer, and bathed my face. I was bruised and exhausted. I thought maybe the worst was over. When I came back I asked Mickey if I could feed the kids now. He said yes, and I went into the kitchen and turned the oven on. A minute later Mickey came in and turned it off. Then he hit me again. I ran into the dining room. We went round and round the table. His eyes were glaring and I believed that if he caught me he'd kill me no matter what I said. I tried to get out the door into the yard. Mickey caught me and pinned me in the doorway. He was punching me, saying, 'I'm gonna kill you this time, you dirty whore! You better say your prayers.' I crouched down, trying to cover my head. The kids were in the yard and I yelled, 'Christy, call the police!' Mickey turned. He must have seen her take off across the yard to Flossie's house. He dropped his hands and went into the living room.

"I went into the kitchen and bathed my face again. I thought he'd probably be quiet until the cops came. He knew better than to let them see him hit me. I turned the oven on again.

"It took the cops about twenty minutes to get there. I was ready to feed the kids when two deputies knocked at the door and I let them in. The cops said, 'Well . . . what seems to be the matter here?' That was what they always said when they arrived. I told them we had been fighting and that Mickey had been hitting me. They looked at Mickey and asked, 'Well, have you?' He said, 'Yeah. That's right.' He was belligerent, but crafty; not drunk enough to get up and hit one of them. He knew talk didn't count.

"The cops stayed about twenty minutes. Mickey cursed and threatened, but didn't make a move. The cops didn't say much. One of them scolded him and told him that talking like that and hitting me was a bad thing to do. Mickey said he was going to kill me. The cop said, 'You're going to kill her? Where do you think that will get you?' I was thinking, 'This is a waste of time; a waste of your time, officer, and a waste of my time; of everybody's time. The minute you leave Mickey can do anything he wants to me. You know it; I know it. Above all, he knows it!'

"One of the deputies asked me if I wanted to go somewhere. I thought of how many times I had run away and how it always ended right back where it began. I had used up all the places to run. I was too tired to run. I said no, that I couldn't go anywhere; Mickey had my car keys and anyway he would follow me wherever I went.

"The cops said if there was a relative within Ingham County I wanted to go to they could take me there, but that they couldn't go out of the county. I said, 'No, thanks.' I explained that my mother and sisters lived in Jackson County. It all seemed like an empty formality. I was grateful they had quieted Mickey. I knew that was all they could do. I said, 'Thank you, officers. Thank you for coming. I'm sorry I took your time.' They said they'd be in the area if I needed them and they left.

"By now the TV dinners were done. I could smell them. I let the kids in from the yard and set the table. Mickey stayed in his chair. I thought, 'Maybe if we're all very quiet he won't start again. Maybe he's worn out, too, and will fall asleep.'

"I set the table and told the kids to sit down and not make any noise. They didn't say a word. I put the TV dinners in front of them, and poured their milk and sat down, too. I had forgotten my hunger, but at the sight and smell of food I felt starved. I picked up a leg of chicken and put salt on it. I tried to take a bite, but my lip was swelled and cut; the salt stung like fire. I had to put the

chicken down. I thought, 'Damn! I want that chicken so!' and tears
rolled down my cheeks.

"At that moment Mickey came into the kitchen. He got a beer
out of the refrigerator. When he turned around he hit me without
any warning, on the side of the head. I jumped up. The kids
jumped up. Milk spilled. Mickey pounded on the table, cursing me.
He picked up my dinner and threw it on the floor. Then he
knocked everything else off the table . . . milk, bread, TV dinners,
silverware. Christy was yelling, 'Daddy, don't! Please, don't!' Nicky
was bawling.

"Mickey turned on her like he was going to hit her, but he didn't.
He yelled at them all to get upstairs to their rooms. The kids ran as
fast as they could. Then he turned on me again. I was standing
against the wall. Mickey came close and glared into my eyes. 'If
you think things were bad before, they're gonna be worse now. I'm
gonna make your life so miserable. . . .'

"I thought, 'How can you? There's nothing more you can do.' But
I was wrong. He grabbed me by the hair and pushed me down on
my knees, so my face was almost into the mess on the floor: the
spilled milk, the TV dinners, mashed potatoes, gravy, chicken. Everything that was so good a minute before he had turned into garbage. He held my face over it and said, 'Now, bitch, clean it up.'
He held me that way until I began to scrape it up with my hands.
Then he let go and left the room.

"I got up and got a dustpan and paper towels and began picking
up the mess. Some of the food was stepped on and mashed into
the rug. I was sobbing and thinking, '*Why?* Why is this happening?
Why am I so helpless? Why can he do anything he wants—*anything*
—and not even the law can stop him?'

"I had put the last of the garbage in the can and was on my feet
when Mickey came back. He said, 'Have you got it cleaned up?' I
said, 'Yes.' He picked up the garbage can and turned it upside
down and dumped it on the floor again. He said, 'Now, bitch, clean
it up again!' I picked up the dustpan and the paper towels and was
bending down, trying to shovel it up, when Mickey picked up a
handful of food and tried to rub it in my face. I turned my head to
get away and he rubbed it into my hair. It trickled down the back
of my neck. Then he hit me two or three times. Somehow I got over
into a corner and raised my arms. I was afraid he would break my

nose or knock out my teeth. While he pounded on me I slumped down, further and further, sinking into the corner. It was the loneliest moment of my life. It wouldn't matter how I yelled and screamed. Nobody would hear me; nobody would help me; nobody cared.

"Mickey said, 'You dumb, mother-fucking whore, do you still think you're gonna go to school?'

"I felt my heart and my spirit break. I said, 'No, Mickey. I'm not gonna go to school.' I'd lost. I was beaten, defeated, broken. He said, 'Say it three times, whore!'

"I said, 'I'm not gonna . . . I'm not gonna . . . I'm not gonna . . .' I was sobbing and couldn't finish.

"Mickey dropped his hands and stood over me, smiling. He said, 'Clean it up. Then make me something to eat.' He went into the bedroom. I cleaned the mess up again. The kids were calling from upstairs, 'Mommy, are you all right?' I went up the stairs and called to them through the door that I was okay, not to worry. Mickey yelled, 'Keep that goddamn door shut and stay away from it! Get your ass down here and do like I said!' I came down the stairs thinking, 'You can't even protect your children. He can do anything he wants to them, too!'

"Mickey came out of the bedroom again. 'Are you gonna do like I say?' He stared at me like he was thinking of killing me right then, as though he was yearning for an excuse. I said, 'Yes, Mickey. I am.'

"He shrugged and said, 'Okay. I want some supper and it better be something I like.'

"I went to the kitchen. There was almost nothing on the shelves. I never had money to buy ahead. I found a can of salmon. I was shaking so I could hardly open it. I had some cooked potatoes. I made patties and put them in a pan.

"Mickey came into the kitchen and looked in the pan and said, 'I don't want that shit! You can just throw that out!'

"I said, 'Okay, Mickey, but it's all I have. If I throw this out there's nothing else I can fix for you.' He thought it over and then he said, 'Okay. I'll eat it.' He took a beer and said, 'I'll eat in the bedroom. Bring it in there.' I fixed his plate as nice as I could and brought it to him. He was lying on the bed looking at TV. He had his own TV in the bedroom.

"I went back to the kitchen to finish cleaning up. I couldn't stand to watch him eat. The kids were quiet upstairs. I didn't dare go to them until Mickey went to sleep. Usually when he had eaten he would go to sleep.

"Mickey yelled for me and I went into the bedroom. He had finished eating. His empty plate was on the floor. He was lying on the bed and he had unzipped his pants. My stomach jumped inside me and I shut my eyes. I thought, 'Oh *no!*'

"Mickey grinned at me. 'How about a little?' he said and began to pull down his pants. He already had an erection. I stood there frozen. I thought I might vomit. I had an impulse to run, but I stopped myself. I thought, 'If you resist, this will go on all night. If you give in, it will be over. He'll go to sleep.'

"I sat down on the edge of the bed. Mickey got up and took off everything: shirt, pants, underwear. God, I hated to look at him sexually aroused. 'Come on,' he said, 'hurry up!' I was wearing slacks. I took them off. 'Everything!' Mickey said. 'I want everything off!' So I took off my sweater and my bra and underpants and stood there naked. He shoved me down on the bed and began.

"I hated it worse than I ever had before. The idea of him inside me, owning even my insides, shoving deep into me, made my flesh crawl. Because he was drunk it took a long time. At one point he wanted me on top. I looked down at him and I had an impulse to put the pillow over his face and smother him, but I knew I wasn't strong enough. I clenched my teeth to keep from screaming. He said nothing; he just went on sawing at me until, after about thirty minutes, he finished. He lay there on his back and I got up and picked up my clothes and went to the bathroom to wash him off me as quick as I could.

"I dressed and went into the living room and sat down. There is no way to describe how I felt: a helpless, frozen fury; a volcano blocked just before it erupts.

"I could hear the kids mumbling and moving around upstairs. I remembered that they had eaten nothing all day. I could almost feel their stomachs hurting. I decided I would wait until Mickey was asleep and then get them down and feed them. I don't know how long I sat there. I wasn't really thinking. My mind was empty, drained.

"After a while I checked and Mickey was asleep, lying on his back, breathing deep. I went upstairs and whispered to the kids, 'Do you guys want to come down?' They said yes, and I said, 'Be very quiet. Dad's asleep and he told me not to let you down.' They tiptoed down the stairs. I asked if they were hungry. They all said no. I guess their stomachs were numb like mine.

"I told them to sit on the couch and watch TV. I thought it would help them relax and they might eat later on. I turned on the set and sat down with them. Nicky lay with her head in my lap. I stroked her and she fell asleep. I have no memory of what show we watched because my thoughts were beginning to stir. They seemed to run like a river, of their own accord. I thought of school. How desperately hard I'd worked—for nothing. What a fool I'd been to think I could make my life better. No matter what I did Mickey would knock it down. I thought of my future: to be at his mercy, all day, every day, day after day, like I had been before but now without hope. I thought about my whole life; how awful it had been ever since I'd met Mickey; how I had suffered, trying to make things better, and how everything I had done was a waste. I thought, 'You don't owe him anything, Fran! *You never did.*' I thought of the children and how their lives were almost as terrible as mine. I thought, 'Don't let him ruin their lives the way he has ruined yours. Take them away! You've got to take them away! How? Just leave! When Mickey wakes up, you and the kids will be gone!'

"My thoughts began to race. I felt very clear-headed, as though I had waked up from a long, refreshing sleep. I thought, 'You *can* take off. There's a car sitting out there with gas in it. You and the kids just get in the car and go. Drive all night. Drive all tomorrow. Don't think about what happens after that! Don't think of anything except going! Go! And never turn back!'

"Suddenly this seemed very simple. I wondered why I hadn't thought of it that way before. I had made a discovery; by losing everything I had been set free! There were no chains around my ankles. All the things that had seemed important before—the house payments, car payments, welfare checks, leaving my mother and sisters, leaving the only place I knew—none of those things mattered. I felt thrilled; scared; elated; the way you feel just before the roller coaster begins to roll.

"I got up and started pacing the floor, telling myself, 'You can do it, Fran. You can do it! Do it quick before you lose your nerve. Don't make plans. It was making plans that always stopped you before.' Suddenly it dawned on me that Mickey had taken my money and my keys. I tiptoed into the bedroom and got them and the food stamps out of his pants pocket. I took what money he had, too. I thought, 'I need it more than you.'

"Now I was ready to go. I was just going to tell the kids to get in the car when it hit me that Dana wasn't there! For an instant I thought the whole thing would crumble. I couldn't leave without Dana. If Dana had been home I would have gone and Mickey would still be alive. I sat down again to wait for Dana. I wasn't sure what time his friends would bring him home, but no matter how long it took, I would have to wait.

"I looked over at Christy and Jimmy. Their faces looked pinched and tired. I loved them so. I said, 'You guys, go get your coats and shoes on. We're going to leave.' Christy said, 'Where are we going, Mom?' I said, 'I don't know, but we can't stay here. We can't live like this anymore.'

"They got their coats and shoes on and sat back down on the couch. Jimmy said, 'When are we gonna leave?' I said, 'As soon as Dana gets here. Just be very quiet! Don't wake *him* up.' Jimmy said, 'We better cover up in case he gets up, so he won't see our coats.' I said, 'Yeah. That's a good idea.'

"Jimmy got a blanket and he and Christy snuggled under it. Nicky was asleep beside them. We were all quiet. I kept looking out the window, wishing Dana would come. It was dark. I was watching for the headlights of a car. Cars went by; none of them stopped. I wondered if Dana were walking home. He should be here by now. I felt more and more scared. I began to pray that Dana would come soon. 'Please, Dana, come home before I lose my nerve!'

"Christy whispered, 'Mom?'

" 'What, Christy?'

" 'This time are we coming back?'

" 'No! Never!'

"She said, 'Good! I don't want to ever come back here again.'

"More minutes passed and Dana didn't come. I was getting very nervous. How could I be sure I wouldn't come back? Hadn't I always caved in, been defeated, been pulled back here against my will? This time had to be different. But how? I got up and walked around the room. Everything I looked at was part of my life with Mickey. I hated it. All of it. I hated my whole past life. I wanted to wipe it out . . . erase it . . . forget it . . . never look back. That was when the thought struck me: I wasn't going to come back because there wasn't going to be anything to come back to—because I was going to burn the house down. What about Mickey? Yes! I decided to burn him, too! Then everything would be gone.

"I became tremendously excited. I forgot everything else—Dana, the consequences, the fact of taking a life, nothing like that occurred to me. I thought of nothing but what I was going to do.

"I bent over Jimmy and asked him the combination to the padlock that Mickey had put on the garage door. Mickey had told Jimmy the numbers, but he hadn't told me. Jimmy whispered them in my ear. I went out in the dark to the garage. I had forgotten how dark it was. I couldn't see the numbers—couldn't make the combination work. For an instant I was stopped and almost panicked. Then, like water flows around a rock, my thoughts flowed right on. 'There's other places to look. Don't turn back. This time nothing can make you turn back.'

"The cellar had an outside door. I pulled it open and went down the steps into the dark. I lit a match and looked around until I saw a gas can that we kept for the mowing machine. That was what I'd been looking for. I carried it up the steps and into the house. I put it down and told the kids to go get into the car. I picked up Nicky, still sleeping, and carried her out and put her on the back seat. I said to Christy and Jimmy, 'Don't come back in the house. Stay in the car. I'll be right back.'

"I went back into the house. I was as calm as though I were doing an ordinary thing. I felt very light, clear-headed, free. This was the easiest thing I had ever done. I picked up the gas can and unscrewed the lid and went into the bedroom. I stood still for a moment, hesitating, and a voice urged me on. It whispered, 'Do it! Do it! Do it!' I sloshed the gasoline on the floor. If I saw Mickey lying there I don't remember it. I don't believe I looked at him at all.

"I went out of the room and put the can down. I had the matches in my hand. I don't remember lighting one, but there was a flame. I stood just outside the doorway and stuck the match into the room. Only then did it hit me. 'My God! What are you doing!'

The fumes of gas caught with a roar and a rush of air slammed the door with tremendous force, almost catching my hand.

"I ran for my life.

"I ran to the car and started it. At the corner I looked back and saw flames shooting out of the bedroom window, a fiery glow inside. I realized what I had done. I felt my mind almost disintegrate with the shock. The kids were looking back, too, and screaming, 'Oh God, Mom, oh God!' I heard Jimmy in the back seat say, 'Dad will be burned up!'

"Christy says I began to scream, but I didn't know it. I didn't even know I was driving a car until Christy, who was beside me, got my attention by beating on my arm and yelling, 'Mom! Where are we going? What are we going to do?' I realized we were on the highway, headed toward Mason. My thoughts were in fragments. All I could think was, 'You've got to get help! Do something quick!' I had a vision of Mickey getting out of the house, following me, killing me, even though he was in flames.

"Christy said, 'Mom! Go to the police. They can help us. Slow down! You're gonna kill us all!' I remember coming to a stop at the gate to the Ingham County Jail. Cops poked their heads in the car window, saying, 'Can I help you?' I couldn't talk. It was like a dream in which you're paralyzed. Every time I tried to speak, instead of speaking I heard myself scream. I heard Christy telling the police that the house was on fire. Then I heard myself say, 'I did it!' Somebody asked if anyone was in the house. I said, 'Yes . . . my ex-husband.'

"I heard men yelling. Cops were swarming around. I felt relief because they were taking charge. I don't remember getting out of the car. Bright lights hit my eyes when I walked into the lobby of the jail. A cop told the kids to sit down on a bench. I didn't want to leave them there. I tried to protest, but there was a cop holding me by each arm, pulling me along. I was led down a hall, to a room with a bare table and straight chairs. I was still crying, not with sobs, but convulsions that choked off my breath. Every time I tried to tell what happened I saw a vision of the fire, flames shooting out of the bedroom windows, and a wave of pain would wash over me; my throat would close and I couldn't talk. I thought of Dana, left behind. Where was he? He would be terrified if he saw the house on fire. He might think the kids and I were inside. I got my voice under control and asked the cops about Dana. They shook their heads. They didn't know. I asked about Mickey. Had they found him? Nobody answered me. They just kept asking me to tell what happened; what I had done. Little by little I began to tell them. With each word, realization would sweep over me like a fiery chill.

"A cop read aloud a legal paper about my rights. I didn't care. I signed where he told me to. There was a policewoman there. Later I learned her name: Patricia Moore. She tried to calm me, telling me to pull myself together, asking if I wanted coffee.

"I needed to go to the bathroom. She took my arm and steered me down the hall. I had a view of the lobby and suddenly saw the kids, sitting close together, looking scared and green under the bright lights. It hit me that they still had not eaten. I started to run to them. Pat Moore held me back. She wasn't rough, but she was firm. She said, 'No! Not now. It will just make things worse!' Perhaps that was the moment I first realized I wasn't free; that the police weren't trying to help me; that I might be under arrest. We had to wait for a key to get into the washroom. Standing there these new thoughts made my mind reel again. If Mickey was dead what would happen to me? Would they put me in jail? Then what would happen to the kids?

"Inside the washroom I washed my face and hands. My face felt burning—scalded with tears. I let cold water run over my hands and bathed my face. It cleared my head, but I still couldn't believe where I was and what had happened. Maybe I had gone crazy and this was all a dream. I saw Pat Moore standing guard over me in her police uniform and I knew it was true.

"When we got back to the room there were a lot more men there, milling around. Phones were ringing. A detective, Lieutenant Tift, asked me questions; asked me to tell the whole thing all over again. I told him about Mickey trying to kill me; about the years and years it had gone on; about the beating and the garbage rubbed in my hair, and burning my books.

"Tift didn't look like a policeman. He was a skinny, older man in a brown suit. His eyes and his voice were cold and hard. When I talked about what Mickey had done I felt my words had no meaning to him, as though Mickey had done nothing at all. All Tift wanted to know was what I had done; how I got the gasoline; how I lit it; did I plan it that way? I told him everything I could remember. I kept asking if Mickey was dead. Tift wouldn't answer. Finally he said, 'If he is, you'll be charged with murder.' *Murder!* The word shocked me all over again.

"Someone interrupted to tell me that Dana was okay; they were bringing him to the jail. I thought, 'Thank God! They'll be together. Christy will take care of him.' Then I thought of how long the kids had been sitting out there, alone, nobody doing anything for them, and how awful they must feel. I asked if I could call my mother. Tift said okay, and Pat Moore led me to a phone. I don't know what time it was, but Mom was asleep. The phone rang a long time. When she answered, hearing her voice was another pang. I said, 'Mom, please come and get the kids. We're all at the Ingham County Jail in Mason. Call Joanne and get here somehow.' She asked, 'Why? What happened?' I didn't want to tell her. I said, 'Please, Mom, just come and get them. *Please!*'

"She insisted I tell her. She was getting more and more upset. I had to say, 'I set the house on fire, Mom.' She said, 'Oh my God! Was he in it?' I said, 'Yes.' She said, 'God have mercy! Oh God, Fran!' I said, 'You've got to come and get the kids. I think they're going to arrest me.' She said, 'I'll be there as quick as I can.'

"I hung up and asked Pat Moore if I would be allowed to speak to Mom when she came. She said no, so I handed her my purse with the money and food stamps and asked her to give it to Mom so she could feed the kids.

"When we got back to the room where I'd been questioned, Tift was talking on the phone. When he hung up he said something to one of the men about getting a dentist to examine teeth. I said, 'A dentist? Why are you doing that?' Tift leaned back and gave me a strange look. He said, 'To confirm his identity; to make sure who he is.'

"I still didn't understand. I said, 'Who? Make sure who *who* is?'

"Tift smiled and said, 'Your husband. We've just got word that they've found his body. He's dead.'

"I think I had known it all along, but when Tift said it I felt suddenly sick. My stomach heaved. I looked around at all the cops in their uniforms. They were unconcerned, busy, doing their everyday job. There wasn't a single sympathetic face. It didn't matter to them what Mickey had done to me. Like always, nobody cared. I was suddenly terribly afraid of everyone in the room.

"Lieutenant Tift sat down at a typewriter and put a sheet of paper in. He said, 'All right, Francine. Are you ready?'

"I said, 'Ready for what?'

"He said, 'To make a statement, a statement of what you did.'

"His voice was curt. There was nothing but contempt in his eyes. My head was clearing up. I thought, 'This man wants to trap you; to make things worse for you than they already are.' I remembered all the TV shows I'd seen about crime and I knew that you're not supposed to say anything until you've seen a lawyer. I decided I wouldn't say anything more.

"Tift was waiting. He said, 'Come on, Francine. You've already told us everything. Just tell me again so I can get it down on paper.'

"I shook my head. I said, 'I guess I better see a lawyer first.' Tift kept trying to persuade me. 'What's the difference? You've already admitted it. Come on, get it off your chest.' I kept on shaking my head. He snapped the paper out of the typewriter. He said, 'You're going to be charged with murder! Murder in the first degree!' He told the policewoman to take me away.

"She led me through corridors, like hospital corridors, only there were locks and bars. At the Women's Quarters, a matron, Miss Lewis, took me in charge. She led me into a big, brightly lit room and told me to drop my clothes on the floor. I asked what for? She said I had to be sprayed in case I had lice. I stood there naked, cringing. Miss Lewis tried to be kind. After she sprayed me she gave me a nightgown and tucked a blanket and a sheet under my arm. Then she led me to a cell. It was a big room with bars opening onto a corridor. While Miss Lewis was opening the door I looked in. In the dim light I could see other women lying on bunks against the wall. There were a table and chairs in the center. I had read about jails and the horrible things that happened in them. I was terrified of going into that cell.

"Miss Lewis gently shoved me in and locked the door behind me. I stood there. I didn't know what to do next. I could feel all those eyes on me. I went over to the table and sat down.

"A voice from one of the bunks said, 'What are you in here for?'

"Another voice answered, 'You know better than to ask a question like that. If she wants you to know she'll tell you.'

"A third person said, 'There's a bunk in the corner if you want it.'

"I went over to it and lay down. I closed my eyes and saw flames shooting out of the bedroom windows, lighting up the sky. I heard Jimmy saying, 'My God! Dad will be burned up!' Was Mickey burned alive? Pain washed over me, as though my own body were in flames."

Ingham County Jail

In the morning Francine was issued a gray sweatshirt and blue cotton trousers, the uniform worn by female prisoners. She was taken from her cell to be fingerprinted and photographed with a number on her chest. She felt a devastating humiliation. She was partially stripped so that the bruises on various parts of her body could also be photographed, and this caused her almost equal shame. When she returned to the cell she lay face down, exhausted, on her bunk. Somewhere a radio poured out ceaseless sound. At intervals, when the news came on, she heard her name as the announcer talked about her in a cheerful patter: ". . . fatal fire in Dansville . . . twenty-nine-year-old wife held in Ingham County Jail . . . Francine Hughes . . . mother of four." The words penetrated her half-sleep and became part of her dreams. She was awakened and handed a document. It was a legal notice of the charges against her. ". . . Did then and there, with malice aforethought, willfully, deliberately and with premeditation intentionally kill. . . ." At the bottom were the words, "Maximum Penalty—Life."

A policewoman, Nancy Kalder, brought her her clothes and told her to dress for a trip to court. In the lobby she casually snapped handcuffs on Francine's wrists. As Francine felt the cold, unyielding metal a wave of panic swept over her. "Do I have to have these?" she asked. Kalder nodded, not unkindly, and led her to a police car waiting outside. It was a short trip to the district courthouse in Mason. Francine knew she was being brought before a judge, but had no idea what it would entail.

Handcuffed and flanked by her guards, she entered the courtroom. Benches on either side of the aisle were crowded, as if at a wedding in which she played the travesty role of bride. Where the altar should be, Judge Bell sat behind a high desk, wearing a black robe. She remembered his face from the day he'd sentenced Mickey to jail.

Francine saw Flossie's tall figure seated among the spectators, flanked by her menfolk. Berlin, stooped and narrow-shouldered, sat on her left; Donovan and Marlin were on the right with their wives. Berlin wore his best suit, Flossie a hat. Until that moment Francine had forgotten Mickey's parents. She thought, "Oh God, Flossie and Berlin must be going out of their minds!"

At her entrance the spectators stirred and murmured; heads turned. Francine had a searing impression of Flossie and Berlin's accusing, suffering faces before she was led past them toward the judge. On the other side of the courtroom she saw her own family: her mother, her sisters Joanne and Kathy, and between them, Christy and Jimmy, staring at her with frightened eyes. To have them see her in handcuffs made her feel sick with shame.

Francine recognized Lieutenant Tift addressing the judge. It seemed to be Tift who was accusing her of murder. She understood the words, "first degree murder and felony murder." What she had done was evidently so terrible that she was accused not once, but twice. Judge Bell asked if she wanted an attorney and she said, "Yes." He asked if she had funds and she said, "No."

The arraignment was over. Francine kept her eyes down as she was led back down the aisle. When she reached the corridor outside she asked if she could speak with her mother. Kalder said, "Sure. Why not?" They waited in the hall. When her mother and the children came, Francine found she dared not speak lest she break down. Her mother was crying. She hugged Francine and said, "Don't worry. We'll help you all we can." Francine could only nod. She exchanged tearful glances with Joanne and Kathy. She raised her arms to hug Christy, but the handcuffs made it impossible. Christy flung her arms around her neck and whimpered, "Oh Mom, what's going to happen to you?" Jimmy was tearless and pale. As Francine kissed him she could feel him trembling. She longed to comfort him, but could think of nothing to say. Deputy Kalder tugged at her arm and led her away.

The following days in the Ingham County Jail were a delirium of blurred impressions. Every sound caused her a painful shudder. She was allowed to lie in her bunk; no one bothered her. She slipped in and out of a sleep filled with vivid dreams.

"I'd be dreaming; I would hear metal clanking on metal. They were sliding the food trays through the slot in the door. I'd wake and it would flash over me, 'You're in jail for murder!' Then I'd think, 'Where are the kids? The kids are with Mom. You can't go to them. You're locked in. You're in jail. Mickey is dead and you killed him. Oh God in heaven, it can't be true!'"

Francine tried to avoid contact with the women sharing her cell, and they left her alone. After a few days their faces and voices became less menacing as one or another of them explained the routine by which they lived. The mechanics of life—washbasin, shower, toilet—were all carried on within the cell without concealment. Bars on one wall of the cell faced a catwalk where the matrons and women trustees went by with mops, trays, and baskets of laundry as they did housekeeping chores. Tall windows opened on the catwalk and allowed daylight into the cell. At night a television set just outside the bars was turned on and filled the cell with sound.

It seemed to Francine that she lay in her bunk for days. She felt as though she had been wracked by a terrible illness. She was unable to eat. The matrons brought her special food—Jell-O and milk and boiled eggs—but she left them untouched. She was allowed to telephone her mother, who told her that the children were all right and that with the help of Francine's sisters she was managing to take care of them. Christy came on the phone and Francine broke down. She went back to bed to reenter a state of half-sleep and fitful dreams.

One morning, after she had waited her turn to wash her face, she looked in the mirror for the first time since the fire. Her face looked gray and haggard, her hair dirty and lank. It was the face of someone who had given up. "I told myself, 'Fran, you are still alive, whether you want to be or not. Mickey is dead, but you are here. You can't change that. You have to go on living and do the best you can.'"

She stepped into the shower, even though public bathing offended her modesty. She brushed her hair, and when breakfast came she made an effort to swallow it, determined to take care of herself as best she could. She opened letters that had accumulated by her bunk and read them in surprise. Some were from strangers who had read about her in the newspapers. Others were from friends and acquaintances. In one way or another the letters expressed sympathy for her. She realized there were people, outside her own family, who did not see her as a monster.

Francine began to talk to her cellmates, learning their names, answering questions, and accepting friendly overtures. "You might as well talk to them," she thought. "You're one of them now."

She had been in jail a week when she was told that an attorney was there to see her. The news unnerved her. She didn't even know his name. What would he be like? How would he feel about what she had done? A matron escorted her to a conference room. Her first impression of the man waiting there was that he was astonishingly tall. She was surprised, too, that he was so young—about her own age. He didn't smile, but greeted her formally. He wore large round spectacles and had gray eyes. When they were seated, facing each other across a small table, he told her his name—Aryon Greydanus—and explained that he had been appointed by the court to represent her. He asked, in a neutral tone, "Well, Francine, do you want to tell me what happened?"

Francine doesn't remember how she began, only that she tried to tell him everything. "I had to pour it out to someone. I wanted to tell the whole truth. There was nothing to hide. I knew I was guilty. I knew I was in terrible, terrible trouble. Maybe he could help, though I didn't really believe anyone could. My head had cleared enough so I understood my crime. I had committed murder and the penalty was prison for life. I didn't think a lawyer could change that, but I wanted someone to know how I could have done this horrible thing."

While Francine talked Greydanus made notes on a yellow pad. His eyes hardly left hers. She began to feel there was understanding, even sympathy, in his gaze. When the interview ended she had formed a feeling of trust. Before leaving her Greydanus explained the next steps in the legal process. She would again be brought before Judge Bell. Witnesses would testify to what they knew of the circumstances of Mickey's death. After this preliminary examination she would be bound over for trial in a higher court. Not until then would she offer a defense or testify. Greydanus promised he would do everything he could to help her. How much he could do was left unsaid.

Ten days after the fire, Francine was taken to court for the hearing Greydanus had described. Now fully aware and filled with apprehension, she cringed as she was led into the courtroom filled with spectators. She was taken to a seat at a table before the judge's bench. Greydanus sat beside her. Francine kept her eyes down, but she had glimpsed the Hughes family and was conscious that they were watching every step in the process of punishment. Greydanus pointed out a young man of slender build with light brown hair and whispered that he was Martin Palus, the prosecutor who would handle the case against her. His manner was mild, but whenever Greydanus rose to argue a technicality, Palus opposed him with a persistence that impressed on Francine that he was intent on prosecuting her to the utmost.

Throughout the long court day Francine heard her crime described from every aspect—sometimes by strangers, sometimes by people she knew. The first witness was Detective Onnie Selin, who recited what he and Tift had found in the burnt-out bedroom. He was followed by Fireman Don Gailey, who told how he had found Mickey's body. Dr. Laurence Simson, who had performed an autopsy, used long, barely comprehensible sentences which Francine finally understood to mean that Mickey had died from smoke inhalation. Simson had found Mickey's nostrils and lungs filled with soot. The burns on his body, Simson said, had occurred after death. As he talked, ghastly images flashed through Francine's mind, so awful that she ceased to listen. Wimpy took the stand briefly. He avoided looking at Francine. Tears rolled down his cheeks as he told how he had seen his brother's body on the porch.

Lieutenant Janutola described Francine's hysterical arrival at the Ingham County Jail. Then Jimmy was brought in. He was trembling visibly. He gave his mother an anguished look and tried to swallow tears. For Francine this was the worst moment since she had come out of her shock. Prosecutor Palus questioned Jimmy carefully about the sequence of events, especially how Francine had asked for the combination to the lock on the garage and how

Jimmy had later noticed the gasoline can by the door to the porch. Jimmy answered reluctantly, as though he knew he was being used to condemn his mother. Sometimes he looked down, in stubborn silence, and Palus had to repeat his question, insisting he answer. When Palus forced Jimmy to describe how Francine had behaved after the fire, Jimmy sobbed and Francine thought her heart would break. Palus decided it was time to let the boy go and a bailiff led him away.

Christy was the final witness. When Francine saw her, again, she felt almost unendurable pain. Christy was more composed than Jimmy. Palus asked only a few questions about the violence preceding the fire. He called it an argument. "Do you remember your mom and dad having an argument that day?"

"Yes."

"Do you remember what it was about?"

Christy groped for words. "It was about almost everything."

"And did your dad hit your mom that day?"

"Yes."

"Did he hit her a lot?"

"Yes."

"Did your father do anything with your mom's schoolbooks that day?"

"He ripped them up and threw them in the middle of the floor."

Palus went on to ask Christy about Francine's behavior just before the fire; how she had gotten the gas can; how long they had waited. When those facts had been established he ended his questioning. Greydanus had no questions and Christy stepped down.

As the session ended Judge Bell gave his decision; Francine would be held for trial on both counts, murder in the first degree and felony murder. Greydanus argued that the felony murder count was unjustified and pleaded to have it dismissed. The plea was denied. Then he asked the judge to grant bail so that Francine could be free during the months that would elapse before her trial. Palus opposed bail, citing the Michigan constitution, which prohibits bail pending trial for a capital crime. Judge Bell looked regretful. "My reaction as a person of compassion would be to set bail, but the prosecutor has objected and I think my hands are tied." As Francine was led away, Greydanus told her not to give up hope of getting bail; he would try again.

A week later Francine was taken to the Mason County Court-house and arraigned before Judge Michael Harrison, who was scheduled to conduct her trial. Waiting her turn, Francine sat in the dock with other prisoners accused of such crimes as robbery, shoplifting, and prostitution. No one else was charged with murder. There were spectators in the courtroom, but to her relief there was no one she knew among them.

When her case was called, she stood before the judge while Palus and Greydanus argued technical points concerning her coming trial. Judge Harrison was an unsmiling man in his forties. His expression struck her as stony and aloof. She watched the judge's face as he shifted his gaze from Palus to Greydanus. Not once did he glance at her. Francine thought, "He has already decided I am too low for him even to look at. He doesn't want to know who I am or why I did what I did."

Her arraignment took no more than five minutes. As it ended, Greydanus asked Harrison to grant bail, arguing that the judge had the discretion to grant it if he chose. Francine heard Judge Harrison curtly refuse. The policewoman escorting her tugged at her arm and led her from the courtroom for the trip back to jail. In the corridor Greydanus caught up with her. He put his hand on her shoulder and told her he would be coming to see her soon.

Greydanus kept his word. He visited Francine every week for talks that lasted two or three hours. He told her Judge Harrison's refusal to grant bail was final and she would have to stay in prison until her trial sometime in the summer; the date would depend on how long it took to prepare a defense.

Francine said that she thought Judge Harrison looked heartless, and as though he had already made up his mind that she deserved no pity. Greydanus agreed that having Harrison assigned to her case was a bad break. He quoted the judge's remark when he denied bail. "After all, what kind of woman would burn up her husband?" It confirmed Francine's feeling that Harrison had prejudged her case.

Greydanus had found the prosecutor equally without sympathy. He told Francine he had spoken to Chief Prosecutor Houk and found him determined to try her for first-degree murder and felony murder as well. Greydanus told Francine he would do his best to put together a defense, but he was not optimistic about her chances of escaping a prison term. The best she could hope for was that a jury would be more compassionate than the judge and the prosecutor had been, and find her guilty to a lesser degree—possibly manslaughter, but more probably murder in the second degree.

In her prison diary Francine wrote:

"My attorney says he has no defense for me. No defense! When he said, 'You know you could go to prison for the rest of your life,' I said, 'No! They can send me, but I won't stay.' He said, 'What do you mean by that?' I didn't answer. I was thinking that I would kill myself."

In one respect Francine was fortunate. The Ingham County Jail is relatively humane. The women's section usually holds no more than thirty prisoners, most of them awaiting trial. Because of a small and mostly transient population the worst evils that beset huge warehouse prisons are absent. Not all county jails are equally benign. Sheriff Preadmore happens to run a good jail.

Francine began to make friends among her cellmates, although she never lost her sense of difference. Prostitution, possession of drugs, bad checks, shoplifting, and theft were the most common crimes. Most of the women were young, and Francine found their way of life as "street people" who habitually broke laws fascinating and bizarre. She wrote:

"While I am lying on my bunk writing, there is a lot going on in the cell. One girl has her head in the toilet bowl. She empties the water in the toilet and talks down the pipe to the guys in the men's prison below. She is nineteen and charged as an accomplice to a murder during a robbery. I have learned something about street people: that they are really just humans but with worse problems. The other girls are building fires in the sink and heating toast left from breakfast. I don't like breaking rules. I guess they know this. I don't think they dislike me; it's just that I am different. I am educated a little more. I don't take drugs. I'm not an alcoholic. I'd rather die than sell my body to a different man every day, and I don't think it's right to steal. The women here throw filthy language around as if it is nothing and I don't do that. They talk back to the matrons and demand things where I don't feel I have the right."

The day in jail began with breakfast at six: cold cereal, milk, two pieces of toast, a two-ounce glass of watered-down orange juice, and a cup of coffee that tasted like hot water. "We take our toast and lay it over the top of the steaming coffee to warm it up because the toast is cold and greasy. Sometimes you keep the cereal so that if you don't like dinner you can eat the cereal with milk from your dinner tray. I had thought I knew a lot about surviving—making do with what you've got—but in prison I am learning a lot more."

In the isolation of jail Francine's psyche, more battered than her body, began to heal. During the first few weeks her emotions were so intense that she feared she would go insane. Then, gradually, she became calm, but deeply depressed. As she always had before, she fought to bring herself out of the depths. She wrote:

"I seem to go up and down in my moods. The last depression lasted five days. I can usually talk myself out of it in about two. I feel this terrible, enormous sense of loss of my children. I miss them so much I have to push thoughts of them away."

The children were living with Francine's mother and going to school in Jackson. Although Francine was allowed a weekly visit—standing up and talking through a window, without physical contact—she decided it would be too painful for her and too frightening for the children to have them brought to the jail. She was allowed one five-minute telephone call to them each week.

"I look forward to it all week, but when I actually talk to the kids it hurts so I can hardly stand it. The matron brings the phone into the cell and hands it to each girl in turn. She sings out, 'Time ya!' and looks at her watch. I talk to each of the kids, trying to sound normal and cheerful. Christy and Jimmy are doing okay, but I can tell they are worried and scared. They understand that I will stand trial and that no one knows how it will turn out. I try to reassure them, but I don't want to give them false hopes. Nicky doesn't understand. She asks me a lot of questions about where I am. She asked, 'Mommy, is your bed hard?' Last week, when it was Dana's turn, I said, 'Hi, Dana, whatcha doin'?' He said, 'Mommy . . .' and there was a long silence. I said, 'Dana, I can't hear you. What's the matter, Dana?' He said, 'Mommy, I'm hugging you through the phone.' It was too much for me. I had to hang up."

A few weeks after Mickey's death, Flossie and Berlin filed a suit asking for custody of the children. Greydanus represented Francine in opposing it, and told her he didn't believe the Hugheses could win, since their suit seemed based more on a desire for revenge than real concern for the children. Nevertheless, the suit was an added nightmare for Francine. Greydanus told her that the Hughes family was so enraged and bitter toward her that even if she could get bail he wondered if it would be safe for her to be out of prison.

The custody suit hung over her for several months. At one point Greydanus was forced to allow the children to visit their grandparents in Dansville for a weekend. Flossie and Berlin took them to their father's grave and reported, through their attorney, that Nicky had cried and kissed her father's headstone. The episode upset Francine; she thought it was a cruel effort to play on the children's emotions. To her relief, Flossie and Berlin made no further effort to see the children, and the suit was dropped.

When she had been in prison six weeks, Francine became eligible to attend high school and college extension classes offered to inmates who would be there a relatively long time. Francine enrolled in them all: math, American history, sociology, arts and crafts. The work did more than anything else to raise her morale and help overcome her despondency. She wrote to Miss Johnson, her psychology teacher at Lansing Business College, and asked if she could complete the course by mail. Miss Johnson replied that she could, and Francine wrote "What I Know About Myself Now" once again. This time she began, 'I know that I am a human being with a mind that isn't as strong as I thought it was . . . I know now that I can't endure everything and anything like I thought I could." Miss Johnson gave her a grade of A-minus for the term. Francine had made good her pledge to Mickey that nothing could stop her from completing the work she had set out to do.

To fight off terrible thoughts, Francine tried to be as busy as possible. In the morning, after the beds were made and the cell tidied, some of her cellmates lay down again and slept half the day, but Francine went to classes until noon. Back in the cell, she read, did her homework, wrote letters, or worked on her autobiography, writing on legal pads that Greydanus supplied. She kept the manuscript under her mattress, hoping no one would read it while she was out of the cell.

But no matter how she tried, guilt and fear were always with her.

"I am no longer afraid I will go crazy, but I am frightened, lonely, sad, ashamed. No matter what happens to me in the future I am being punished right now. They are not mean to me here, but I know every minute that I am in prison. There are heavy steel doors with big brass keys that lock me in a cell about thirty feet by twenty feet with eight or nine others. I feel I am worse than the other people here because I murdered. I murdered! Such an awful, awful thing! It hurts me even to write that word. How I ever came to do it I'll never know. Sometimes I think this is all a dream and that I'll wake up. It seems so impossible. Me, Fran, in jail for murder! I am not a person who hurts other people. I get sick when I hear about crimes of violence. How could I do it? I still can't understand. Was I crazy? When the reality of it hits me I feel sick to the core.

"I have awful visions. I see graveyards. I see a headstone with Mickey's name on it. I see him running, his body on fire. They said they found him between the living room and the dining room. Was he running to save us? Was he running to save himself? Was it painful for him? What were his thoughts when he died? I've never hurt anyone before, but I know that doesn't justify this crime that is so enormous I think it will swallow me. The pain, the awful shame, are getting larger and larger. I can picture him hitting and hitting me, his fists coming at me—me sinking down lower and lower, but the guilt won't go away."

Twice Francine thought she heard Mickey talking to her. She was lying on her bunk, awake, staring at nothing, when she heard his voice whispering, "'Fran! Fran! Fran!' I thought, 'God, I'm going crazy! I'm hearing voices! I'm going to lose control!' I shook my head. I put my fingers in my ears, but the voice went on. Then I decided, okay, I'll listen! Mickey talked. His voice was quiet and nice. He was telling me that everything would be okay; that he knew I was suffering, but not to worry. He said, 'I understand why you did what you did.' He wasn't angry with me. He wanted to comfort me. He said he loved me. Then his voice faded away. The first time it happened it left me shaking. When it happened a second time I wasn't scared. I lay still and listened. Mickey said he would watch over me, protect me, and that he knew everything would be all right in the end. When his voice faded away I felt calm, more at ease with myself. I never heard his voice again."

Little by little Francine's feelings became less punishing. She faced with honesty the fact that she was not sorry Mickey was dead, but never ceased to believe that what she had done was wrong. She told Greydanus that the letters she was receiving in increasing volume—as her story continued to be carried in the newspapers—comforted her by letting her know that people cared about her, but did not alter her attitude toward her crime. She was grateful, too, for the way she was being treated. She wrote in her diary: "Almost everyone here is so sympathetic toward me. The turnkeys and just about all the staff. They say things like, 'You shouldn't be here,' or, 'I wish there was something I could do to help.' They say I'm 'personable,' that I act like a lady. Mrs. Preadmore [Sheriff Preadmore's wife] said yesterday when we were talking that anyone could see that I was a refined lady. *Me* a refined lady? Is it because I hold everything inside and try to remain calm and in control? Is that what a lady is?"

Francine's loneliness was intense. "I feel so cut off, so far away. Every day I wait for something from the outside—a letter, a visit, a piece of news—anything to give me hope, to make me feel I'm still part of the world." Francine's mother and sisters visited, and occasionally her brothers, but Dansville neighbors and friends she had known with Mickey did not. They were no more anxious to be involved now than they had been when Mickey was alive and abusing her. Francine, therefore, was tremendously touched when Betty Cover, her vivacious Brazilian friend from Lansing Business College, became a regular visitor. Betty was not only sympathetic, but she also brought news that made Francine feel giddy with sudden longing. Betty told her that George Walkup had sent word that he loved her and would wait for her, no matter how many years it might be before she was free. George, Betty said, had started coming back to the lounge and asked her to transmit the message. He didn't dare write, Betty reported, for fear of causing Francine trouble, but he wanted her to know how he felt. Betty and Francine discussed George over a series of visits; each time Betty relayed a more passionate message. Francine confided in Betty that she had broken off with George because she discovered he was living with his wife. Betty said she thought Francine had misunderstood—and that in any case his marriage was over now.

Francine found her mind filled with fantasies. Once again she pictured George as strong, protective, gentle, wise. She decided it was her own sense of guilt that had made her judge him so harshly; she should have given him a chance to explain. Among the women in her cell, thwarted sexuality permeated the atmosphere. A number of them wrote hotly erotic letters to their boyfriends—letters they shared with their cellmates. Francine decided to write to George. "Sweetheart," she wrote, "this is a very hard time for me. . . . It is natural for me to want and dream of a man's arms around me. When I dream of being with someone it is always you that comes to my mind. . . . I'm not sure of your feelings for me. I don't want to open myself to this kind of relationship only to be hurt. I was told you said you would wait for me for many years. Do you realize what a statement like that could mean to someone in my position. I miss you terribly. . . ."

Because she knew the mail was censored, Francine didn't mail the letter, but gave it to Betty Cover to give to George. Betty reported that he was thrilled by it and wanted more, but thought it too dangerous to answer. Francine wrote two more long letters to George, pouring out love, longing, and pent-up desire. Each time Betty delivered the letter. After the third letter Betty reported to Francine that George no longer came to the lounge. When there were no more messages, Francine's fantasy faded. For the second time she put George Walkup out of her mind.

Greydanus visited Francine weekly. He told her that he wanted to know her life story as intimately as possible; almost any detail could be important in the picture he would present to the jury. He still refused to predict the outcome, but Francine could see that he was doing his utmost for her. "That a decent man believes in me means so much!" she wrote in her diary. Greydanus told her that he thought the prosecutor was utterly wrong, both legally and morally, to insist on prosecuting her for murder in the first degree.

A number of newspapers were carrying stories in the same vein. A reporter for the *Lansing Star*, Laura Segar, had interviewed Greydanus and he had pointed out that the case raised the question of how women subjected to violence and abuse could protect themselves. Segar's story attracted the attention of the local chapter of the National Lawyers Guild—a liberally oriented organization of law students. Several women's-rights organizations joined Guild members in forming a Francine Hughes Defense Committee. The committee hoped to use Francine's case to focus attention on battered wives as the case of Joanne Little—the black woman who had killed her white jail guard in North Carolina—had focused it on women abused in prison. The committee held press conferences asking that the charges against Francine be dropped on the ground that the police, the courts, and society had failed her, leaving her no alternative but to kill in self-defense. The committee was able to stir up a controversy that was widely reported in the press. Greydanus was careful to point out to Francine that in the courtroom it would be the jury and not the press or the public who would decide.

Francine's trial had been scheduled for June, but postponement followed postponement as Greydanus worked out the strategy of his defense. Francine finished all the courses that were given at the jail. Rather than be idle, she enrolled again and repeated them. She searched the bookshelves in the classroom and discovered Shakespeare's sonnets, which she read for the first time, with perplexity and delight. In the evenings she studied a textbook on self-taught French in her cell.

"But no matter what you do, jail is still jail. Your longing for freedom becomes so intense it is like an ache. We'd go out for exercise in the yard back of the jail. I would hear a car go by on the highway and the sound would stab through my heart. The thought would come . . . Maybe I'll never be free to get in a car and drive . . . never again go where I want. . . . Things that I had accepted as a normal part of life now seemed priceless: to walk down a street; to buy a pack of cigarettes or an ice-cream cone; to pick up a telephone; to look at trees and birds and clouds; to watch kids playing.

"Sometimes I think of my life with Mickey. In a way I've been in prison—locked up—for many years. At least here I can go to sleep at night and not be afraid that tomorrow I'll be beaten or killed. Now I'm in a different hell behind bars. Deep down I don't think it can happen, but I can't help praying for a miracle that will set me free."

Aryon Greydanus is an imposing man: big-boned, six feet five inches tall, with blunt features and light brown hair. His parents came to the United States from the Netherlands in 1953, when Aryon was seven, and settled in Grand Rapids, Michigan, where his father continued his trade as a meat cutter and Aryon went to school. He speaks English with no trace of an accent. A determined and competitive young man, Greydanus graduated from Wayne

State University Law School, and for several years worked in a private law firm in Detroit. He moved to Lansing in 1974, when Prosecutor Houk's predecessor in office, Ray Scodeller, offered him a job on his staff. For three years Greydanus was an assistant prosecutor. He was tough and effective, losing only one major case.

Scodeller left office the December before Mickey Hughes died, and Peter Houk was elected in his stead. Greydanus stayed on, but shortly found himself at odds with the new regime. His aggressive, outspoken style had offended several of the other prosecutors on the staff. They asked Houk to get rid of Greydanus. In February there was a showdown and Greydanus left, bitter about what he considered shabby and humiliating treatment by Houk.

There were two murders reported in the Lansing newspapers the week that Mickey Hughes died. The second involved a woman who had shot her husband. Greydanus read brief accounts of both cases. Judging by the addresses given, it seemed unlikely that either woman would have the funds to pay a lawyer, and Greydanus wondered if one of the cases might be assigned to him. Court-appointed lawyers are chosen by the presiding judge from a list of qualified attorneys. To be chosen to defend a man or woman charged with murder indicates the court's confidence in a lawyer's abilities and thus, though it brings little money, it pays off in enhanced prestige. At that moment prestige was what Greydanus needed. He was still smarting over his departure from the prosecutor's office and wondering if he would succeed in private practice in a town already well supplied with lawyers. He was, therefore, gratified to get a call from the administrator of the court, Tom Gormely, who said, "Hey, Greydanus. I've got a case for you."

Greydanus answered, "It's a murder case, right?"

"That's right," Gormely said. "How did you know?"

"I didn't," Greydanus replied, pleased as punch. "I just had a feeling." His first thought, as he hung up the phone, was that the case would pit him against his former colleagues only a month after their acrimonious parting. He found the prospect interesting.

That evening he went to the jail to see his client. What Francine told him of her life with Mickey Hughes struck him as so horrifying that he could hardly believe Houk would go on with the prosecution. It was obvious that a formal defense would be difficult, but he thought that by any standard of mercy, justice, or common sense,

Mickey's death should be termed justifiable homicide or at most manslaughter, and Francine released on probation. The next day Greydanus made an appointment with Houk to discuss a plea bargain. As he prepared for the meeting, Greydanus thought it unlikely the case would ever come to trial.

Houk was cool and polite as Greydanus outlined the facts surrounding Mickey's death. When Greydanus asked that Francine be allowed to plead guilty to manslaughter, Houk replied with a flat no. He said that in his opinion a woman who burned a sleeping man was a cold-blooded murderer and he intended to prosecute her to the fullest extent of the law. After a few moments of vain argument, Greydanus left. "It was obvious," he has since said, "that they just weren't going to do any deals with Greydanus." He had no idea how he was going to defend the Hughes case in court, but if he had to do it, by God he was going to win.

His first step was to learn everything possible about his client, checking her story to make sure Francine had told him the truth. As a prosecutor, Greydanus had gotten to know a good many men in the sheriff's department. Now he found that acquaintance useful. When he visited the jail he was able to talk casually to deputies who had dealt with Mickey. They confirmed that the Hughes home was a well-known trouble spot. "That guy was a real bastard," several of them said.

Greydanus made it a point to drop in to see Lieutenant Tift, the detective in charge of the case. Tift offered him a chair and talked freely about the Hughes brothers and the trouble they had caused his department over the years. Mickey Hughes, Tift commented, was a violent son of a bitch who deserved everything he got. However, in Tift's view, this made no difference in the case against Francine; he saw it as open-and-shut murder in the first degree; nothing that had happened gave her the right to kill. Greydanus left with the impression that Tift, a zealous professional, was looking forward to winning the case.

With some misgivings about entering hostile territory, Greydanus made the first of several trips to Dansville to see what information he could pick up in the neighborhood. He hoped above all to find witnesses willing to testify to Mickey's abuse of Francine. He drove down Grove Street, toward Adams, and found the scene of the crime just as the firemen had left it. The house, with its clapboards mottled gray by smoke and a jagged hole where flames had eaten out the bedroom wall, struck him as macabre. At the edge of the porch, early spring flowers that Francine had planted made bright spots of discordant cheer. Greydanus parked and, using Francine's key, entered the house. The acrid smell of burning still hung in the chill air. Debris littered the floor. Greydanus quickly made what notes were necessary and left. At the home of the elder Hughes, next door, no one was in sight. Greydanus was glad to get back in his car unobserved.

Greydanus turned the corner and drove slowly down Adams Street. He parked at a distance from the Hughes house and got out to survey the lay of the land. He noticed that behind the house on Adams and Grove was an open area that gave neighbors a good view of each others' backyards. He knocked on door after door. Each time the person he spoke to denied knowing anything about Mickey and Francine Hughes. No one volunteered to come to her defense. Greydanus went back to his car considerably discouraged. Getting witnesses is never easy, but it seemed that getting them in Dansville would be more than usually difficult.

When Greydanus described his fruitless trip to Francine, she expressed no surprise. She had always felt that the neighbors wanted to avoid trouble with the Hughes family. She told Greydanus she believed she could have been beaten to death in the middle of the street and most people would have shut their eyes and ears. Even those who sympathized with her, she said, would probably be afraid to testify; their attitude would be, "We have to live here. It's not our business."

Without much real hope, Francine suggested Greydanus talk to the Eiferts, the Quembys, and Donna Johnson—the families who lived opposite the duplex on Adams Street, where she and Mickey had lived immediately after his accident. Betty Cover also was a possible witness, Francine said. She had seen bruises on Francine and was an independent, spunky girl, not easily intimidated.

Greydanus talked to Laura Eifert. She seemed both eager and nervous as she told Greydanus what she knew. Her husband, Chris, she said, was a good friend of Donovan Hughes and "ran around" with the Hughes brothers. It was Chris who had once intervened when Mickey was beating Francine in the yard. Laura described other episodes, confirming what Francine had told Greydanus, but when Greydanus asked her if she would be willing to repeat her story in court, Laura hesitated. She asked if her testimony was important in the outcome of the case. Greydanus told her it was—that unless witnesses were willing to tell a jury that Francine was a good person and Mickey a violent one, it was very likely that Francine would serve a life sentence. Did Laura think Francine deserved that? No, Laura said, she did not. She'd always felt sorry for Francine and knew she was trapped in a terrible situation. Though it was clear the prospect frightened her, Laura consented to testify for Francine. A few days later Greydanus called Laura again. With some embarrassment, Laura confessed that she had changed her mind; she wouldn't take the stand unless she was forced to. Greydanus asked how Laura's husband felt about Francine. Chris felt very strongly, Laura admitted. He hoped Francine would go to prison for life. Greydanus scratched the Eiferts off his list of witnesses for the defense.

Greydanus made his second trip to Dansville to see Donna Johnson, who had sometimes baby-sat for Francine. A tall, thin woman with dark hair and eyes and an air of quiet dignity, Donna answered his questions candidly and deliberately. She told him she had never known Francine well, but had felt sorry for the way she had had to live. She described the violence she had seen, including the time Mickey burst into her house in search of Francine.

"Will you testify?" Greydanus asked.

Clearly troubled, Donna considered the question. She said that it would be a difficult thing to do and she understood why many people in Dansville didn't want to get involved. Nevertheless, she felt it was her duty to tell what she knew. "Someone has to do it," she said. "Someone has to stand up and tell the truth or there can't be a fair trial." More than that, she said that wife-beating was a hidden evil, more widespread than most people knew, and that it had to be exposed.

Alice Quemby, next door to Donna, was as excited and talkative as Donna had been deliberate. She pointed out the picture window in her living room and told Greydanus how she had sat by it and seen terrible things happening in the Hughes apartment across the street. She said the thought of testifying made her shake in her boots, but she would do it because, like Donna, she knew that unless people had the courage to speak up Francine would not get a fair trial. Francine, she said, was a nice, quiet person and it shocked her that though everyone in Dansville knew what went on, no one had volunteered to speak up for her. Yes, Alice said, she would take the stand.

Donna Johnson's two sisters, Connie Feldpausch and Debbie Brown, who lived in Lansing but had grown up in Dansville, also agreed to testify. When Greydanus told Francine that the four women were willing to help in her defense, she was quietly amazed. She told him she hadn't realized they had known and sympathized that much. As Francine had predicted, Betty Cover was eager to do all she could. When Greydanus interviewed her she described how Francine had often come to class with marks and bruises she tried unsuccessfully to hide.

From his experience as a prosecutor Greydanus knew that each time the police had been called to deal with Mickey, whether or not he had been arrested, a detailed report of the incident had been filed at the Sheriff Department. Greydanus wanted those reports. He asked Houk to provide Mickey's police record. The prosecutor refused. Finally Greydanus resorted to the Michigan Freedom of Information Act. As a result, the County Attorney instructed the Sheriff Department to produce whatever records it possessed and Sheriff Preadmore provided Greydanus with a thick stack of reports. Reading them over, Greydanus found they not only corroborated Francine, but gave exact information as to dates, circumstances, and the presence of other witnesses, Flossie and Berlin for instance, that Francine could no longer recall. Greydanus interviewed the officers who had been involved in these incidents, including those who had come to the house on the day of the fire. They were matter-of-fact as they told what they had seen. None expressed any sympathy or desire to help with the defense, but as police officers they would testify to the facts in their reports no matter what their feelings might be.

Finally Greydanus interviewed Francine's mother and sisters, and decided they would not be helpful on the witness stand. None of them had actually seen the worst of Mickey's behavior and, in any case, their testimony would be suspect in the eyes of the jury. Mrs. Moran brought the older children to Greydanus' office several times. He found Christy a bright and forthright little girl who did not hesitate to express her hatred for her father. She would be a good witness for her mother. Jimmy struck Greydanus as a child full of conflict and suffering. It was clear that he loved his mother, but talking of his father and the scenes he had witnessed seemed excruciating for him. Both of them told the story of the fatal day in the same way Francine had. Greydanus thought that the children could help win sympathy for their mother, but there was also danger in their testimony if the prosecutor used it skillfully to underline the time that elapsed while Mickey slept and Francine waited for Dana to come home. It was this lapse of time on which the prosecutor would undoubtedly base his case that Francine had premeditated her crime.

Even though Greydanus had more than half a dozen eyewitnesses and sheaves of documents to prove that Francine had been horribly abused, he recognized that these alone would not constitute a defense. Greydanus was convinced that ultimately Mickey would have killed Francine, and he could see that she had tried one exit after another—flight, the police, the welfare office, the mental-health clinic, the judge who had granted her divorce, and, ironically, the office of the prosecutor in which Greydanus was then working—and found every door closed. "Every time I tried and failed I just sank lower; I felt more beaten down," she told Greydanus, and it was clear to him that Mickey Hughes was a problem that no one had known what to do about. His family, and the social agencies and courts who dealt with him, invariably shunted him back to Francine. Now society was punishing her for taking the only way that remained to save her own life. Greydanus believed that a plea of self-defense would be legitimate but legally shaky. Self-defense is traditionally defined as occurring in the context of immediate danger. In Francine's case the prosecutor would argue that to save her life she had only to leave while Mickey slept, requiring Greydanus to prove that her entire history, her situation as a woman, her children, and her psychological state after years of abuse, made flight impossible as long as Mickey lived. Yet, searching the law books, Greydanus could not find a single precedent for such an argument for self-defense.

Another possible defense was "temporary insanity." Greydanus believed Francine's description of her trancelike state as she prepared to burn the house. Whenever they discussed the fatal moments, Francine insisted, "Mr. Greydanus, I must have been crazy.

I must have been out of my mind. There is no other way I could have done what I did." But in Michigan, insanity is a perilous defense. A defendant acquitted by reason of "temporary insanity" is set free, but a defendant found "guilty but mentally ill" serves the same term in the same prison as a convicted criminal who is sane. The only difference is token psychiatric treatment provided for the insane.

In either defense, temporary insanity or self-defense, expert testimony on Francine's state of mind would be important. Greydanus arranged to have Dr. Arnold S. Berkman, an associate professor in the Department of Psychiatry at Michigan State University, who was experienced in legal psychiatry, examine Francine. Berkman visited Francine in jail and talked to her for a total of six hours. In a report to Greydanus Berkman wrote:

"Mrs. Hughes is an attractive woman, who was neat and well groomed despite her prison attire. She related easily and non-defensively, being frank and candid about the events of her life and about the incident in question. She seemed eager to talk to me, and spoke about events with much detail, even those events which were painful for her to remember. Mrs. Hughes' style was both subtly seductive and self-effacing. She spoke articulately and intelligently, and although she gave an initial impression of sophistication, there was also a quality of naiveté and ingenuousness which at times made her seem like a starry-eyed adolescent perceiving life through Hollywood-tinted glasses. The totality of Mrs. Hughes' demeanor and the general tone of her interactions made her at one and the same time likeable, pitiful, believable, intelligent, refined, graceful, and dignified.

"This present psychological examination revealed no evidence of psychosis. Mrs. Hughes was coherent, was well oriented to person, place, and time, and was very much in contact with reality.

"At present Mrs. Hughes is deeply remorseful. The genuineness and depth of her remorse are impressive and are certainly not similar to the shallow remorse found in most criminals."

So far Berkman had told Greydanus nothing that would help acquit her, but in the final pages of his report he offered an opinion that gave Greydanus something to work on: he had found significant "psychopathology," and "maladaptive patterns of behavior" in Francine. Her behavior at the time of the fire, Berkman wrote, represented a psychological breakdown, during which she had been overwhelmed by her most primitive emotions and unable to make a rational judgment or decision. She had been, in short, totally out of control.

Dr. Berkman told Greydanus he wanted to help defend Francine and would be willing to testify that she had been pushed beyond the bounds of sanity when she set fire to the house. Greydanus and Berkman talked over the legal implications of his findings. Berkman said he thought Francine suffered from what recent psychiatric literature terms a "borderline syndrome," meaning that extreme pressure could cause her to have a temporary mental breakdown.

The fact that Francine's irrational state could be scientifically described—and had been brief—gave Greydanus hope that he could offer a "temporary insanity" defense without falling into the trap of having Francine found "guilty but mentally ill." He decided to find a second expert to back up Berkman. He and Berkman talked to Dr. Anne Seiden, a psychiatrist at the University of Chicago, an expert on the psychology of women, who agreed to see Francine. Both experts would be paid out of state funds.

As Berkman had, Dr. Seiden found Francine appealing and was anxious to help her. She described Francine as "a quietly attractive person . . . Her words indicate an intelligence greater than her educational level would imply, but at times she showed evidence of considerable naiveté. She is like a bright little girl who is desperately trying to be a good little girl in a world which has become more complex than she was prepared for." Seiden summed up Mickey's behavior as "exquisitely targeted sadism," pointing out that by forcing Francine to burn her books he had forced her to destroy herself—what Seiden called "her personhood"—since it was in school that she had "begun to feel like a person for the first time in her life." As with Berkman, Francine had responded to Seiden with complete candor. "In fact," Seiden wrote in her report to Greydanus, "she appeared to be using the interview as part of her attempt to understand herself and how she could have come to do what she did, which obviously concerns her greatly." Seiden agreed with Berkman that Francine had exhibited symptoms of a mental breakdown consistent with "borderline syndrome," and told Greydanus she would be willing to testify that on the day Mickey died,

Francine was temporarily mentally ill and not criminally responsible for what she had done.

Greydanus told Francine what the doctors had found and
discussed the odds involved. If the jury believed she had been temporarily insane, she could be acquitted and get off scot-free. The
law required only that after the acquittal she be certified presently
sane, and Greydanus had no doubt she would be. On the other
hand, the temporary insanity defense opened the door to the terrible verdict "guilty but mentally ill" and a mandatory life sentence.
Francine answered without hesitation. She told Greydanus she
wanted to tell the truth in court, regardless of the consequences.
She believed she had been temporarily insane when she set the fire
and it was on those terms that she wanted to be judged.

From the moment he began to prepare Francine's defense, Greydanus had been worried by the fact that she was charged not with
one offense, but two. The charges against her read:

"Count I, March 9, 1977, did then and there with malice afore-
thought, willfully, deliberately, and with premeditation, intentionally kill James Berlin Hughes, contrary to compiled law. . . .

"Count II, did then and there murder James Berlin Hughes
while perpetrating or attempting to perpetrate the crime of Arson,
contrary to compiled law. . . ."

Count II seemed to Greydanus a clear case of legal overkill. It
was also the more dangerous of the two charges. In deliberating on
Count I, first-degree murder, the jury would have the option of
finding Francine guilty to a lesser degree—second-degree murder or
manslaughter were possible verdicts—but Count II allowed no middle ground; the only possible verdicts were innocent or guilty. If
she were found guilty, a life sentence would be mandatory, with
parole possible only after twenty years.

Several times Greydanus brought motions before Judge Harrison
asking him to dismiss Count II, arguing that it was a repetition of
Count I. If Francine's intention had been to kill her husband, the
fire that resulted was not a felony, but part and parcel of the
murder with which she was charged in Count I. Each time Harrison refused to dismiss the second count. Greydanus had never forgotten the remark that Harrison had made—"After all, what kind of
woman would burn up her husband?"—and it seemed to him to

demonstrate prejudice against Francine. When Harrison had ruled against him a number of times, Greydanus became convinced that any other judge would be preferable to Harrison and decided to make an effort to get rid of him, taking the risk that if the move failed the judge would be even less sympathetic as he conducted the trial. Greydanus filed a motion asking that Harrison disqualify himself on the grounds of prejudice, quoting the remark he had made about Francine as evidence of his preconceived opinion about her crime. Judge Harrison refused to disqualify himself and also denied that he had ever made such a remark. Since he had said it while he and Greydanus talked off the record, the court stenographer had not taken it down and Greydanus couldn't prove the incident had occurred. Nevertheless, Greydanus refused to give up. He asked the Chief Judge of the Circuit Court to review Harrison's refusal. This motion was also denied, and Greydanus resigned himself to trying the case before Harrison.

All during the summer, publicity on the Hughes case built up. Silvia Chase, an ABC reporter, picked up the story as holding particular interest to women. Her TV broadcasts spurred on the local papers. The Defense Committee was also creating a considerable stir, even holding a rally on the steps of City Hall. Greydanus was bothered by the Defense Committee's desire to shape Francine's case in order to prove their point that the social system had failed her. The Defense Committee believed that by pleading temporary insanity she dodged the issue of a woman's right to defend herself. Greydanus thought that making her trial a test case on a social issue could be disastrous for her, and he and the committee wound up at odds. Nevertheless, the committee had been effective in getting attention, and Francine's trial was building up to an event of the first magnitude—the biggest news story Lansing had seen in years. For Greydanus the publicity raised the stakes to an uncomfortable degree. If he won his case the victory would be all the sweeter, but if he failed he was, in his own words, "going to take a very deep dive."

The publicity was also putting pressure on Houk, but if he had any second thoughts about Francine's prosecution, he gave no sign of it. Greydanus guessed that the prosecutor had a bear by the tail; he couldn't let go and still save face. When the Defense Committee issued a statement attacking the prosecutor as "incredibly callous" to the needs of battered women, a spokesman, Assistant Prosecutor Lee Atkinson, retorted, "I view the case as . . . a very straightforward case of premeditated murder. Francine is not the first person ever to be afraid. . . . The best personal advice I could have given her is that, while I don't know the answer, the alternative is not to commit murder."

After several postponements Greydanus saw no use in further delay. Palus agreed, and the trial was set for October 17. As the trial neared, Greydanus was under tremendous tension. His sense of responsibility was the heaviest he had ever felt. If Francine should be convicted and spend a long term in prison because of his error or omission, he would find it hard to live with. He also knew that when he walked into the courtroom he would be putting his career on the line.

By October Francine had spent seven months in the Ingham County Jail, and Greydanus had come to know her better than he had ever known anyone except his family and closest friends. He believed that only if he and she together could make the jury see her life through her eyes, and make it as vividly real as it had become to him, would there be any chance of winning her freedom.

As Francine shook off her initial anguish and despair, Greydanus became aware of a complex and, in some ways, mystifying personality. She was trusting, compliant, and thoughtful. When he asked her a question she seldom answered quickly, but sat silent, sometimes for minutes, searching her memory and framing her answer as exactly as she could. It occurred to Greydanus that in the course of their sessions she was evaluating her past in a way that she found new and astonishing. But though fully cooperative, she refused to be led, deciding for herself where the truth lay. Greydanus began to recognize that beneath her docility lay hidden strength: an ego of whose power she seemed unaware.

After each session it would seem that she must have exhausted what she could tell him, yet when Greydanus returned for another visit he would learn something new: another anecdote or detail that made her story either more credible or more horrifying, adding to the effect he wanted to achieve when they came before a jury.

As the weeks went by Greydanus had seen Francine develop and change, becoming less humble and tentative, more self-possessed and independent. Now and then, beneath her willingness to please,

Greydanus glimpsed iron determination to reach whatever goal she set. Sometimes she displayed her quick wit, an ability to detect the ridiculous and expose it with a quick, audacious question. She could be exasperating, too, and there were moments when Greydanus had an inkling of how she might have goaded Mickey with subtly stinging words.

One day, toward the end, as Greydanus instructed her on what to wear in court—skirts rather than slacks, earth tones rather than pastels, no earrings or other jewelry—she gave him a speculative look and asked, "Are you making me over? Am I your Fair Lady?" Greydanus laughed and said, "If so, I hope I'm not Henry Higgins. That's not the kind of person I want to be," but he knew there was truth in what she said. She had never before had so much attention from intelligent, educated people, and she seized every opportunity to learn from them.

By mid-October, with the trial only days away, Greydanus felt that he had done everything that could be done, but that only a miracle could bring an acquittal. Dr. Berkman and Dr. Seiden would testify that Francine had been temporarily insane. The prosecutor had had Francine examined by their own expert, Dr. Lynn W. Blunt, Clinical Director of the Center for Forensic Psychiatry in Ypsilanti, Michigan. Greydanus had a copy of Blunt's report to Houk, which described the horrifying circumstances with which Greydanus was so familiar, but concluded that in a legal sense Francine was sane when she killed Mickey Hughes. The jury would have to choose between these conflicting opinions, and Greydanus believed that sympathy would be the most important factor in their choice. He also expected Judge Harrison to conduct the trial in a lofty, arrogant style that would exclude sympathy as much as possible. He had had no dealings with the judge since his motions alleging prejudice had been turned down, but he assumed that the episode had done nothing to improve their relations.

Five days before the trial was scheduled to begin, Greydanus was in his office making last-minute notes when his secretary told him Judge Harrison was on the telephone. "What on earth . . . ?" Greydanus wondered as he picked up the phone.

The judge was brisk. He wanted to talk to Greydanus in his office at eight o'clock the following morning and he wanted Greydanus to bring Francine. Greydanus asked what the meeting would be about. "I want to talk about this prejudice thing," the judge said. "And I want to discuss it with your client." Greydanus agreed to be there. When he hung up he knew that a crucial encounter was in the making. He decided that under no circumstances would he allow the judge to talk to Francine. Every word uttered might be important and he would take no chances that a naive response from Francine would compromise her position. Furthermore, Greydanus decided, he wanted the prosecutor present and he wanted the meeting to be on the record.

Greydanus telephoned Palus and found that he knew nothing of the private meeting the judge had proposed. Greydanus reminded Palus that it is improper for a judge to talk to one party in a case unless the other is present. Palus said that he would be in the courthouse on other business that morning and would be available. Greydanus called the Sheriff Department and asked to have Francine brought to the courthouse the following morning, but specified that she should be kept in an anteroom unless he sent for her.

In the morning Greydanus presented himself at Harrison's office. "Where is your client?" the judge asked. Greydanus decided to defer a showdown on that point, so he replied mildly that she was on her way. However, Greydanus said, Mr. Palus was in the adjoining courtroom and he would like him to be present. The judge looked surprised, but it would have been difficult for him to refuse. Palus appeared and Harrison ushered both men into his office to wait for Francine. Then Greydanus politely remarked that he wanted whatever took place to be on the record. The judge looked even more surprised, but had no choice but to send for a court stenographer. When everyone was seated, Greydanus began. "Your Honor, I don't want my client to appear at this meeting." He went on to point out that a defendant has the absolute right to remain silent. Furthermore, he said, Francine might construe the meeting as further evidence of the judge's bias against her.

Harrison, obviously taken aback, said that he had given a great deal of thought to the allegation that he was prejudiced. The allegation was, he said, untrue. However, there had been a new development in regard to the remark that Greydanus had quoted. The judge said he himself had no recollection of saying anything of the sort, but the clerk who had been sitting within earshot had recently told him that she had heard the judge say something similar to what Greydanus recalled. Therefore, Judge Harrison said, he would like to talk to Francine to find out if she actually believed him to be prejudiced against her.

Greydanus said that Francine's sworn statement asking Harrison to disqualify himself should be sufficient. "I'm sorry, Your Honor," Greydanus said, "but my client has a right to say nothing more."

Harrison looked disconcerted. "Well," he said slowly, "it seems we are at an impasse."

For several long moments no one spoke. Then Harrison rose from his desk. "I have decided to disqualify myself," he said. "I am not prejudiced in any way, but since doubts have been raised I believe it would be best if I did not conduct this trial."

Greydanus, concealing his jubilation, thanked the judge and the uncomfortable meeting was over.

As a result of Harrison's decision to withdraw, the trial was postponed for a week, to October 24, and Judge Ray C. Hotchkiss was selected to preside. Hotchkiss, forty-eight years old and a former Navy officer, customarily ran his courtroom with good-natured efficiency, squelching histrionics and taking an active role in keeping affairs on the track. While a legal hot potato like the Hughes case might bother a less confident judge, Greydanus guessed that Hotchkiss would find it just his dish. It was said around the courtroom that he enjoyed adding to his increasingly thick scrapbook of newspaper clippings. Greydanus had no clue as to how Hotchkiss would feel personally about Francine's case, but considered him a fair and open-minded man. For the first time in eight months of hard work and worry, Greydanus thought that he and Francine had a fighting chance.

Four days before the trial was to begin, Greydanus received a call from Martin Palus. Palus was not one of the group on Houk's staff that had forced Greydanus' departure, and the two men were on politely friendly terms. Palus told Greydanus that some new evidence in the Hughes case had just turned up and suggested Greydanus come to his office to discuss it. Mystified, Greydanus agreed. He was confident that he knew everything about Francine that could matter. When Greydanus entered his office, Palus asked him to sit down. "Do you remember reading about a guy who killed himself recently? A security guard at the capitol?" he asked.

Greydanus shook his head.

"His name was George Walkup," Palus said.

Greydanus looked blank. "I've never heard of him as far as I know."

"Francine Hughes has heard of him," Palus said with a cryptic smile.

"Tell me what you mean," Greydanus said, and Palus did. He said that some months earlier George Walkup had been charged with a sex offense involving the rape of a child: that Walkup was a very kinky guy. He faced trial and probably a long term in the penitentiary. On October 5, while talking on the telephone to his wife, George Walkup shot himself. A week later his superior officer at the capitol cleaned out Walkup's locker and looked through his personal effects. At the bottom of the locker he found letters signed "Francine." At that moment "Francine" was the most famous first name in Lansing. He had given the letters to Tift. Palus opened a file on his desk and handed Greydanus Xeroxed copies of a sheaf of handwritten pages, and leaned back contentedly in his chair. Greydanus recognized Francine's neat handwriting on lined tablet sheets. As he read the salutation, "Sweetheart," his heart sank. Palus waited as Greydanus, trying not to show his consternation, read on. "Well . . . here I am again, trying to write you. This is just about the tenth I've written and torn up. . . ." The letters, dated in late April, six weeks after Mickey's death, were an outpouring of intimate thoughts coupled with girlish flirtation and amorous references. "I just can't seem to close this letter. It's just like I felt when I was near you. I didn't want to ever leave you. I just kept thinking of things I want to tell you. Like right now I feel warm all over, like when you looked at me the way you used to. You know, when you did that to me with your eyes, I felt like the closest I could get to you wouldn't be close enough! Well, just the thought of you does that to me now."

Greydanus glanced grimly at Palus, who shrugged in sympathy. He knew how an attorney feels when an important case blows up in his face. Greydanus continued to read until he had finished the dozen pages, using the time to take control of himself, determined not to show his surprise. The letters made it perfectly clear that Francine had had a sexual relationship with another man before Mickey died and that she was still in love with him several months later. In all his hours of searching talk with Francine, she had never given the slightest hint of such a relationship. There was no doubt Francine was the author of the letters; she had written freely of her situation in the Ingham County Jail. In addition to the amorous passages were others that told of her loneliness, grief, and fear. Greydanus knew he would have to say something. He seized on this aspect.

"Marty, these are pathetic," he said, putting the letters down.

Palus waited expectantly. Greydanus thought, "I don't know what it is but there's got to be some explanation for this." After a few moments of guarded talk, Greydanus put the photocopies Palus had given him in his pocket. "Thanks, Marty," he said. "I guess I've got a problem." He took his leave.

Walking back to his office, he found himself seething with rage at Francine. Then it occurred to him, "That's why Marty called me over. He didn't have to show me the letters. He did it hoping I'd blow up, hoping I'd tell Francine I've lost faith in her and advise her to plead guilty. He and Houk think they've got me nailed to the wall!"

Greydanus' first impulse was to storm over to the Ingham County Jail and demand an explanation from Francine, but it was late in the day. He decided to go home to supper first. As he drove he struggled to keep his anger under control and think the situation through. He could see that even though Palus was totally confident of victory, he would prefer to avoid a controversial trial. He could also see that on the face of it the letters could make a shambles of Francine's insanity defense and put him, as defense attorney, in a highly embarrassing position. Yet, in spite of the evidence in his pocket, he could not believe that Francine was merely an adulteress who had killed her ex-husband to get him out of the way of an illicit love affair. When he reached home he told Rosemary, his wife, what had happened and what he had decided: "I'm going out to see Francine and I'm going to be calm. If I lay into her about this it will destroy our relationship. Then there'll be no way to get the truth and retrieve what we can. I'm just going to let her explain this."

In the conference room at the jail he waited for Francine, rehearsing his first words. When she had been brought in and was sitting opposite him he said quietly, "Well, Francine, tonight our talk isn't going to be so pleasant. I've been to the prosecutor's office and this is what they gave me." He handed her the Xerox sheets. Francine looked at them in disbelief. For a moment she said nothing and Greydanus watched her face. She showed the shock of surprise, but no guilt or shame. Looking straight at him, she said simply, "These are some letters I wrote."

"I realize that," Greydanus said. "But you never told me about them and you never mentioned this person."

"I meant to tell you," Francine said, "but I just didn't want to at the time. Later it wasn't important."

Greydanus said, "Well, Francine, I could be very angry about this, but I'm not going to be. I'm upset because you may have really hurt yourself. These letters may put you in prison for the rest of your life. Do you understand that?"

Francine nodded. She cried in her quiet way. Greydanus changed the subject to give her time to recover. Then he said, "Now you'd better tell me everything about this guy—everything you didn't tell me before."

Francine described her meeting with George Walkup in the lounge at Lansing Business College and how she had built up romantic notions that had been extinguished by the discovery that George Walkup was married and living with his wife. She told how, during her second month in jail, when her morale was at its lowest ebb, Betty Cover had relayed messages from George that rekindled her feelings. It was obvious that Francine found it embarrassing and difficult to discuss sex, but she confessed that in jail, along with her other frustrations, she had suffered from sexual privation as long-repressed erotic feelings came to life. Even as she wrote to George she knew the letters were foolish, and when there was no response she forgot them. It had never occurred to her that they might come to light, and she naturally wanted to know how the prosecutor had got them. Greydanus told her that Walkup was dead. He tried to postpone telling her about his suicide and the reason for it, but Francine insisted. When he told her the whole story she was appalled.

At the end of the talk Greydanus felt much better. Everything she told him was consistent with what he already knew about Francine. She hadn't lied to him; she had merely omitted something of which she was ashamed. As she described how she had felt when she wrote the letters—how desperately lonely, abandoned, longing for comfort and for love—he began to see how the letters could be woven into the character sketch he intended to draw for the jury: a woman of deep emotion who was too trusting in her judgments and had been victimized once again.

Greydanus knew that when he and Francine were in the courtroom a relationship of trust between them would be vital. They would have to work as a team and Francine would have to do her share, keeping her head, responding to his cues and even prompting him as the testimony unfolded. It would be fatal if she were demoralized by fear. He told her that the discovery of the letters was a bad break, but that if she handled them as candidly in court as she had with him he believed they would not damage her case. When he left the jail that night he felt their trust in each other was as solid as ever.

Two days later there was an event that more than balanced the setback of the Walkup letters. When Judge Hotchkiss was appointed in Harrison's stead, Greydanus had prepared a new motion asking to have Count II, the arson charge, dismissed. As he had with Harrison, Greydanus argued that the fire and Mickey's death were a single event and did not constitute two distinct crimes. Hotchkiss agreed. He dismissed Count II. Greydanus was jubilant. He had a sudden feeling that the tide was turning his way.

The People *vs.* Francine Hughes

The case of *The People* vs. *Francine Hughes* opened at ten o'clock in the morning on Monday, October 24, in a courtroom on the mezzanine floor of the City Hall in Lansing. Long before the courtroom doors opened, the lobby and corridors were crowded with people hoping for a seat. In the week before the trial, daily newspaper and TV stories whipped up public interest. The Defense Committee had continued to describe Francine as the victim of a heartless system. Houk had reiterated that she was a common, cold-blooded killer and promised that the prosecution would unveil a blockbuster surprise. Dozens of newspapers, several national wire services, and TV networks had sent reporters and cameramen to cover the trial. ABC reporter Silvia Chase brought an artist to sketch the scene inside the courtroom, where photographers would not be allowed. Mickey's brothers were there with their wives. Dexter Hughes, who was divorced from Cleo and living in Nashville, had come north for the occasion accompanied by a gaudily dressed country singer. A number of Francine's neighbors from Dansville, including the Eiferts and her former landlord, were in the crowd, but her old friends, Sharon and Bill Hensley, had decided not to come. Sharon had written Francine a note: "I won't be at your trial. I'm sorry. I just can't." Flossie Hughes was also absent. She would be a witness and therefore would not be allowed in the courtroom except when she testified. Berlin had been excused from testifying on his doctor's advice. He had been taken ill after Mickey's death and spent weeks in the hospital. He did not come to the trial.

For a fortnight before the trial Francine found it difficult to eat or sleep. She fought to keep her emotions steady, but the nerve-wracking events in the last days, as Harrison was replaced by Hotchkiss, her letters were discovered, and Count II was dismissed, made it impossible. Her reactions, whether of new hope or added despair, were as intense as physical pain. Even before these episodes, the buildup of tension was so increasingly hard to bear that she wanted above everything to get the trial over with.

"I was tired of thinking about it. I was tired of being scared. I was tired of not knowing what would happen. I was tired of everything. I had prayed a lot. The way I prayed was not for God to let me out, but for Him to make me strong enough to face anything . . . even the worst . . . a long term in prison. I asked for strength to face that possibility. I prayed for it nightly, daily, and He gave it to me. I knew that when I walked into the courtroom I might very well be sent to prison for the rest of my life and that with God's help I could face it."

On the morning of the trial Francine woke at dawn. She got up and washed and dressed while the other women still slept. When breakfast came at six, she found she couldn't swallow solid food. She drank the juice and the coffee and stored the rest in a paper bag in her bunk. She thought, "It's a weird life when a little box of cornflakes is so important. Will it be that way for the rest of my life?"

At seven a matron brought her court clothes and Francine put on a brown jumper and a beige turtleneck sweater. Following Greydanus' instructions, she used very little makeup. Her cellmates gathered around her, telling her how nice she looked, offering advice and encouragement, and trying to quiet her nerves with jokes. When her best friend, Melanie, still facing trial herself, hugged her, Francine had to fight back tears. At eight Francine was escorted to the lobby and put in the custody of Deputy Nancy Shelton, a burly woman about Francine's age. Shelton had two other women in tow. She snapped handcuffs on Francine, linking her to the others, and herded them to a waiting police car.

There was little said on the twenty-minute drive to Lansing. Francine stared out the window at the woods, bright with color in the autumn sun, and the cornfields that stretched peacefully to the horizon. She remembered that only a year before she had driven this road every weekday on her way to school. After this week she might never see it again—or not until she was very old. A year ago could she have imagined that she would make the trip in a police car, handcuffed to two other criminals? It would have been beyond her wildest dreams.

At City Hall the police car drove down a ramp to the basement, where the prisoners were unloaded. Shelton took the handcuffed women to an elevator. They rode in silence to an upper floor where the Lansing Police Department maintains a small cellblock for prisoners waiting to appear in court. Francine and the others were locked into a single cell. Court would not convene for an hour.

The cell, used for transients including overnight drunks, had a foul, dank smell. It was furnished with a steel bunk lacking mattress or pillow, a toilet, and a sink from which rusty water trickled. Beyond the bars were a catwalk and a window that faced a brick wall. A fluorescent light gave a strange cast to the prisoners' faces. Not far away Francine could hear the voices of men prisoners; some sounded drunk or crazy as they cursed or shouted. There were already two women sitting on the bunk, smoking. Francine sat down and lit a cigarette. It made her dizzy and she put it out, carefully saving the butt. The two women who had ridden in with her paced up and down. No one had much interest in conversation. Francine read the graffiti scratched everywhere on the black walls. Amidst long skeins of obscenities someone had written, "If you can't stand the time, don't do the crime."

While Francine waited she felt an attack of panic coming on and fought it down. When Shelton returned, Francine had forced herself into an almost dreamlike calm. Shelton told her to hold out her wrists for handcuffs. "Do I wear them into the courtroom?" Francine asked. Shelton nodded and snapped them on. She led Francine to the elevator and they rode to the mezzanine floor. The doors opened on a short ramp. Beyond was a corridor jammed with people. As Francine was recognized, a wave of excitement and noise rippled through the crowd. Greydanus was standing near, waiting for her. He took her arm and led the way. She was blinded by photographers' flashguns and nearly tripped up by cords, as reporters thrust microphones in front of her face. "Don't say anything," Greydanus told her. "Look straight ahead." They entered the courtroom through a door at the rear. Francine had seen the room before—a large windowless theater with rust-colored walls, rows of benches, and, flanking the judge's bench, the flags and seals symbolizing his awesome authority. Every seat was taken, and as she and Greydanus appeared as though from the wings of a stage, the audience stirred and murmured in recognition of the stars. There was a long narrow table in front of the bench, and a number of straight chairs. Greydanus and Francine took seats at the far end—on the audience's right.

Francine saw that Palus and Lieutenant Tift were already sitting at the opposite end of the table. Palus avoided glancing at her, but Tift gave his strange, smirking smile. Shelton, who was taking the cuffs from Francine's wrists, smiled back at her colleague, then took a chair against the wall behind Francine. Greydanus and Francine faced the empty jury box. Greydanus had already explained that he wanted Francine to sit where the jury would have a full view of her. Francine, in profile to the audience, was grateful she didn't have to look in that direction. One sideways glance over the rows of expectant faces, some familiar, brought such an attack of stage fright that she tried not to look again. A court attendant announced the judge. Everyone stood as Hotchkiss swept in, wearing a black robe, and mounted to the bench. A short, vigorous man, partially bald, he wore an expression that struck Francine as businesslike, but not grim. He looked over the crowd with an open, friendly gaze, glancing at Palus, at Greydanus, and at Francine. Then, with a rap of the gavel, Judge Hotchkiss took charge of the courtroom and the trial began.

The first step was the selection of a jury. A bailiff opened a rear door and escorted fourteen men and women to the jury box for questioning. Greydanus explained to Francine that the defense and the prosecution were each allowed a certain number of challenges and could use them to eliminate jurors they suspected might be hostile or prejudiced one way or the other.

When a juror was asked to step down, another was brought in from a pool of prospective jurors waiting outside. Francine tried to follow the proceedings, but found herself confused by the intricate maneuvering. Greydanus wanted no older men on the jury, especially none who worked in law enforcement or a rigid profession such as engineering or banking. He settled for a young, unmarried man with long hair and a married man who was a student at the university in Lansing. Among the women he considered middle-aged women who had happy marriages and children more likely to be sympathetic, and challenged unmarried professionals or women who might themselves have been beaten.

As the prospective jurors were questioned, strongly opposing opinions emerged. A number of people believed there could be no excuse for killing except in the face of immediate danger to one's own life. Others confessed they were horrified by the manner of Mickey's death. They said they might understand stabbing or shooting, but fire was utterly abhorrent. Those who admitted such feelings were excused for prejudice favoring the prosecution. No one admitted favoring the defense, though Palus used his challenges to get rid of those he suspected of feminist views.

When half a dozen jurors had been accepted, court adjourned for lunch. Shelton handcuffed Francine and returned her to the upstairs cell, where a matron served a meal of bread, water, and a chicken pot pie frozen in the middle and burned at the edges. Francine ate the bread, washing down each swallow. She gave the pie to a cellmate. When Shelton returned and brought her down in the elevator, Greydanus was waiting as before to lead her through the crowd.

By four o'clock, two men and twelve women had been selected. A panel of fourteen would hear the evidence. At the time of the verdict, two jurors would be eliminated by drawing lots. Greydanus still had challenges left, but he thought the panel a good one. Only two jurors worried him—an unmarried woman who worked in a bank and a housewife whose son was a policeman—but he feared that if he eliminated them Palus would seat others even worse. He asked Francine how she felt about the jurors. She shrugged helplessly. All day she had sat rigid, expressionless, almost dazed, and Greydanus worried that she wouldn't be able to help him when he needed her. He touched her hand. "Come on, Francine," he whispered, "you've got work to do, too." She managed a faint smile. "They look okay," she said. "Ordinary, decent people, I guess."

Greydanus told the judge that the defense was satisfied. Palus was also. The jurors took their seats in the box. Then, as though moved by a single impulse, all of them turned toward Francine. To her, their faces appeared blandly expectant, like an audience waiting for the lights to go down and the film to begin, and she thought, "What is reality for me is just a show for them and for everyone else here." She had to fight an impulse to stand up and shout, "Look, everybody, let's call this off right now. Send me to prison and get it over with. I apologize for causing all this trouble. Don't make me sit here, scared to death, wondering what you'll do with me. Don't torture me for days. What for? You'll never know the truth!"

She heard Hotchkiss announcing that in the time that remained he would hear opening arguments by the opposing attorneys, and saw Palus, dressed in a light-colored, sharply tailored leisure suit, get to his feet. "Your Honor, Ladies and Gentlemen . . ." he began in his well-mannered, low-keyed voice, and Francine found herself listening as he began to describe what purported to be her life.

More in sorrow than in anger, Palus outlined the case he intended to prove. He told how two deputies had broken up a domestic dispute on the afternoon of March 9, and afterward Hughes, the victim, had gone to bed. The dead man's children would testify that their mother had sat down calmly while their father slept and after an interval told them to get ready to leave. The children noticed a can of gasoline by the bedroom door before their mother led them to the car. Then, with the house in flames, she had driven them to the police station and cried out a confession of her crime. At the end of his address to the jury Palus partially unveiled the letters to Walkup. Francine's motive, he said, was "an intimate relationship" with another man—a man she wanted to be with more than anyone else in the world. Such clearcut evidence, Palus said, could add up to nothing less than murder in the first degree.

When he sat down, Francine thought, "Yes. That's how it all must seem. It makes more sense than the truth."

Greydanus got up and slowly walked over to stand before the jury. He was wearing a dark gray business suit. His manner was serious and sincere. "Some people argue better than others," he began. "It is the evidence that counts and you must weigh it in the context of your whole experience in life and what you know to be right and wrong. . . ." For a moment more he talked in generalities in order to give the jury time to become accustomed to his presence and style, his tall figure and the sound of his voice.

"In listening to the prosecutor," Greydanus went on, "I get the impression this is a very simple case. Very simple." He paused and let his glance rest on each of the jurors in turn. His round spectacles gave his boyish features a professorial look. He noticed that the courtroom was quieter than it had been when Palus spoke, and hoped it was a sign that his listeners were more interested in Francine's version of events than the prosecutor's. "Mr. Palus," he continued, "is going to present some fifty witnesses to you and yet it all boils down to that simple case he explained to you. . . ."

Greydanus went on to point out how much Palus had omitted: that the police had been called to Francine's house not once, but countless times; that the police "assistance" mentioned by Palus had amounted to nothing; that the house was Francine's, and Mickey, her ex-husband, lived there because she knew no way to make him leave; that he had repeatedly threatened to kill her if she ran away. There would be no denial, Greydanus told the jury, that Francine had set the fire. What was deniable was the charge that she had done it deliberately; that she had planned her actions on the fatal night. As for the "intimate relationship" Palus had mentioned, Greydanus promised that it, also, would appear in a quite different light.

When Greydanus finished, the session ended. Francine was returned to the upstairs cell to wait for transportation "home" to the Ingham County Jail. She was not offered food and her stomach hurt miserably. The women who had shared the cell earlier had been taken elsewhere. Her single cellmate, a black woman, lay face down on the naked bunk, crying. Utterly exhausted, Francine sat silently on the floor, staring at the black graffiti-scratched walls, listening to the sounds of the cellblock—footsteps, cries, curses, fists or shoes pounding on metal doors as inmates sought to attract the attention of their jailers. The place reeked of desperation and degradation. Would state prison be like this? She dared not think of what would become of her if it were.

As court convened on the second day of the trial, Francine was again led through the packed corridor while flashbulbs flickered along her path. Some of the spectators held newspapers with front-page stories of the previous day's events. MRS. HUGHES ACCUSED OF ILLICIT AFFAIR was the headline in *The State*

Journal. "Francine Hughes was having an intimate relationship with an unidentified man, and that was the key to her actions last March when she set a fire that killed her ex-husband, the prosecution contended yesterday. . . ."

Inside the courtroom Judge Hotchkiss rapped for order and the day began. It was Mr. Palus' first move. He had chosen as his opening witness one of the deputies who had come to 1079 Grove Street in response to Christy's call for help on the day of the fire. His name was Steven Schlachter. A blond man, about thirty, he took the stand with the nonchalance of a professional who feels at ease with the law. After preliminary questions establishing his arrival at the house, Palus asked him to describe what he had found. Schlachter gave his answers in a dry, matter-of-fact tone.

"What condition was Mrs. Hughes in?" Palus asked.

"She was upset. She looked like she had been crying."

"Do you recall your conversation with Mrs. Hughes?"

"She said that he, Mr. Hughes, had been hitting her on the head but he stopped when I pulled up . . ."

"What did Mr. Hughes say?"

"He said it was true."

"And what was Mr. Hughes' attitude during this conversation?"

"Very disrespectful. Very obscene. Both to me and Mrs. Hughes."

"And did Mrs. Hughes respond?"

"She didn't argue. She was relatively calm."

"Do you remember what condition her clothing was in?"

"A little bit disrupted . . . not ripped."

"And did Mr. Hughes make any threats?"

"He told her it was all over for her now that she had called the police. He said he was going to kill her and then he made threats to me."

"Did Mrs. Hughes indicate she wanted to sign a complaint?"

"No, sir. She did not."

Greydanus listened to the questions and answers, surprised that Palus had chosen this opening. He could only suppose that Palus had decided that since the "domestic quarrel," as he insisted on calling it, was certain to be described, he had decided to get it over with, hoping that whatever sympathy for Francine it aroused

would be dissipated by later testimony. Unfortunately for the prosecutor, Deputy Schlachter's testimony was giving the jurors their
first glimpse of what Francine had endured that day, and his blood-
less tone and laconic answers made that glimpse all the more tantalizing. Greydanus could sense surprise and tension in the jury box—
an eagerness to know more.

When his turn came to cross-examine, Greydanus drew out details that filled in the picture—Mickey's foul language, for instance:

"Was this common, ordinary swearing, sir?"

"Common gutter language, yes."

"*Gutter* language? Is that worse than ordinary?"

Schlachter shrugged. "I don't know."

There was a ripple of laughter and Greydanus, smiling, looked
incredulous that Deputy Schlachter was not acquainted with
swearing of all degrees. Greydanus knew that small hypocrisies can
erode credibility. He went on to draw from Schlachter the fact that
Francine had wanted very much to leave the house, but had told
the officers she had no place to go. Then, after underlining Mickey's
threats, he asked, "Mr. Schlachter, why didn't you take *him* away?"

Schlachter hesitated. "Because he had made the same threats to
me. They seemed like . . . just words. He had an opportunity when
he was threatening me to back it up and he didn't."

Greydanus looked baffled. "Mr. Schlachter, did you think that
you, in uniform and with a gun on your hip, were in the same position as Francine? Are you equating your position with hers? Wasn't
it obvious to you, sir, that he wasn't going to do anything while you
were there?"

Schlachter looked uncomfortable. "No. I didn't assume that."

"Mr. Schlachter, you were informed that he stopped beating her
when you pulled up. Wasn't it very possible that after you left the
beating would begin again?"

"That would be possible," Schlachter agreed.

When the witness stepped down, Greydanus felt an exhilarating
glow. The opening couldn't have been better if he had planned it
himself.

As his second witness Palus called Deputy Dean Malm, who had
accompanied Schlachter to the house on March 9. Palus led Malm
through essentially the same testimony that Schlachter had given,
also minimizing the more violent aspects of the scene. When Palus

finished, Greydanus took over and again drew out details that enlarged the picture.

"You indicate Mr. Hughes was abusive and called Francine foul names."

"Yes, sir."

"Like what?"

"Do you want me to repeat the terminology?"

"Certainly."

"He called her a son of a bitch and a whore. It's hard to recall all of it."

"You mean there was *more*?"

"Yes, sir."

"And all of this time Francine sat there and basically just responded 'yes' or 'no'?"

"Yes, sir. Or else she ignored the comments."

"Now you also heard him making threats?"

"Yes, sir."

"And what was the nature of these threats?"

"That once we left he was going to get even with her."

"I see. Did that cause you any concern?"

"Yes, sir."

"Did she at any time threaten Mr. Hughes in any way?"

"No, sir, she did not."

When Greydanus had finished questioning Malm, the clear and simple picture Palus had drawn in his opening address had already taken on a different tint. Palus' next witnesses were the officers who had seen Francine arrive at the jail: Gate Guard Simons; Lieutenant Janutola, to whom she had given the gas cap; Deputy Hidecker; and Sergeant Nye, who had also come out to the gate. Greydanus questioned Nye about the normal procedure of the police in dealing with domestic quarrels, drawing out the surprising information that even if a woman had been badly beaten, her assailant would not be arrested unless the officer had seen the assault.

Switchboard operator Patricia Moore took the stand and described Francine washing her hands like Lady Macbeth and moaning, "My God, what have I done." However, when Greydanus questioned her, he forced Moore to recall that Francine had also said, "I don't know what made me do it," making a point that would be important later when Francine's state of mind would become the central issue.

When Patricia Moore left the stand, court adjourned for lunch. Shelton came for Francine and she obediently held out her wrists to be manacled. Being led, handcuffed, through the crowd, made it seem to Francine that even before being convicted she was being punished with public degradation. Perhaps the same thought occurred to Judge Hotchkiss. He appeared in the corridor in his shirt sleeves and halted them.

"Officer," he said to Shelton. "I don't want bracelets on in the courtroom."

"Oh?" Shelton exclaimed in surprise.

Hotchkiss turned to Francine. "You're not going to make any trouble, are you?"

"No, sir."

"Okay," Hotchkiss said. "No more handcuffs, do you understand?" With a pleasant, impersonal nod, he walked away. Thereafter Francine was handcuffed only during the ride to and from the courthouse.

When court reconvened Palus called Flossie Hughes to the stand. This would be Greydanus' first view of her, and she was the first witness whose testimony he feared. A bereaved mother can be a powerful instrument with which to arouse sympathy in a jury.

Flossie entered through the front door of the courtroom, escorted by a bailiff. Tall and dignified, wearing a plain cloth coat, she swept down the aisle, looking straight ahead. She unhesitatingly stepped into the witness box and looked over the courtroom with fierce dark eyes. It was the anger bottled up inside her that impressed Greydanus most. He thought, this is a proud old country woman who isn't scared of hell itself. She'll do anything to avenge her son. As Flossie took the oath, her high-pitched mountain voice and hillbilly accent rang out like a foreign tongue.

Palus approached Flossie with deference.

"Mrs. Hughes, do you see the person known to you as Francine Hughes in the courtroom here today?"

Flossie inclined her head for a brief glance in Francine's direction and replied, "Yes, sir. I do."

"She was married to one of your sons?"

"Yes, sir."

"Which son was that?"

As Flossie tried to say Mickey's name her face reddened with emotion and tears filled her eyes. She put a handkerchief to her face and struggled to control herself. Greydanus watched in dismay. Glancing at Francine he could see she was deeply upset by the spectacle of Flossie's grief. There was no doubt her tears were genuine and no doubt of the effect on the jury.

Still crying, Flossie answered, "My son James. We called him Mickey." Palus hovered over her solicitously. Flossie straightened up and wiped her eyes. "I'm sorry," she said. "I'm all right. I'm fine." Palus continued his questions. When he asked what she recalled of the day Mickey died, Flossie told of coming home with Berlin at six o'clock, parking the car in the garage, and going into her house.

"Did anything unusual happen at that time?"

"When we drove into the garage I thought I smelled gasoline and I insisted that I smelled gasoline and I asked my husband if he had been working on the tractor in the garage. He said no, he hadn't been messing with no gasoline in the garage. Before I entered into the house the odor was so strong I felt like we was going to have something to explode. I went into the house and I set down, but I couldn't set there."

Greydanus was momentarily baffled. Six o'clock, the time Flossie had mentioned, was more than two hours before Francine had fetched gasoline from her own cellar and even then the odor could not possibly have reached Flossie. As Flossie continued to elaborate her account of smelling gasoline, Greydanus wondered if she were lying in an effort to establish six o'clock as the time at which Francine began to plan the fire, and thus imply several hours of premeditation.

"All right. What happened then, ma'am?" Palus asked.

"I kept going out on the back porch checking and out in the garage checking to see if there was any danger of any explosion out there."

"And then what happened, ma'am?"

"Well, I kept that up for a whole hour. I couldn't set and watch television. I was so uneasy about that gas odor. I couldn't figure out where it was coming from. Before dark the kids had been in the yard. The last time I went out into the garage the kids was in the house. I glanced over to their house and I could see the children setting on the couch."

"Do you know about what time of the day that was, ma'am?"

"It had to be just before eight o'clock."

"What happened then?"

"I saw Fran come out of the bedroom. She went toward the television and I drawed on my own imagination that she was going over to turn the television off and put the children to bed. So I walked back in the house and set back down and I didn't go back out until the fire whistle blew."

Palus asked Flossie to describe her experiences during the fire. She told of her panic when she thought the children were in the house; how she had screamed at the firemen to save them and tried to get in the house herself, but had been held back by the police. Palus moved on to question her about Francine's relationship with Mickey.

"Around the time of March ninth, 1977, how would you say Mickey and Francine were getting along?"

"I thought everything was just as good with them as anybody else. I knew they had a few problems, you know, like anybody they have disagreements or maybe financial problems or stuff, but nothing out of the, you know, usual. Nothing that bothered or concerned me."

"Was there ever an occasion, Mrs. Hughes, when you saw your son strike Francine Hughes?"

Flossie drew herself up ramrod straight. She looked at Palus with the gaze of an outraged queen. "*Never!*" she declared. "*Never* did I ever see any of my sons strike one of their wives!"

Greydanus could hardly believe his ears. He had expected Flossie to whitewash Mickey's behavior, but not to go this far. In the stack of papers under his hand was evidence that could prove her an outright liar.

Blandly, Palus continued as though he were unaware that there was irrefutable proof that Flossie had seen Mickey beat Francine.

"Was there ever a time, Mrs. Hughes," Palus continued, "when Francine came running over to your house for help?"

Contemptuously Flossie replied, "She was constantly doing that."

"Was there ever a time when James followed Francine to your house?"

"Yes, he has."

"And in what condition was James when he followed Francine?"

"Well, I don't know what condition he was in. Sometimes he seemed as normal as anybody. Sometimes he would seem to be mad. Sometimes he would seem upset. A lot of times I think he was drunk. Later I would find out that he wasn't drunk."

"Did you, Mrs. Hughes, ever observe Francine Hughes strike her husband?"

"I have seen her throw things at him. I never see her deliberately strike him. But I have knowed of it."

"All right, Mrs. Hughes, when was the last time you saw Francine throw something at your son?"

"I don't know exactly how long it's been, but it's not been in the past year. They got along good as far as I knew. She was all the time, though, coming over for some kind of help. Wanting something. She always got what she come after." Flossie's voice was sharp with malice as she spoke of Francine.

"Your Honor," Palus said, "I have no further questions of this witness." He sat down. It was Greydanus' turn to cross-examine. He moved toward Flossie with the caution due a coiled rattlesnake. It would be an easy matter to show that she had committed perjury, but he wanted more than that. He wanted the jury to see her as a vindictive liar who would go to any lengths to punish her daughter-in-law, but if he were not careful, if he badgered her to the point where she became tearful or collapsed, the effect might be quite the opposite—Flossie would become pathetic to the jury and her perjury would be forgiven. Greydanus' tone as he addressed Flossie was as quiet as Palus' had been. "Mrs. Hughes," he asked, "when did your son and Francine marry?" Flossie gave the date— November 4, 1963—but the very sight of Greydanus seemed to anger her and she spat out the words.

"Do you recall the grounds for their divorce, Mrs. Hughes?"

Flossie bridled, sensing the trap. The divorce had, of course, been granted for extreme cruelty.

"All I knowed about it," she said, "was what she told me."

"Did you read that order of divorce?"

"Absolutely did, but I can't remember what it said. It sure didn't say what she told us."

"How do you know that, Mrs. Hughes?"

Flossie's face flushed. "Because I know what she told me and the divorce papers read different!"

Greydanus turned away satisfied. In only a few sentences Flossie had contradicted herself. She had also become more defiant the harder he pressed her, and that emboldened him. He guessed that she wasn't going to cry, but would flare into anger, and that could do him no harm. He decided to raise his voice and moved a little closer.

"Mrs. Hughes, before 1971, were you ever aware of your son beating up on Francine?"

"You don't have to shout at me!" Flossie shot back. "I'm not hard of hearing!"

"I'm sorry, Mrs. Hughes," Greydanus said more quietly. Then his voice hardened. "*Were* you . . . ?"

"No!" Flossie said defiantly. "I wasn't *ever* aware of him beating up on her!"

"*Never?*" Greydanus' voice was gently incredulous.

"Well." Flossie raised her chin haughtily. "I have knowed of them having fights, but I don't know what was the cause or who was afighting who. I didn't see nobody hit the other. Afterwards she would tell me, 'It's more my fault than his.' *He* was the one that would have the bruised places and the cut places. I never seen none on her."

"Anything else you would like to tell us, Mrs. Hughes?"

Flossie's answer was an angry silence.

"Okay. Did the children ever tell you about their father beating up on their mother?"

"Yeah. The kids thought their father was beating up on their mother, I guess. The way she would run out of the house and scream, she had all of us thinking he was killing her. Probably sometimes when he hadn't even touched her."

Again Greydanus was crowding Flossie, leaning a little closer when he spoke, raising his voice ever so slightly with each question, and Flossie's voice was rising in response.

"And the children told you he was beating her. Isn't that correct, Mrs. Hughes?"

"The children has come over a couple of times when Fran and Mickey would be racketing and yelling." She paused. "*She* would be the one that was doing the stuff!"

Suddenly Greydanus held up the police reports.

"Isn't it true, Mrs. Hughes, that *you* called the police . . . and that was because your son beat up on *you*?"

Flossie reared back in anger. "My son *never* beat up on me! How dare you?"

Greydanus, surprised, asked, "*Never* beat up on you?"

"No, sir!"

"Do you recall an incident in 1972, Mrs. Hughes, when you called the Ingham County Sheriff Department and Francine hid in your house?"

"Yes, she hid in our house sometimes. She done that even before they got married. I didn't know if they was playing games or they was fighting or what was going on!"

Greydanus glanced at the report in his hand. "On August seventeen, 1972, at fourteen minutes after seven, don't you recall that the police came to your house because your son hit you in the face?"

"I most certainly do not!"

"Don't you remember the police coming to your house when Francine was hiding because Mickey had been beating on her?"

"I do not remember no such occasion as him beating on her!"

"Do you recall him breaking down the door, trying to get into your house to get after her?"

"He didn't break down no door! He did not!" Her voice was shrill and trembling with anger.

Greydanus dropped his voice. "Mrs. Hughes, I am merely asking you."

"You better ask something else. . . ."

She half rose from her chair and was continuing to scream at Greydanus when Judge Hotchkiss' gavel came down and cut her off. "Mrs. Hughes!" he admonished. "Silence, please!" He called a recess and dismissed the jury. The courtroom broke into a hubbub. Hotchkiss quieted it and told the attorneys he wanted to talk to them and the witness in his chambers. A court attendant led Flossie from the witness stand in the wake of the judge.

In his office Judge Hotchkiss seated Flossie and lectured her briefly on courtroom decorum. He would allow no screaming, he said. Mr. Greydanus, the judge went on, had a right to ask certain questions and she was required to answer. Flossie glared, but held her peace. She acknowledged that she understood. When they returned to the courtroom there was an interval while the jury was recalled. Greydanus sat down beside Francine. "What did you think of that?" he asked. "That was the most blatant perjury I ever heard in my life!"

"I felt bad for her," Francine said simply. "She didn't know what else to say."

When the jury returned Greydanus asked only a few more questions. Flossie continued to deny incidents that were described in the police reports Greydanus held in his hand. When Greydanus let her leave the stand he was satisfied that her testimony had tarnished the integrity of the prosecution. More than that, in seeking to defend her son, Flossie had put him on trial.

Flossie Hughes' testimony had been a debacle for the prosecutor. On the third day of the trial he sought to regain lost sympathy by bringing to the stand a succession of police and firemen to describe the burning house and the discovery of Mickey's body.

Although Palus managed to bring grisly details before the jury—the smell of burning flesh that permeated the house, Mickey's skin sloughing off in a fireman's groping hand—Greydanus was not troubled by their testimony. He could detect no strong reaction among the jurors, and since he did not intend to dispute the official version of the fire, he asked few questions. However, when Palus attempted to show the jury half a dozen vastly enlarged color photographs of Mickey's naked corpse, Greydanus objected that the prosecutor's sole purpose was to horrify the jurors. Judge Hotchkiss compromised the issue, eliminating the most gruesome pictures and allowing one that showed only the upper half of Mickey's body to be entered as evidence.

When the business of the photographs was finished, Palus announced that Christy Hughes would take the stand, and the courtroom stirred with interest. That Christy was a prosecution witness was merely a technicality—in fact, Greydanus preferred it since it would give him greater latitude in questioning her—but some of the audience undoubtedly thought it meant that Christy was willing to condemn her mother, an inference that hurt Francine. When Christy was brought in, demure and neatly dressed in a sweater and skirt, she gave her mother a yearning look so eloquent that Francine drew in her breath and impulsively rose in her chair.

Greydanus touched her arm and Francine slumped back. She covered her face with her hands and wept. It was the first time her composure had cracked in public.

Judge Hotchkiss cautioned Christy that she must answer questions and tell the truth. She said she understood, and Palus began: Did she remember March ninth? What time had she come home from school? Who had been at home? What had happened when she and her mother and the other children returned from the store? After the TV dinners were in the oven what had her father done?

"He turned the oven off," Christy answered.

"How many times did he do that?"

"About three times."

Puzzled, the audience and the jury tensed with interest. Hotchkiss, leaning forward, watched the child intently.

"How was your father talking?" Palus asked.

"Well, he was in an angry mood and he was mad because we were having TV dinners."

"Okay. And how was your mom speaking to him?"

"Very calmly, trying to talk some sense, you know, trying to get him to calm down and get him to quit turning the oven off and on and all that."

This was the jury's first view of Francine's daily life with Mickey and they listened with rapt interest as Christy, in her clear, unemotional child's voice, described the prelude to her father's death.

"We were playing and then all of a sudden Mom comes popping out the back door with Dad having ahold of her shirt. And she is yelling and screaming, 'Christy, call the police! He's going to beat me to a bloody pulp.' And so I ran over to my Grandma Hughes."

When Christy had described the visit of deputies Schlachter and Malm, Palus asked, "What kind of a mood was your mom in?"

"She was nervous. She was sad. You could tell she had been crying and she was sort of, you know, how you act, how you breathe when you get done crying? You just gasp . . . gasp. She was doing that. Sort of whimpering, I guess."

Palus tried to pin Christy down on the crucial point of how much time elapsed from the moment her father went to sleep and Francine sat down in the living room—perhaps to plan his murder—until she lit the match. Christy gave no definite answers, but Palus was able to establish that Christy noticed the gas can by the back door and that it had not been there earlier in the day. Then Palus asked Christy to describe how Francine led the children to the car, left them for a moment, returned, and got in the driver's seat.

"What happened then?"

"She started the car."

"Did she start it in a normal manner?"

"There is only one way to start a car," Christy replied, and the tension of the dialogue was broken as laughter swept the audience. Palus grew pink and allowed himself a slight smile.

"I know that you turn a key, right? But did she do it slower or faster?"

"Faster."

Christy described their panic-stricken flight. "Mom was crying really bad! And screaming! She was screaming, 'Oh my God!' and shaking really hard. She kept looking out the back window and screaming, 'I didn't mean to do it!' and 'Oh my God!' I said, 'Mom! Where are we going? What are we gonna do?' She says, 'I don't know . . .'" Christy's voice trembled with remembered excitement and terror. Palus broke in.

"Do you remember she said something like, 'I burned him up'?"

Christy hesitated, as though she understood the intent of the question was to convict her mother. She looked down and, in a small voice, reluctantly answered, "Yes."

Palus stepped back and turned Christy over to Greydanus for cross-examination. Palus' questioning had already sketched an outline of the day's events; now Greydanus began to fill in the colors.

"How much beer did your dad drink in a day, usually?"

"Over twelve cans."

"What was his normal mood when he was drinking?"

"Mean!"

"That day did your mom seem depressed or happy or normal or what?"

"Depressed. She's always depressed."

"Christy, what kind of meals does your mother prepare?"

"Big meals."

"Do they taste good to you, Christy?"

"Yes."

"So it isn't like you had TV dinners every day?"

"Right."

"Christy, do you think your mother is a good mother for you children?"

"Yes!"

Greydanus reminded Christy that when she was questioned at the jail on the night of the fire she had demonstrated for the police how Mickey had twisted her mother's arm behind her back, forcing her to her knees. "Could you show the jury how that was?" Greydanus asked. Christy scrambled out of her chair and, with her arm behind her, crouched before the jury, until her head almost touched the floor. It was a startling tableau. "Was he hitting her with his open hand or his fist?" Greydanus asked. Christy held up a clenched fist. Back on the stand, Christy imitated Mickey's gesture as he snapped his fingers and pointed to the door, ordering the children outside. While they were in the yard, she said, she had heard her mother's screams and the sound of breaking glass. Nicky had begun to cry. When the deputies arrived, the children ran to the police car; then Christy followed the officers inside.

"What was your father saying?" Greydanus asked.

"He was yelling, 'If you ever call the police again I'm going to kill you!'"

"Do you remember him saying that in the past? Before this day?"

Christy nodded. "Yes." She told of seeing the pile of torn books and papers in the middle of the floor and her mother picking them up. Greydanus asked her to repeat the language that Mickey used. "I'm sorry I have to ask you this, Christy, but I want you to tell us what he said."

Christy answered without hesitation, "He called her a fucking bitch and a whore." The impact of the words coming from the mouth of a sweet-faced little girl was exactly as Greydanus had planned.

As the dialogue between Greydanus and Christy continued, the courtroom was perfectly still. Christy spoke with a spontaneous candor that made it impossible to doubt a word she said. Relentlessly, Greydanus continued to pile outrage upon outrage.

"How many times did your father beat up on your mother?"

"Too many times to count."

"Once a week?"

"Yes. About once a week. But he would also, like, push her around, every day. Every day."

"Christy. Do you remember seeing your father use a weapon?"

"Yes. A couple of times."

"What happened?"

"I came into the dining room and Dad had Mom pinned down. . . ."

"Was she on the floor?"

"Yes. And he was saying he was going to kill her and I was awful afraid. He got up and got a knife. A big butcher knife. While he was getting it Mom got up and ran. She got out the back door."

"Where did she run?"

"Like usual, over to Grandma Flossie's."

"A lot of times?"

"A lot of times."

Christy described her memory of a terrifying time when Francine and the children hid in the basement of Flossie's house. Christy could hear her father's voice through the floorboards as he searched for them in the rooms upstairs. "I heard him saying, 'All right, where is she?' and Grandma was saying, 'I don't know. I ain't seen her. I ain't seen her at all!'"

"Christy, was your Grandma Flossie out there, was she watching, when your dad beat your mom out in the yard?"

"Yes."

"Did your mom ever hit your father first?"

"No. Never."

"Did she try to defend herself?"

"Well . . . once she threw a plant . . . a flower pot. Dad put up his arm and got cut."

"What was the reason she threw it?"

"Because he was coming at her."

"Had he been beating her?"

"Yes."

"Christy, do you remember hearing your father tell your mother what he would do if she tried to leave him?"

"He said if she left with us kids he would kill her."

Greydanus had come to the climax of his interrogation. He stepped back, framing one single question that would sum it all up. He knew he would not be allowed to ask Christy if she hated her father. "Christy," he asked gently, "are you glad he is gone?"

Palus leaped to his feet and appealed to the judge. "That's irrelevant, Your Honor. How she feels is not an issue."

"Objection sustained!"

Greydanus tried again. "Christy, have you missed your father?"

"No!"

Greydanus had achieved his effect. "That is all the questions I have, Your Honor," Greydanus said and sat down. Christy left the stand. As she walked down the aisle to the door there was something like a sigh from the audience as the tension relaxed.

Palus announced that his next witness would be James Wade Hughes, and Jimmy, an appealing boy wearing a starched white shirt and bow tie, was conducted to the stand by the bailiff. His face was deathly pale and he looked very small as he sat stiffly in the witness chair and faced the courtroom. Palus informed Judge Hotchkiss that Jimmy was eleven years old. Palus began his questions about what happened on the day of his father's death. As Jimmy answered he squeezed his hands between his knees, a picture of reluctance and misery. He confirmed the story Christy had told.

"Now, Jimmy," Palus asked, "what was happening when the police were there?"

Jimmy stared at his feet for excruciating seconds. "My mom was crying and my dad was talking mean."

"What happened when the police left?"

"My dad started hitting my mom again."

Such answers must have seemed to the prosecutor a thorny thicket through which he had to pass in order to reach his goal—the testimony that would show that Francine had ample time in which to plan the death of her husband.

"Jimmy, do you remember what time your dad went to sleep?"

"No."

"Was it still light outside?"

"It was still light."

Palus moved on to establish how Francine had prepared for the crime.

"Before you went out in the car, Jim, did your mom ask you a question?"

"Yes."

"What was the question?"

Jimmy looked as though he might cry. "She asked for the combination to my dad's garage."

"Were there any cans out there with liquid in them?"

"Yes."

"Do you know what kind of liquid?"

Jimmy sat in silence for seconds. Then he said in a low voice, "Gas."

"All right, Jimmy," Palus said. "I know this is hard for you, but we have to keep on. Now, as you went out to the car, did you notice anything unusual in the house?"

Jimmy nodded. "Yes."

"What was that?"

"A gas can sitting by the back door."

Palus asked Jimmy to recall what had happened as Francine drove to the Ingham County Jail.

"Did your mom say anything?"

"Yes."

"Do you remember what it was?"

"She was crying . . . and she said, 'Oh my God' . . . and . . . she said . . ." Jimmy looked imploringly in the direction of Francine. "She said, 'I did it!'"

"Did she say anything more?"

"Yes."

"What was that?"

"She said . . . if he ever got out of the fire . . . if my dad got out . . . he would kill her."

"Do you remember her saying it was wrong to take someone's life?"

"Yes."

"Do you remember her saying she threw a match in the bedroom where your dad was sleeping?"

"Yes." Jimmy's voice was almost inaudible.

"So she did say that?" Palus insisted.

Jimmy nodded wretchedly, in tears, and again answered, "Yes."

"Thank you, Jim," Palus said. "I have no more questions." As he sat down the prosecutor looked cheerful for the first time. He had at last shown the jury the key facts in the open-and-shut case of premeditated murder, as he had promised in his opening address.

Greydanus rose to question Jimmy. He ignored the topics that had interested Palus and asked Jimmy about the scene Christy had already described, when the children saw their father hold Francine pinned to the floor and then get up and pick up a knife. Jimmy also gave his story, similar to Christy's, of how his father had forbidden Francine to continue school and then destroyed her books and papers.

When at last the wretched little boy was excused and a bailiff led him away, Francine watched his retreating figure and tears streamed down her face. Then she put her head down and silently sobbed.

"It was the worst moment of the trial. It hurt so to see my children up on the stand; to know what they must be going through. Jimmy looked so pitiful. So scared. He would look at me and I could see he knew he was being used against me. It was a cruel, terrible thing to do to a child. Christy tried so hard to be grown-up and be honest and help me. I knew she was terribly afraid of saying something wrong that would hurt me. I could feel her wanting me to tell her she was doing okay. I wanted to jump up and run to her—take her in my arms and tell her everything would be all right. When Jimmy cried, I almost got out of my chair. But I knew cops would grab me and handcuff me and everything would be worse. So I sat quiet and thought, 'Maybe you'll never be able to hold them again.' When they led Jimmy out I thought, 'My God, I love that child.' That was when I had to hide my face and cry."

The testimony of the children added to that of the deputies created considerable excitement in the corridors of the City Hall. Reporters covering the trial wondered why prosecution witnesses sounded more like defense witnesses. Some asked why Houk had decided to prosecute the case in the first place. Houk beat a retreat, saying that while he realized Francine's story stirred sympathy it was the duty of the prosecutor "to let the people decide."

Greydanus was elated that in the first three days the jurors had been given the facts he wanted them to have and, if the reaction of most spectators was an indication, Francine was winning tremendous sympathy. Not that everyone agreed; law-enforcement people and "hard liners" still believed that murder must be punished no matter what the extenuating circumstances. Greydanus dared not become overconfident; there were still high hurdles ahead. The letters to George Walkup remained to be dealt with. Francine would have to testify and would face risky moments when Palus questioned her on such crucial points as her thoughts while she waited for Dana to come home. Greydanus was counting on the testimony of the psychiatrists to show that Francine's behavior was consistent with temporary insanity, but here too, there were risks. Would their technical language make sense to a jury of lay people? Greydanus felt that no matter how well the trial went in the early stages, the jurors would not make up their minds until the final moment.

On the morning of the fourth day of the trial, the largest crowd so far gathered at City Hall. Would-be spectators stood in line for hours hoping for a seat in the courtroom, which could accommodate only a fraction of them. A fist fight broke out at the doorway and was quelled by guards. As a spectacle the Hughes case was a smash hit.

This was the day Palus intended to present evidence of Francine's affair with Walkup. His first witness was Lieutenant LeMar Erb, Walkup's superior officer on the State Police Security Force, who described finding certain letters in Walkup's locker and delivering them to the prosecution.

Palus' next witness was Betty Cover, Francine's friend from Brazil. Greydanus had originally planned to call Betty as a witness for the defense, but when the letters were discovered Palus had subpoenaed her as a witness for the prosecution. Nevertheless, there was no doubt where Betty's sympathies lay. She would do her best to help Francine. It was her unpredictability and lack of judgment that bothered Greydanus.

Greydanus was still furious at Betty. He had talked to her a number of times while the letter-smuggling was in progress and she had never given him any clue to what was going on. Greydanus believed she was responsible for reviving Francine's emotions about George and in the end it might be their girlish conspiracy that would tip the balance against Francine. When the letters were discovered, Greydanus had called Betty and told her how angry he felt. Betty expressed regret, but no repentance. She said she had only been trying to cheer Francine and hadn't thought it would do any harm.

Betty came to the stand, a pert, dainty woman, exotically pretty, who answered Palus' opening questions in a strong accent. Her manner was disdainful and she forced Palus to struggle for every scrap of information. Palus asked Betty to identify the three envelopes he held in his hand. Betty fenced, avoiding direct answers. "I don't know why I should recognize them. I never opened them. I never read them. What do you expect me to do?"

Shrugging, tossing her head, and rolling her eyes, she repeatedly drew laughter at Palus' expense, but ultimately she admitted that she had received letters from Francine while Francine was in prison and had given them to Walkup. Palus tried to draw out details of the romance, but Betty refused to be drawn. She insisted she did not recall how often she had seen Francine and George together in the lounge at school. Frustrated, Palus gave up.

Now it was Greydanus' turn, and he knew that Betty had specific information that would help Francine. Betty willingly testified that twice she had seen Francine come to class with noticeable bruises and that when Betty asked about them Francine admitted that her husband had beaten her. Though he knew Palus would object, Greydanus managed to bring out a description of the bruises. "They were purple . . . and pink . . . and red. . . ." Betty wrinkled her nose.

"Horrible?" Greydanus prompted.

"Horrible!" Betty agreed, as Palus leaped to his feet to object that she was improperly inflaming the jury.

Betty testified that the second time she saw Francine's bruises she had asked, "Again, Fran?" and Francine had answered, "Yes. Again."

Greydanus' questions permitted Betty to make it clear that Francine's meetings with George were in the midst of a group of students in the Business School lounge and that, as far as Betty knew, the flirtation went no further. Her most important contribution to the defense was the information that Francine had broken off her relationship with Walkup because she discovered he was living with his wife, and that months later it was Betty who had persuaded Francine, by then in jail, that George was no longer married and wanted to hear from her—that it was Betty who had rekindled the romance.

When Betty left the stand, Palus had given the jury all the evidence he had of Francine's affair with George Walkup except the letters themselves. He proposed to read them aloud in court. Greydanus objected, and Hotchkiss said he would hear arguments on the question on the following day.

As his final witness, Palus called Lieutenant Tift. Tift's function was largely the routine one of identifying more than thirty objects—ashes, bits of carpet, the gas can, and so forth—that Palus was introducing as physical evidence. Each day of the trial Tift had placed large plastic cannisters containing these grim relics in a conspicuous position on the table. When the moment came to unveil the contents, it fizzled. The jury showed scant interest, and when the cannisters were handed into the jury box, the jurors passed them on without opening them. As his final question of Tift, Palus asked him to describe how Francine looked when he first saw her at the Ingham County Jail on the night of the fire.

Tift glanced across the room at Francine and replied, with dry understatement: "Pretty much as she does now—except she had apparently been crying and was somewhat upset."

From the first Greydanus had believed that the zealous little detective had been a prime mover in the prosecution of Francine. Greydanus had also been struck by Tift's offhand remark, when they talked in Tift's office about the case, that Mickey Hughes was known to him as a mean, violent son of a bitch. As he began to question Tift, Greydanus decided it would be instructive to the jurors to know Tift's informal opinion of the victim. When Greydanus asked him if he remembered the remark, Tift tensed with irritation and replied that he could not recall it. Greydanus badgered him while Tift, increasingly flustered and angry, dodged, at last admitting that it was "possible" he had said something of the sort. Tift left the stand with his composure badly ruffled and once again the prosecution had appeared as something less than candid and fair.

With Tift's testimony the trial had come to the halfway mark. Hotchkiss called a recess for a long weekend. Francine was taken upstairs to wait in the grim detention cell until late in the day, and then was driven back to the Ingham County Jail. She was still feeling nauseated, and the jail doctor ordered a special diet that eased her stomach pain. For Francine the three-day recess was both a rest from the tension of court and an extension of the agony of suspense.

Greydanus came to talk to her over the weekend. He told her the first week had gone better than he had hoped; he thought Palus seemed in a state of embarrassment and disarray. Inexplicably it seemed that Palus had not foreseen the reaction of sympathy and outrage that the testimony of his own witnesses would evoke. As for the letters, Greydanus thought that the prosecutor's failure to produce any other evidence that Francine's affair with Walkup was the motive for Mickey's murder made them less damaging than they seemed at first. How the jury ultimately felt about them would depend on how fully Francine could explain them when she took the stand.

At the mention of her own testimony Francine froze. She took a deep breath and asked if Greydanus knew what day he would call her. He said no, he would have to play it by ear. He promised to give her warning and urged her not to worry about it; it was still several days away.

On Monday morning, when court convened for the fifth day of the trial, Judge Hotchkiss sent the jury out of the courtroom while Palus and Greydanus argued the question of whether Francine's love letters should be read aloud in court or given to the jurors to read for themselves in the privacy of the jury room. If Palus read them aloud it would be acutely embarrassing for Francine to listen to them, accompanied by inevitable gasps and titters from the courtroom audience. Greydanus argued that reading them aloud would unfairly impress the jurors, and Hotchkiss agreed. He denied Palus' request. His decision was a tremendous relief to Francine. If the letters had been read aloud, every newspaper in the country would have been free to reprint whatever excerpts they chose.

When the matter of the letters had been settled, it was time for Greydanus to begin the defense. As his first witness he had chosen one of the deputies, Mohammad Abdo, who had been called to Dansville to subdue Mickey six years before, when Mickey had first recovered from the accident and beaten Francine in Flossie's yard. Abdo had since retired from police work and now ran a bar and grill—Abdo's Lounge—in Lansing. Greydanus had found his name signed to one of the reports he had gotten from the Sheriff Department and looked him up. Abdo had told Greydanus that he remembered the episode. Since he was no longer connected with the police, he had no hesitation about testifying for Francine. As Abdo described his recollections, Greydanus knew the testimony would draw a vivid picture for the jury.

When Abdo, a tall, heavy man, took the stand Greydanus asked him about the episode during which he and another deputy wrestled Mickey to the ground and strapped him to a stretcher.

"Was his mother, Flossie Hughes, present?" Greydanus asked.

"Yes, she was," Abdo replied.

"How many of you had to fight Mickey Hughes to subdue him?"

"Two of us to start with and then two ambulance drivers pitched in."

"Did you try to hold him yourself?"

"Yes, sir. He was on his back and I was holding down his right arm and holding his head. He was so violent that he was banging his head on the ground. I was holding his head trying to keep him from banging it. He turned to bite me. I grabbed his arm and he picked me up off the floor with one arm. I held his shoulders, his right arm, and his head, and when he tried to bite me, apparently his mother thought we were going to hit him and tried to interfere . . . I kept telling her we weren't going to hurt him. . . ."

Greydanus broke in. "Excuse me. You said he picked you up *with one arm*?"

"Yes, sir."

"How much did you weigh at that time?"

"About two hundred and twenty-five pounds."

Greydanus paused and looked over at Francine, silently comparing her with Abdo's burly figure, and he could see the jury doing the same.

Another point that Greydanus wanted to make was that Mickey's violent nature was well known to the Ingham County deputies, but those he had questioned so far had evaded him. Now he asked Abdo:

"Could you tell me if there was any standard procedure you patrolmen followed when you dealt with a call to the Hughes home?"

"Well, there were certain individuals who were known to all of us on road patrol and if the call came and one of these people was named it was just common practice to respond knowing you could find a violent situation."

"Was Mickey Hughes one of those persons?"

"Yes, he was."

Greydanus thanked Abdo and he left the stand. His next witness was Mason City Police Officer Leon Langridge, who had been parked at the Majik Market when Francine drove in with Mickey in pursuit. Langridge testified that Francine, shaking with fear, had told him that her husband had been choking her in her house and when she fled in her car, he had tried to run her off the road. Then Deputy Richard Dral of the Ingham County force testified that he had helped Langridge arrest Mickey, who was yelling obscenities and cursing the officers.

"Did you hear him say anything directed to anyone else?"

"Yes, he looked at a lady parked there and yelled, 'Just wait until I get my hands around your throat!'"

Greydanus' fourth witness was Deputy Barry Kingsley, who had gone to Adams Street in the summer of 1972 when Flossie Hughes had telephoned for help. Kingsley had written a report at the time and Greydanus had the report in his hand, so he knew just what details Kingsley could supply. Greydanus asked Kingsley to describe his conversation with Flossie Hughes after Mickey had been arrested.

"We took an assault-and-battery complaint from Flossie Hughes," Kingsley said. "She told us she had been struck by her son several times in the face. She said he had also struck his ex-wife."

Greydanus looked at the jurors and waited, giving them time to recall Flossie's denial that Mickey had ever struck her. Then he asked, slowly, "Mrs. Flossie Hughes told you that? At that time?"

"That is correct," Kingsley replied.

Greydanus asked if Mickey had threatened anyone.

"Well," Kingsley recalled, "he said something about cutting their throats. He used abusive language. I tried to calm him down. I tried to get him to leave, but he wouldn't. We ended up arresting him."

"Did Mrs. Flossie Hughes say anything about damage?" (This, too, was in Kingsley's report.)

"She said her son had broken through the screen door and broken the lock on another door to get into her house."

Greydanus thanked Kingsley. Palus had no questions and the officer left the stand.

Greydanus' final police witness was a deputy named Albert Looney, who had been called to Dansville in 1973 by Berlin Hughes. This was the occasion when Francine had been taken to the hospital in Mason after Mickey had beaten her and chased her into Berlin's house. Looney testified that Berlin told him how Mickey had broken a storm door and said he might get a warrant against his son for malicious destruction of property. Looney recalled how Francine, sitting in the kitchen describing how she'd been beaten, had turned faint and vomited. It was Looney who had called an ambulance.

Greydanus turned the witness over to Palus, who had no questions. Presumably the prosecutor had read the officers' reports and been prepared for their testimony. He had listened, arms folded, with no expression, as though these events added up to nothing more than a motive for Francine to kill Mickey Hughes.

Now Greydanus turned to the four women who had agreed to testify for Francine. The first was Connie Lee Feldpausch, who had been Mickey's classmate in school. Connie, small, red-haired, and pretty, took the witness chair and squared her shoulders as she looked out over the packed courtroom. Greydanus knew she was confronting the Hughes family, at least in her thoughts, and he admired her courage. His first questions established that she had lived in Dansville and known Francine and Mickey when they were first married.

"Were you friends with Francine?"

"Yes. As close as you could get to Francine."

"What do you mean by that?"

"Well, she wasn't allowed to have real close friends. We talked to her. We seen her. We were as close as anybody could be to her."

"Why wasn't she allowed to have friends? Who didn't allow it?"

"Her husband didn't."

"Do you know why?"

"He said she didn't need friends."

Greydanus turned to the question of Mickey's reputation. Connie said that it was well known he beat up his wife and was not the only one of the Hughes boys with that reputation.

"What kind of character did Francine Hughes have?"

"She is very nice and a very good mother. An exceptionally clean housekeeper."

"Did you ever see Francine Hughes behave in a violent manner?"

"No. I have not."

"Did you ever hear Francine Hughes use bad language against anyone?"

"Never."

"Did you ever hear anyone say anything bad about Francine?"

"Never."

"Can you recall a specific time you saw Mickey Hughes beat Francine?"

"There was a time I saw him out in the yard beating her with his fists and kicking her."

"Was that before the accident?"

"Yes."

"Did you ever see Francine with bruises?"

"Many times. I have seen her with black eyes and a cut lip. With bruises all over her face."

"Did Mickey have a reputation for going around with other women?"

"Yes, he did."

"Have you ever seen Mickey Hughes strike his mother?"

"Yes."

"Was that before or after his accident?"

"Before. I was coming down the street and Mickey came out of the house and his mother right after him. She was yelling at him. He turned around and slapped her in the face and told her to go back in the house and mind her own goddamned business."

"What would you do if Francine and Mickey were fighting?"

"I didn't like it, but I couldn't do anything about it."

"Did you leave?"

"Yes."

"Why?"

"Because I was afraid of Mickey."

"Did Mickey try to hide the fact he beat his wife?"

"No. He would do it in front of people and brag about it afterwards."

"Actually *brag* about it?"

"Yes. I would ask where Francine was and he would say she's home mending her wounds from the night before."

When Connie had first told him of Mickey's remark, Greydanus had thought it spoke volumes. He decided to end Connie's testimony with that quotation from Mickey still ringing in the jurors' ears.

Connie was followed by her sister, Donna Johnson, who told of witnessing the violent scene when Mickey, newly recovered from his accident, had beaten Francine. "Some way Francine got out of the house," Donna said, "and Mickey went out looking for her. I was at my neighbor's, Alice Quemby. I believe Mickey thought I was Francine because he came right in Alice's front door and started after me. I ran out the back door. Then Alice's husband came and put Mickey out. Mickey followed me to my house and my husband called the police."

Donna had also seen the episode that ended when Chris Eifert held Mickey down until the police came. Donna spoke highly of Francine. She had never heard a word against her, Donna said, and though she didn't know her very well, had always thought her a very nice person. Donna's quiet, dignified presence and her evident sincerity, added to Connie's equally convincing testimony, were tremendously effective, Greydanus felt.

Evidently Palus felt the same. He tried to minimize the effect by cross-examining Donna. She had testified that she had lived in Dansville twenty years. "You saw Mickey Hughes strike his wife twice in twenty years. Is that correct?"

"That's all I saw. Yes."

"Only those two occasions?"

"Yes."

The prosecutor sat down, but Greydanus returned to question Donna again, making clear that both episodes had been within the past six years, and continued. "It was known in the community that this was going on, isn't that so?"

"Yes."

"Did you see the police at her house many times?"

"Yes."

"Was Francine the kind of person who would complain to you about what was going on?"

"No."

"Could you tell, though, that something was bothering her?"

"Yes."

Palus had no further questions and Donna left the stand. She was followed by Alice Quemby, who elaborated the story Donna had just told. When Greydanus finished, Palus had no questions.

Debbie Brown, the youngest sister of Donna and Connie, was a small blonde in her mid-twenties. Her answers were forthright and to the point.

"Debbie, how did Mickey treat Francine?"

"Bad."

"Have you seen Francine with injuries?"

"I've seen her with two black eyes and her mouth busted up."

"Did Francine tell you why she didn't leave?"

"She was too scared of him."

"Have you ever heard anyone say anything bad about Francine?"

"No. Never."

When Debbie Brown was excused the day ended. In cross-examination, Palus had tried to imply that the four women had gotten together to tailor their testimony, but Greydanus doubted his efforts had had much effect. He was, however, angry that Deputy Shelton, sitting behind Francine and facing the jury, had made faces and exchanged incredulous glances with Tift during testimony favorable to Francine. Greydanus considered protesting what he thought were low tactics, designed to distract the jurors, but decided against it for fear of upsetting Francine, who hadn't seen what was going on. At the end of the day, after so much helpful testimony, Francine seemed a little more relaxed, her face less taut and somber. Greydanus decided not to tell her that in the morning he would call her to the stand.

Greydanus had given a great deal of thought to his promise to warn Francine before calling her to testify. He looked upon her testimony as the linchpin of the defense; all the rest, no matter how overwhelmingly sympathetic, could not prove that she was innocent of planning the death of Mickey Hughes. Only Francine could tell the jurors what she had thought and felt.

Greydanus intended to lead her through virtually the entire story of her life with Mickey, hoping to reveal to the jurors the special qualities of her emotional makeup that had held her fatally enmeshed. Her testimony would require all her resources of eloquence and control. He would guide her from topic to topic with his questions, but unless her answers were fully thought out—as candid and vivid as when he talked to her at the jail—the jurors would not see the full picture.

Francine had shown increasing panic at the prospect of testifying and Greydanus decided that, rather than give her time to become unnerved by anticipation, he would take her by surprise. On Tuesday morning, the sixth day of the trial, he opened by calling to the stand Dr. Jon Desquin, who told, in dispassionate terms, what he had observed when Francine consulted him for symptoms he believed were due to stress. His testimony was brief and Palus had no questions. Watching him leave the stand, Francine wondered who Greydanus would call next. A moment later she heard Greydanus make the announcement. "Your Honor," his voice rang through the courtroom, "the defense will now call to the stand Francine Hughes."

Francine turned white. She seemed frozen, unable to move. Greydanus went to her and guided her to the stand. She obediently raised her hand to take the oath, and sat down as Judge Hotchkiss instructed her to do. She looked out over the crowded courtroom, then turned to Greydanus with a beseeching glance. Judge Hotchkiss leaned toward her and asked her to state her name. For an instant she seemed unable to answer. Greydanus' heart was sinking. He was inwardly praying, "Dear God, don't let her collapse now!"

Her voice was tight with near-hysteria as she answered, "Francine Hughes." Greydanus moved close to her, encouraging her with his voice as he led her through a series of simple opening questions.

"Francine, where do you live?"

"Where do I live now?" She looked confused.

"Where is your home? Do you own a home?"

"Yes. In Dansville."

"And right now you are incarcerated in the Ingham County Jail; isn't that correct?"

"Yes."

"I am going to show you a document, Francine. You tell me if you recognize this?"

"Yes. That's my divorce certificate."

"Could you read to me from this document, Francine? What was the basis for the divorce?"

Francine glanced down at the paper he had put in her hands and then looked up silently. Her eyes were beginning to brim.

"*Francine!*" Greydanus snapped at her, hoping to bring her to herself. "What was the basis for the divorce?"

"Extreme cruelty," Francine replied and then burst out, "I don't think I can do this!" She covered her face and sobbed.

Hotchkiss brought down his gavel to silence the noise in the courtroom and ordered the jury to leave. Greydanus watched in dismay while Francine huddled, crying, in the witness chair. Unless she pulled herself together, all might be lost. Tears at appropriate moments could do no harm, but if she remained a weepy, hysterical witness it would be impossible to bring out the testimony he planned.

"Francine." Hotchkiss spoke to her and Francine looked up. The judge leaned over, put an arm along the back of her chair, and began to talk in a confidential tone. Greydanus couldn't hear what was said, but he saw that Francine was listening. As the judge talked she visibly recovered, nodded, and wiped her eyes. A moment later she managed a small smile.

"Judge Hotchkiss began to talk to me. His voice was friendly and calm. I don't remember what he said at first, but it gave me time. I began to listen. He said he knew this was a hard thing for me to do, but I had best get it over with. If I didn't do it now it would prolong the trial for me and everyone involved. I thought, 'He's right. It won't be any better another day. Get it over with! Isn't that what I want?' I pulled myself together. I told Judge Hotchkiss, 'Okay, I'll try. I'll do the best I can.'"

Hotchkiss turned from Francine and addressed the lawyers. "The witness has advised me she is ready to proceed. Any exception you want to make, Mr. Palus?" Palus said he had none. Hotchkiss recalled the jury and they took their seats. Greydanus waited in front of the witness box while the judge quieted the courtroom. When Greydanus began his first question the silence was absolute.

"Francine, when did you first meet Mickey Hughes?"

Francine frowned in thought. After a moment she answered, "Well, it was around 1962. I was still going to school." Her voice was controlled and determined. Greydanus' confidence in her came surging back. He went on with the questions he had planned and

Francine gave simple, coherent replies. Her moment on stage was under way.

Greydanus used no notes. He knew the narrative of her life by heart and had long before selected the details that would most vividly symbolize the larger picture. He moved smoothly from episode to episode, letting each fact fall naturally into place.

Francine responded simply, gathering confidence as they moved along. When a question struck her as complex she paused, sometimes for seconds, as though carefully sorting out her thoughts in order to answer as accurately as possible. She refused to exaggerate what Mickey had done. Sometimes, in answer to a leading question from Greydanus about some outrage, she would consider carefully and then correct him, saying the situation hadn't been quite as he put it. Nor did she retreat at moments that were embarrassing to herself. Francine kept her eyes on Greydanus and, as her testimony went on, became more and more evidently absorbed in her memories, reliving her experiences and forgetting everything else. The courtroom was utterly still. Francine was succeeding in what had seemed impossible: telling her listeners what it had been like to be Francine Hughes.

Greydanus framed his questions to bring out the emotions that had propelled Francine along her disastrous course; she had given herself to Mickey because he loved her so much, more than anyone else ever had, and then she had married him because, having given herself, she believed she belonged to him. She described Mickey's jealousy: how he was angry and suspicious of any friendship, tore off her clothes if they made her too enticing, and forced her to quit her job in a restaurant because of a brassiere that allowed her to "jiggle." When Francine said the word Greydanus waited for the laughter he supposed would inevitably follow. There was not a sound.

Francine described how Mickey had beaten her at the beginning of their marriage; how she had felt like a prisoner, isolated in one tiny apartment after another, not allowed to go out or see her family or friends.

Greydanus moved on to Francine's divorce and her struggle to keep the household going while Mickey lived with another woman, and then the accident that had been a turning point in both their lives. Francine told of spending forty days by Mickey's hospital bed

and consenting to move to Dansville because his family wanted her
to. "Flossie said Mickey wouldn't be able to live without me if I
left and took the children away. Then Mickey moved into the
apartment with me and the kids."

"Why did you let him stay, Francine?"

"I just couldn't hurt him more . . . more than he had already
been hurt. If you could have seen him, seen the condition he was
in, you would have understood."

Francine sketched the next phase of their life together as Mickey
began to drink more and more and to use his physical power over
her without reason or restraint.

Francine told of the times Mickey had come close to killing her:
of being strangled until she blacked out, threatened with a knife,
forced out of the house in her nightgown, and kept prisoner for
hour after hour of verbal and physical abuse. She told of how the
pressure had increased and increased—the small sadistic tyrannies
and the blood-curdling threats—until she believed it was only a
matter of time before she would be killed. "Day after day it got
worse. I felt like I couldn't breathe. I had a tight feeling in my
chest. I don't think I could ever make anyone understand how
much I have been through and how much I have hurt."

Greydanus asked Francine to tell the story of their pet dog,
Lady. As Francine described Lady's death a shock wave of emotion
swept the courtroom. The simplicity of the event—a helpless animal,
a female, left outside to freeze while struggling to give birth—held
no ambiguity, no shadings of motive; it left no room for doubt. The
impact of the story was as strong as anything Francine had told so
far.

Greydanus moved swiftly to the day of Mickey's death. Francine's responses were as even as before. She seemed to draw no line
between that day and any other. The jury had already heard part
of the story from Christy and Jimmy, and the deputies, Schlachter
and Malm. Francine filled in what they could not have known.

She told it all—the torn books, the beating, the respite when the
deputies came, and the renewed abuse when they left. She told
how she had felt as she scraped up the food from the floor, and
when Mickey rubbed it into her hair, then beat her into submission.
Again the entire courtroom audience seemed spellbound with
shock. Francine went on, oblivious. She told of bringing Mickey his

food and the sexual bout that followed, about Mickey falling asleep and her return to the living room where she sat with the children in a deep reverie.

She had reached the pivotal point in her testimony. It was time to tell the jury how she had killed Mickey Hughes.

Greydanus paused, deciding on his next question, and the audience held its breath.

"Francine. You sat there thinking. What did you decide to do?"

"I decided the only thing for me to do was to get in the car and drive . . . drive west . . . just go. I told the children to get their shoes and coats on . . . as soon as Dana got there we would leave."

"Now, Francine, at that point did you have any intent, any thought of killing Mickey Hughes?"

Francine answered as though the question were no more important than any other. "No. I didn't. I was just going to take the kids and leave."

"And what happened next?"

"I remember sitting in the chair, waiting. Nicole was asleep. Christy was saying, 'Mom, where are we going? Mom, let's not come back this time. Please.' And Jimmy says, 'Yeah, Mom. Let's not come back this time.' And I said, 'Don't worry, we won't.' And then I asked Jimmy for the combination to the garage."

"What were you going to do in the garage?"

"I had decided there wouldn't be anything to come back to. I was going to burn everything."

"From that point on, Francine, how did you feel?"

"I didn't feel anything at all. It was like I was watching myself do the things I was doing." She paused for thought and then slowly continued: "I remember telling the kids to go to the car. I remember picking up Nicole and going out to the car . . . I went back to the house . . . I walked into the bedroom with the gas can and I started pouring it around on the floor. There was an urgent whisper saying, 'Do it! Do it! Do it!' over and over, and I just kept on . . . I was at the door of the bedroom . . . I stuck my hand out with the match . . . there was a swish and the door slammed and just before it did I thought, 'Oh my God, you can't do this. My God, what am I doing?' I ran to the car. I looked back and saw the flames."

Francine fell silent, and closed her eyes. She was thinking, "I've done it. I've told them. I've told them everything I can tell them. Now they can make up their minds what I deserve."

The audience sighed as the tension relaxed. After a moment Greydanus went on. "Now, Francine, tell us what happened then."

"I just remember being scared to death. I remember Christy told me, 'Mom, please slow down. You'll kill us all.'"

"What do you remember after that?"

"Going through a traffic light in Mason . . . and then being at the Guard Gate . . . and screaming."

"Were you booked that night?"

"I think so. I can't remember very well."

"And you've been in jail ever since?"

"Yes. I have."

The story of Mickey's death was finished, but one more thing remained: Francine would have to explain why she had written love letters to George Walkup.

"Now, Francine," Greydanus began in a new tone, "you have told the jury that you felt intense fear and felt unbelievably lonely living with Mickey Hughes. During that time did you ever have an opportunity to strike up a relationship with another man?"

"Yes, I did."

"Who was he?"

"His name was George Walkup."

"Where did you meet?"

"In the student lounge at school."

"You believed he was a policeman?"

"Yes. He had a uniform and a gun."

"How did this relationship start?"

"At the beginning it was just people around a table talking and having coffee and we were introduced."

"And later on did he tell you anything about his marital status?"

"We talked, off and on. And he told me he was single and living with another man; that he shared an apartment. He told that to other people, too."

"Francine, would you deliberately have developed a relationship with this man if you knew he was married—had a family and children?"

"No. I wouldn't."

"And what happened then?"

"I went out with him one night and he told me that he wasn't divorced; that he was getting divorced, but was still living at home because he and his wife had financial problems to work out."

"Did that bother you? Did that change your feeling about him?"

"Yes. The way he talked about his wife and kids bothered me. It bothered me a lot. Even though he kept insisting he was getting a divorce."

"What happened the next day?"

"He telephoned me and I told him I could not and would not see him anymore."

"You never saw him again."

"No."

"Did you think of George Walkup at all on the day of the fire?"

"No. Not once. He had nothing to do with the things I thought and did that day."

"Now, Francine, the prosecutor, Mr. Palus, states that certain letters show a motive in this case; that you wanted to be with this person more than anything else in the world. But in your mind there is no such situation; isn't that correct?"

"That's right. I didn't love him. I didn't know him that well."

Greydanus picked up copies of the letters from the defense table and held them before Francine.

"Yes," she said. "I wrote them. Messages were coming to me in jail that this man loved me and would wait for me for twenty years. I just let my imagination go. I was lonely. I was afraid. I had lost everything: my kids, my freedom, everything. And here was someone sending messages saying no matter what I had done, he loved me . . . he cared . . ."

"Francine, would you describe what it's like to be in jail?"

Francine shook her head. "I can't describe it. You have to be there to know what it is like. You feel a hurt . . . and a sadness and a being alone . . . there is no way I can tell anyone."

"Did you have a real hope that George Walkup cared about you? Did you have a real hope that you could finally have a relationship with a decent man?"

"It wasn't really a hope; it was like a dream. I didn't know what was going to happen to me. I couldn't really hope for anything. This dream was sort of like hanging on to something, trying to hold on to something out there in the real world."

Greydanus handed her the letters and asked her to read aloud passages he had marked. She began, " 'I am so frightened at times I know what I really need is a strong man to hold me for hours and hours. Would you like to volunteer?' "

"Okay." Greydanus stopped her. "Does that sentence, Francine, begin to explain how you felt . . . how you reached out?"

She shook her head. "I was afraid . . . so afraid . . ."

"Francine, how long had it been since you had a strong man to hold you in his arms lovingly?"

She returned his gaze with a steady look. "A long time," she said slowly. "Someone who would really care." She shook her head. "A long, long time."

Greydanus picked up another letter and read aloud: " 'Sometimes I am afraid to tell you things; I don't know why, but I am. I guess I have got to know first that I can trust you. Why did I hear all those conflicting stories about you? Did you lie to me about your marital status and all that? . . . I told you that I wanted you to be honest.' Why did you write that, Francine?"

"Because I still wondered. I wanted so much to believe in him, but I still had doubts deep down."

Greydanus picked up the third letter. "Francine, you wrote here, 'I don't want to open myself to this kind of relationship only to be hurt.' What did you mean?"

"I just . . . I just can't explain how I felt." She shrugged hopelessly. "I had been in jail so long . . . I had been through so much . . ." She broke off as though finally exhausted.

"Francine, at the time you wrote those letters, and even now, do you feel you are capable of loving someone in a genuine way? That you have a lot of love to give?"

"Yes. I feel like I do. With the right person."

"Really, really love someone?"

Francine nodded.

"Yes?"

"Yes."

"And isn't it true that that is what you have been wanting and aching to do for a long time?"

"Yes."

"Is that what you meant when you said, 'And someday I will find someone to give all this bottled-up love to'?"

"Yes. Someday, perhaps."

"Francine, you have told the jury some things that have happened in your life—something of what your life was like. You have given them some idea of the living hell you existed in. Let me ask you one single, vital question: Did you premeditate and plan the death of your ex-husband, Mickey Hughes?"

"No."

There was a silence in which no one spoke; no one moved. Greydanus stood still, his eyes fixed on Francine while her answer seemed to hang in the air. Then he relaxed and turned to the judge. "Your Honor, that's all I have to ask." Hotchkiss announced a recess of fifteen minutes as the courtroom broke into a roar of noise.

Greydanus took Francine's hand and helped her down from the stand. She looked exhausted, too tired even to feel relief. Sitting at the council table Greydanus told her she had done wonderfully. Then he reminded her that she wasn't quite finished yet. Though she had testified for almost four hours, enough time remained for Palus to begin his cross-examination. "Just remember," Greydanus said, "that you have no reason to be afraid of him. You're telling the truth and when you tell the truth there is nothing he can do."

As Palus approached Francine in the witness chair he wore the look of a man resolved to make the most of his last chance. In the six days of the trial the clean-cut, sincere young prosecutor in his modish suits and polished boots, who had entered the courtroom representing righteousness, had been unable to conceal his dismay as witness after witness testified not against Francine, but against Mickey Hughes. Sometimes Francine had felt almost sorry for him; it was evident how intensely he wanted to win and that every reverse increased his nervousness.

"Mrs. Hughes," Palus began, "did Mickey Hughes ever tell you that he loved you?"

The question was bold and unexpected. Francine felt a wave of fear. Would he be able to twist her answer to this—and other questions about her feelings—and use them in unexpected ways? She remembered Greydanus saying, "Just tell the truth." She answered, "Yes."

"Did he tell you that he loved you within a year of the day that he burned to death?"

"Yes." She was thinking of the spring and Mickey's vain attempt to rehabilitate himself.

"Within a month?"

Francine considered. "I don't remember."

"Did *you ever tell him* that you loved him?"

"Yes."

"Did you tell him that within a year of his death?"

"Probably."

"Isn't it a fact, Mrs. Hughes, that on March ninth, while the police were there, you called Mickey Hughes a bastard at least once?"

"I might have."

"Isn't it a fact, Mrs. Hughes, that on March ninth when the police officers were there and Mickey threatened you, you turned to him and said, 'Oh shut up!'"

There was a low laugh in the courtroom. Francine ignored it. "No. I don't remember saying anything like that."

"Isn't it true that you told the officers not to worry about threats because Mickey Hughes was always making them?"

"No. I don't remember saying that."

"Isn't it true that you told the officers you could handle the situation?"

"Yes."

"Now, Mrs. Hughes, after these beatings that you've described, wouldn't Mickey apologize to you?"

"He did a long time ago, but he got to the point where he didn't. No." After several more questions in the same vein, Palus turned to the letters to Walkup.

"Now, did you write to him . . ." Palus picked up a page from his desk and read it. "Did you write, 'You have to keep that body of yours in shape for me, you know'?"

"Yes, I did."

"Did you write it because you *didn't* want to have a relationship?"

Francine appeared momentarily puzzled. "I wrote it because I remembered him telling me that he worked out at the gym."

"Do you remember writing, 'It's just like I felt when I was near you, I didn't ever want to leave you'?"

"Yes. I remember writing that."

"Did you mean that? You didn't want to ever leave him?"

"When I first met him and he was so nice to me and everything I . . ." Francine paused as though to think of the right words in which to explain a difficult concept to a child. "When I was in jail I let my imagination go. I was imagining what it would be like to be near someone who was kind to me and cared about me."

"But you are telling us you never thought about that between the time you stopped seeing him and the time that you were in jail; is that correct?"

"That's right; I didn't."

"Do you remember writing to George Walkup, 'Like right now I feel warm all over. Like when you looked at me the way you used to. You know, when you did that to me with your eyes, I felt like the closest I could get to you wouldn't be close enough'?"

"Yes. I remember. I read the letters just the other day."

"Did you mean that when you wrote it?"

"I am trying to tell you that the things in that letter were written six weeks after I had been in jail."

"Do you remember writing, 'Since you, no one measures up'? Did you mean that?"

"There wasn't anyone else."

Now Palus tried to tie her relationship with Walkup to a motive to get rid of Mickey.

"While Mickey Hughes was around you couldn't have George Walkup or anyone else, could you?"

Francine shook her head in contradiction. "I could have, if I wanted. Mickey would go off with other women. He'd even tell me he was going. I could have."

Palus dropped Walkup and tried to establish that there had been a normal married relationship between Mickey and Francine.

"Did you and Mickey go out together at night?"

"Yes. We'd go out sometimes."

"What would you do?"

"Oh. It wasn't very often, but sometimes we would go to the movies; sometimes we would go down to the bar and I would watch him play pool."

"Did you have a good time when you did that?"

"No."

Palus had equally little luck with a series of questions asking if

Francine had attacked Mickey on a number of occasions. She said she had not and Palus was unable to produce any evidence that she had.

At last Palus gave up efforts to discredit Francine and went to the heart of the case for the prosecution: the time in which she might have premeditated murder. He questioned her about her thoughts while she sat with the children.

"Were you thinking about how tired you were of Mickey Hughes?"

"I was thinking about how tired I was of living the way I was living. Yes."

"And the person making you live that way was Mickey Hughes."

"Yes."

"And when you decided to leave you decided you didn't want to leave anything behind; is that right?"

"Yes."

"Is that when you decided you didn't want to leave Mickey Hughes behind?"

Francine sat in silence. As she had when Greydanus questioned her, she seemed to look inward. There was a long pause. Her face became a mask of pain as she answered slowly.

"I don't know. So many things went through my mind." She paused again. "The kids said, 'Let's not come back this time, Mommy.' I remember thinking that we wouldn't because there wouldn't *be* anything."

"Okay!" Palus raised his voice and confronted her with her own words. "Did that thought, 'there won't *be* anything,' include a person, Mrs. Hughes?"

Francine nodded. "*Everything!*" she said. Tears appeared in her eyes. She wiped them away and raised her head, waiting for the next question.

Palus went on to question Francine about her actions after Mickey went to sleep and for the second time she described going out to the garage and being unable to open the door, going to the basement instead, bringing up the can of gasoline and placing it by the door.

"How long after you brought the can upstairs did you pick up Nicole and say, 'Now, it's time to go'?"

"I don't know."

"Did you do any more waiting before you did that?"

"I remember being at the window. I remember being in the chair. And at the window again. But I don't know how long."

"Now you took the children out to the car. Is that correct?"

"I carried Nicole because she was sleeping."

"And then you went back inside?"

"Yes."

"Now what did you go back inside for, Mrs. Hughes?" Francine thought for several seconds. Her answer was plain and vehement.

"To get rid of everything! To destroy everything that had anything to do with my life up to that point!"

"Including Mickey Hughes?" Palus' voice was vibrant with triumph.

Francine nodded. "Yes," she replied slowly, with evident pain. "Yes. Including Mickey Hughes."

"You went into the bedroom?"

"Yes."

"Where Mickey was sleeping?"

"Yes."

"Then what did you do?"

Francine looked down. She was crying as she answered, "I started to dump the gasoline around on the floor."

"Where? Under which bed?"

"Under his bed."

"Where he was sleeping?"

"Yes." Francine wiped away the tears as rapidly as they appeared, as though determined to complete her task. In brief sentences she told once again of holding the match inside the door, the wave of panic that swept over her as the fumes caught and the door slammed; then running to the car and driving away.

Palus circled back in time. "Were there ever *other* times when you wanted to kill Mickey Hughes?"

"No. I can't remember any."

"Okay." Palus looked stern, as though evidence to the contrary were in the palm of his hand. "Now, the time he gave you two black eyes and a split lip twelve years before this time, did you want to kill him then?"

"No."

"The time he got you down on the floor with a knife, did you want to kill him then?"

"No."

"What was different about this time than the other times, Mrs. Hughes?"

Francine considered the question: the question by which Palus hoped to show the jurors that her motive to kill Mickey was revenge and that it had smoldered in her mind for years. Seconds went by while Francine stared at Palus and the courtroom hung in suspense. Finally she said slowly, "I don't know, Mr. Palus. I just . . . it was just everything over the years; everything that had happened. . . ." Again tears ran down her face. Ignoring them, she leaned toward Palus. "Don't you understand, Mr. Palus," she said earnestly. "It wasn't like you are saying. It wasn't because twelve years ago he gave me a black eye. It was *everything* that happened. *Everything! Everything!*"

Palus wouldn't give up.

"But *this* time he made you burn your schoolbooks, didn't he, Mrs. Hughes?"

"Yes."

"And you enjoyed going to school?"

"Yes."

"And if you didn't go to school you wouldn't get to be with people you wanted to be with, couldn't get the job that you wanted, right?"

"That wasn't the reason. . . ."

"And on March the ninth, Mrs. Hughes . . ." Palus paused to emphasize that he was coming to the climax of his cross-examination. "On March the ninth, you were tired of your life?"

Francine looked back steadily and answered with quiet scorn. "Mr. Palus, I was tired of my life long before March the ninth."

"And you were tired of Mickey Hughes?"

"Yes. I was."

"You wanted to leave that life behind you?"

"Yes. I did."

"You wanted to leave Mickey Hughes behind you?"

"I wanted a different life."

"And so you left that life and that man behind you?"

Francine closed her eyes for a moment. After a pause she said slowly, "Yes, Mr. Palus. But you see what kind of a life I have now."

Palus turned away and announced that his cross-examination was ended. Greydanus came forward and led Francine from the stand. The audience, which had been utterly still during Francine's testimony, broke into a tumult of noise. To Greydanus' ears it sounded like applause. Francine's performance had been superb.

Although it was midafternoon when Francine finished testifying, Greydanus decided to bring on his next witness before the mood Francine had created could slip away. He called Dr. Arnold Berkman, the clinical psychologist who would explain Francine's act in terms of temporary insanity.

Berkman, a small, serious-looking man with glasses and a shock of dark hair, conformed perfectly to the popular image of a learned doctor. He described visiting Francine in jail and giving her a battery of tests. When Greydanus asked for his evaluation of Francine, Dr. Berkman read from his report: "My examination revealed no evidence of psychosis but did reveal defects in psychological functioning and personality development which reflect significant psychopathology . . . characterized by deeply ingrained maladaptive patterns of behavior which have brought her tremendous pain. . . ."

Greydanus feared that much of this technical language would confuse the jurors, but as the doctor went on his meaning became plainer. "Mrs. Hughes has a strong need for approval, developed in response to her lifelong feelings of vulnerability and powerlessness. . . . She experiences little sense of competence, self-confidence, or autonomy, making it easy for her to be overwhelmed, tremendously threatened, and easily controlled by those whom she perceives as more powerful than herself."

Dr. Berkman explained that Francine's strong need for approval, coupled with her belief that to be a "good wife" meant to be a slave of one's husband, and her well-founded fear of retribution if she angered Mickey, caused Francine to suppress her own anger year after year, until the marriage became "a horror show," in which she was almost literally imprisoned. Berkman testified that her terror of Mickey's revenge if she tried to leave him was vividly real, and was constantly reinforced by his beating her if she dared even to visit a friend or her family. "She believed he would find her and kill her wherever she went. She was hopelessly trapped both by her own profound psychological conflicts and by her realistic fear of her husband."

Berkman described how much it had meant to Francine to go to school. By forcing her to burn her books, Mickey "was forcing her to kill that part of herself which was on the threshold of independence . . . to symbolically kill herself and all that she had invested and suffered in trying to be a person."

When Francine killed Mickey, Berkman said, "she was overwhelmed by the massive onslaughts of her most primitive emotions. Emotions she had suppressed for so many years overwhelmed her. . . . She experienced a breakdown of her psychological processes so that she was no longer able to utilize judgment . . . no longer able to control her impulses . . . unable to prevent herself from acting in the way she did.

"Anger is an emotion which creates considerable distress for her and since anger runs counter to her quest for approval she is unable to express anger directly. In terms of her life, particularly her marriage, it is appropriate she should be enraged. It is part of her psychological sickness that she could not get angry, feel angry, react with anger to a situation that was so deeply humiliating, dehumanizing, and physically cruel. . . ."

When Berkman finished reading his report, Greydanus asked, "Dr. Berkman, is Francine a person who could plan a murder?"

"No."

"Why do you say that?"

"The ability to plan a murder would require an ability to think ahead, wait, plan for the proper time. Francine is not good at doing those things. Her style is to behave very impulsively, sometimes with very poor judgment. Also, it is not in her character to plan something with such a degree of violence. Something like this would be abhorrent to her if she thought about it in advance or tried to plan it."

It was time to ask Berkman for the diagnosis that could win Francine's freedom.

"Dr. Berkman, at the time Francine committed this act was she mentally ill?"

"Yes, she was."

"Was she mentally ill to the extent that she could not conform to the law, or control her behavior? Was she operating under an irresistible impulse?"

"Yes, she was."

"And at the time you examined her subsequently she was *not* mentally ill?"

"That is correct."

Greydanus could only hope he had sufficiently underlined the distinction between temporary insanity and mental illness. He thanked Berkman and the session ended. The jury would have all night to mull over Berkman's words.

When court convened the following morning, the seventh day of Francine's trial, Palus questioned Dr. Berkman in an effort to construe his diagnosis in a way that would, under Michigan law, make Francine criminally responsible for murder.

"Dr. Berkman, would you tell us what your diagnosis of Francine Hughes was?"

"Borderline syndrome with hysterical and narcissistic features."

"Isn't it true that many people with borderline syndrome can tell the difference between right and wrong? Can understand the nature of their acts?"

"Yes. That's true. However, you are leaving out a crucial point. People with borderline syndrome, when a certain kind of stress impinges on them . . . at that particular time those people can fall apart. It's what we call psychological decompensation. It's very typical of these people."

"Now, Doctor, isn't it a fact that lots of people who are not mentally ill do things that are wrong and that they know are wrong?"

"Yes, that's true."

"And lots of people who are mentally ill do things that they know are wrong when they do them?"

"True."

"The fact that the defendant may have done some wrong things doesn't prove that she didn't know they were wrong, does it?"

"No. It doesn't prove that; it doesn't show that she necessarily did or didn't know that they were wrong."

"All right. In your opinion when did Francine Hughes recover from borderline syndrome?"

"She has not as yet recovered from it."

"So, borderline syndrome is not a psychosis; is that correct, Doctor?"

"My diagnosis is not a diagnosis of what she was like during those moments on March ninth, 1977. It is a diagnosis of her entire personality."

For several minutes Palus chivied Dr. Berkman in an effort to pin down the moment when Francine's psychotic state began and ended, and challenged Berkman to name the facts, aside from Francine's own account of hearing voices and feeling "unreal," that would show that Francine was insane at the moment the fire was lit. Berkman could only repeat that her fragile personality made her vulnerable to becoming temporarily insane under certain types of stress.

With a skeptical shrug, Palus went on. "Let me ask you a hypothetical question, Doctor. Someone waits for two or three hours while a person sleeps before she sets fire to the bedroom where that person is. Would you say she had waited for the proper time?"

"No. I would not say that."

"Is going to a police station immediately after committing an act and confessing to the police, evidence of a consciousness of guilt?"

"Yes. It would be."

With that Palus allowed Dr. Berkman to step down.

As his final witness Greydanus called Dr. Anne Seiden to the stand. Dr. Seiden, a small woman in her early forties, gave the court her extensive credentials, including her current position as staff psychiatrist at Michael Reese Hospital in Chicago. In a firm, quiet voice she described Francine's moment of "decompensation" in much the same terms Dr. Berkman had used.

"On the basis of that, Dr. Seiden," Greydanus asked, "did you make any findings concerning Francine's criminal responsibility at the time she committed this crime?"

"Yes," Dr. Seiden said. "I believe she was mentally ill at that time. She was unable to form a criminal intent because she lacked the capacity to appreciate the difference between right and wrong."

"Dr. Seiden, could she have stopped herself from doing what she did?"

"I don't believe she could have. She was in a state of ego fragmentation."

"What do you mean by ego fragmentation?"

"By that I mean that the part of the personality which ordinarily keeps one's understanding and impulses under control was not functioning. She was, in other words, acutely psychotic."

"Is that what we laymen call insane?"

"That's right," Dr. Seiden replied, and, as Greydanus questioned her, went further than Berkman had in pinpointing the moment Francine's mind snapped. The psychotic state, Dr. Seiden said, began at the moment of Francine's surrender: when she crouched in the corner of the kitchen with garbage smeared in her hair and told Mickey she wouldn't go to school any more.

Greydanus' final question for Dr. Seiden was designed to deny Palus' implication that Francine had acted in cold blood.

"Dr. Seiden, is Francine what we would call a compassionate person?"

"Yes. I think one might say excessively so."

Greydanus thanked Dr. Seiden and stepped aside. It was Palus' turn to cross-examine her. As he had with Berkman, Palus badgered Dr. Seiden about the terms she used to define Francine's lack of criminal responsibility. Seiden stuck to her guns, and as she finished her testimony Greydanus was satisfied that whether the jury fully understood the complex distinctions involved was less important than the fact that Seiden had firmly reiterated her professional opinion that Francine had been temporarily out of control.

Dr. Seiden was the final witness for the defense. When she finished Judge Hotchkiss called a short recess. The trial would close with the testimony of Dr. Blunt, the expert in legal psychiatry engaged by the prosecution to refute Berkman and Seiden. The brutalities of the life that Francine had endured with Mickey had been as clear to Blunt as to Seiden and Berkman, and in his written pretrial report Blunt had cited very similar details.

Where Blunt differed with Seiden and Berkman was whether, at the moment she poured the gasoline and lit it, Francine was legally insane. Michigan law defines insanity as "a substantial disorder of thought or mood which significantly impairs judgment, behavior, capacity to recognize reality, or ability to cope with ordinary demands of life." At the conclusion of his report, Dr. Blunt wrote: "In my opinion, Mrs. Hughes shows no evidence of any disorder that would render her mentally ill in accordance with MCL 330.1400a [the statute defining mental illness], either at the time of the inci-

dent or at the present time." When he read Blunt's report Greydanus had wondered how Blunt could have understood Francine's
situation as fully as he seemed to, and yet consent to give testimony that might send her to prison for a long term.

Now, walking down the corridor by the judge's chambers, Greydanus spotted Blunt, a tall, sandy-haired man in a light blue suit,
waiting to go on the stand. On an impulse Greydanus walked over
to him. "Dr. Blunt," he said, "I want to talk to you for a minute."
Taking the surprised doctor by the arm, he led him into a vacant
office nearby. "I've read your report," Greydanus told him. "I want
to know what you're going to testify. How are you going to answer
questions on premeditation? How in the world can you take the
stand and say that Francine planned this thing?"

Looking acutely uncomfortable, Dr. Blunt defended his opinion,
reiterating that Francine had been legally sane. Greydanus
persisted in his questions, pointing out that Blunt had agreed with
Berkman and Seiden in almost every other respect. Beads of sweat
appeared on Blunt's upper lip. "What are you going to answer,"
Greydanus demanded, "if I ask you if Francine premeditated this
crime?"

Blunt hesitated and said, "I can't say she premeditated it. I will
have to say to the contrary. I don't think she was capable of planning it."

For Greydanus that was enough. Premeditation is an essential in-
gredient of murder in the first degree. He thanked Blunt and
walked out of the room. In the corridor he encounted Palus.
"Marty," Greydanus said, "I think you'd better go talk to your doctor. He's got something important to tell you." Palus hastened to
confer with Dr. Blunt. Only a few moments later Judge Hotchkiss
returned to the bench and the session resumed. Greydanus could
imagine how Palus must feel as he called Dr. Blunt to the stand; if
he asked Blunt the question Greydanus had, he would torpedo his
own case. If he didn't ask it, Greydanus surely would.

Palus did not ask the question, but led the doctor through the
other points on which he differed with Dr. Seiden and Dr. Berkman.

"Did you, Dr. Blunt, examine Francine Hughes for purposes of
evaluating criminal responsibility?"

"Yes. I did."

"Did you arrive at an opinion concerning whether or not Francine Hughes had a mental illness?"

"It is my opinion that Mrs. Hughes does not suffer from mental illness as defined by the Michigan statute."

"On the evening of March the ninth, 1977, was Francine Hughes criminally responsible?"

"It was my opinion that she was criminally responsible on the night of March nine, 1977."

"You, sir, have heard of the term 'temporary insanity'?"

"Yes, I have."

"Did you find any temporary insanity in this case, sir?"

"I did not feel there was any temporary insanity. I felt that Mrs. Hughes was extremely frustrated by the situation, by the particular episode that day. I would think this was more of an episode that caused her to finally just explode because of the things she was going through."

Palus asked Blunt to give his views on "borderline syndrome," and Blunt agreed with Seiden and Berkman that such a category of illness exists, "but I question it very highly unless there is a pattern of this kind of thing—evidence of it in the past."

"Dr. Blunt, did you, sir, find Francine Hughes was a borderline syndrome type of person?"

"No. I did not."

Prudently, Palus ended his questions there and turned the witness over to Greydanus for cross-examination. As he rose to address Dr. Blunt, Greydanus felt like a card player with an ace up his sleeve. He intended to play it last.

"Dr. Blunt," Greydanus began. "How long did you examine Francine Hughes?"

"For one hour and forty minutes."

"And you have testified that she gave you her entire history, all the background, an explanation of what her character is like, and her motivations?"

"Yes. I think she did."

"Do you feel you acquired all the information you needed in that hour and forty minutes?"

"Yes, I did." Dr. Blunt bridled. "Or I would have taken longer."

Wasn't there a possibility, Greydanus insisted, that deeper examination might have turned up the "previous episodes" that Blunt

had said would be needed to convince him that Francine was subject to borderline syndrome?

"Yes," Blunt acknowledged after considerable hairsplitting. "You
could always miss something." But he continued to maintain that
Francine had not "decompensated" into an abnormal state of mind.
He considered the voice she had heard urging her to "Do it! Do it!"
to be evidence of a conflict of feeling rather than a hallucination.

Greydanus turned to Blunt's report on Francine.

"Doctor, on page six you indicate that her pent-up hostilities
reached a stage where she 'chose' a course that would 'end the situation forever.' My question is, how do you know she could make a
choice at that time?"

"By my interview with her. By talking with her about it."

"Well, Francine is the one who told you she heard voices; isn't
that correct?"

"She told me she heard a voice saying, 'Do it! Do it! Do it!'"

"And you just sort of concluded that that wasn't the case; that
she actually didn't hear those voices?"

"I did not feel it was an attempt on her part to feign hallucination. I felt it was her way of explaining how she felt at the time—
of expressing her strong conflicting impulses."

"But despite your statement that you didn't feel she would make
it up, or feign it, you are making the end judgment that she didn't
really hear those voices?"

"I am making a judgment based on my clinical experience and
training."

At least the doctor had admitted that Francine hadn't feigned
hearing a voice. Now Greydanus asked if Dr. Blunt hadn't contradicted himself when he said that Francine "chose" a course, but at
the same moment her "pent-up hostilities broke forth."

"No, I don't think so. I think that some things happened that
night that were particularly devastating to her, and this brought a
level of hostility which she was no longer able to keep under
wraps."

"Did Francine have an immense fear of her ex-husband?"

"Yes. She did."

"And isn't it true that there is an element of self-defense in what
she did?"

"Yes. Yes. She was defending herself in a sense. Not directly, because he was certainly not attacking her at that instant, but he had told her he would always follow her if she tried to get away—find her and harm her. I think she believed that was a real possibility; that wasn't an idle threat on his part."

Dr. Blunt had made a concession of great value to Francine's defense. Now Greydanus decided to play his big card.

"Let me ask you, Doctor, in studying Francine's character and everything that happened that night, in your opinion did her actions that night indicate premeditation and planning?"

"In my opinion," Blunt replied, "I do not think that her actions represented premeditation and planning. In other words, she did not sit back and think, 'I'm going to kill my husband now!' It was an impulsive thing that happened."

Greydanus felt a rush of triumph as he repeated the doctor's words, nailing them down.

"It was an *impulsive* thing? There was *no* planning? *No* premeditation?"

"I see no evidence of that."

"Thank you very much, Doctor," Greydanus said with sincerity, and sat down.

"Further questions, Mr. Palus?" Judge Hotchkiss inquired.

"No redirect. Thank you, Your Honor," Palus replied, and the testimony in the case of *The People* versus *Francine Hughes* was at an end.

The following morning Francine was brought to court for the eighth and final day of the trial. The crowds and excitement in the corridors of City Hall were greater than ever. Greydanus had to fight his way through photographers and reporters to lead her into the courtroom, where she took her usual seat. A moment later she glanced up and her heart lurched. The children, including Nicole, were sitting with her mother and sisters in the second row. Greydanus had forgotten to warn her that he had asked to have them brought for the benefit of the jury. Francine quickly looked away. At that moment she knew her self-control was fragile as spun glass.

The trial had moved faster than anyone expected. Nothing remained but the closing statements by the opposing attorneys and the judge's instructions to the jurors. Then the case would be theirs to decide. Hotchkiss opened the proceedings with his usual briskness and called on Mr. Palus to begin. Looking serious and more than a little nervous, Palus rose and stood before the jury box.

"Members of the jury, good morning. Those of you who have sat on a trial before know this is the time we argue our positions and try to convince you to rule in the way we would like. . . . Let's consider the evidence. . . . First we have shown that there was a death. You have seen the body of Mickey Hughes. . . . We have shown you that he died as a result of acts committed by Francine Hughes. . . . Have we shown you that there was malice afore-thought, or intent? We have indeed done that! There can be no question that Francine Hughes knew that as a result of lighting a match to that gasoline Mickey Hughes would die."

Palus reminded the jurors of other evidence that Francine had acted deliberately and premeditated her crime. On the afternoon before the fire she had told the deputies she could handle Mickey and needed no further help; Christy had testified that her mother was calm, "acting normal," as she made her preparations to burn the house. Francine's own testimony, Palus said, showed that she had had ample time to cool off, but instead had sat for a long time and thought about "how tired she was of living with Mickey Hughes."

Palus dismissed Mickey's abuse as a prime motive. "It is claimed that these beatings went on for thirteen years until suddenly, on this day, Francine decided to stop it." Palus shook his head. "We have heard testimony that Francine Hughes received more severe beatings than this one. . . . What made this day different? What made it more compelling, more necessary to get rid of Mickey Hughes? We have a couple of suggestions for you. One is that she wanted to go to school and Mickey Hughes had told her she couldn't do it. Isn't it interesting that he burned her books and she burned him? The other suggestion, members of the jury, is George Walkup!"

Palus picked up Francine's letters and read torrid bits aloud. "Consider those letters very carefully . . . there are things in there such as 'I have loved you since the first day I saw you. Since you there has been no one else.' There are also such things as 'And that night you were bowling, God, I couldn't keep my eyes off you.' And 'Did you know that your eyes are so sexy? Everytime you looked at me I got heated up. Our time together just wasn't long enough. It was like having something you have wanted all your life and only having it for five minutes.'"

Palus laid the letters down. "I am asking you to consider whether those letters were written by a woman who saw a man just once or twice and then completely forgot him. Or did she want to be with him the rest of her life?"

Now Palus tackled the question of Francine's mental state and the opinion of Dr. Berkman and Dr. Seiden that Francine had crossed the borderline of insanity and then recovered after the murder had been committed. "Isn't that a little bit too convenient?" Palus asked.

In conclusion Palus again stated The People's case: "We submit, members of the jury, that Francine Hughes acted in the cool of reflection: that she decided to get rid of Mickey Hughes. We ask that you find Francine Hughes guilty of first-degree murder. Thank you very much."

As Greydanus rose to answer Palus, he knew this was the most important moment in what had become the most important case in his professional career. He touched Francine lightly on the shoulder, and then walked over to stand before the jury box. His first words came from the heart. "Ladies and gentlemen of the jury, I have become terribly aware of the tremendous burden that I carry in this particular case. The prosecutor has presented it to you as being a simple case, but we are talking about much more here than Mr. Palus wants you to believe."

Greydanus reminded the jury of facts Palus had ignored. "Mr. Palus admits there were beatings and then, incredibly, he skips over the fact that these beatings went on for twelve years. *Twelve years* of abuse of every conceivable kind!" He listed the worst atrocities of Francine's life with Mickey. She had put up with them, he said, because of a fatal combination of personal traits: her compassion, her tendency to accept guilt, her resolve to be a good wife and mother, no matter how impossible the circumstances.

Greydanus picked up Francine's letters to Walkup and held them before the jury. "I submit that the prosecution has operated in bad faith," Greydanus said. "She was charged with first-degree murder months before anyone knew these letters existed. Now Mr. Palus says that these letters are the focal point of this entire trial. These letters show that Francine broke off with George Walkup before

March nine, 1977, but Palus doesn't tell you that. He says these letters are evidence of Francine's motive. I don't understand how he can say that in good faith when what these letters really show, ladies and gentlemen, is what a pitiful creature Francine Hughes had become as a result of her husband's inhumanity. Francine in her helplessness, in her absolute agony, when someone reached out a hand to her, responded in an almost pitiful manner."

Greydanus faced the crucial question of Francine's sanity. "Mr. Palus placed a psychiatrist on the stand and what does he say? Something that Mr. Palus obviously must have known. Dr. Blunt said that Francine could *not* have planned and premeditated this crime! In spite of that, in spite of Dr. Blunt's opinion, Mr. Palus insists that she did! Mr. Palus insists that these letters, and the sequence of events that evening, prove premeditation. But Dr. Blunt, the psychiatrist for the prosecution, says her act was impulsive—utterly spontaneous. Our own witnesses, Dr. Seiden and Dr. Berkman and Francine herself—and even the prosecutor's witness, Dr. Blunt —have testified that Francine was compelled by an irresistible impulse. I submit to you, based on that testimony, that Francine Hughes was temporarily insane. The testimony has also shown that she was acting against an evil force that was threatening her life. She was acting in self-defense, protecting herself. Even Dr. Blunt indicated that."

Finally Greydanus asked that the jury exercise mercy. "A life has been lost. No one denies that. That is a tragedy. But this woman has suffered immensely. She feels a deep guilt. Within your hands is the destiny of Francine Hughes—the destiny of her children. I am appealing to your mercy, your compassion. If you can't understand how anything like this could have happened, at least try to understand how horrible it was.

"Ladies and gentlemen, I am convinced that justice will be done if you return a verdict of Not Guilty. I ask you to bring in those two words that will set her free, 'Not Guilty.' Thank you very much."

When Greydanus sat down, Judge Hotchkiss asked Palus if he had anything to say in rebuttal. Palus rose and for a moment seemed to grope for words. "May it please the court, members of the jury, now is my last time to speak to you and I will try to keep it brief. First, as to the statements of the psychiatrists. They were here to aid you. I urge you to consider what they told you in the context of *all* the evidence. *You* have to decide whether or not you are convinced Francine Hughes was temporarily insane." Palus turned to the letters. "It is *not* our position that the letters are the focal point of the trial. It is our position that you must consider all the evidence. . . ."

As Palus talked on, repeating that phrase again and again, Greydanus believed the prosecutor was floundering; that he had been unprepared for the way in which Greydanus had moved from the defense to the attack, putting not only Mickey Hughes but the entire prosecution on trial.

"I think what you should remember," Palus continued, "is that the main issue here is whether or not Francine Hughes in fact committed murder on March the ninth, 1977. A person claiming self-defense cannot be a person committing assault at the same time. When Francine Hughes poured gasoline under Mickey Hughes' bed and lit the match, which was the aggressor? Which one of them was assaulting the other with deadly force?

"As for 'temporary insanity,' I ask you to consider that during that day Francine Hughes appeared calm and normal. I would like you to consider the convenience of her claim that after all those years of stress, she has a breakdown on the night that she set fire to Mickey Hughes! Rely on your own experience and decide!

"The question before you, members of the jury, is did this woman, Francine Hughes, did she, on March the ninth, 1977, did this compassionate, fearful, beaten woman wait for two hours after Mickey Hughes went to sleep, think about her life and what he was doing to her life, decide she didn't want that to happen anymore, decide that she wanted to get rid of him, decide that she would burn Mickey Hughes to death? Did she plan that? Did she premeditate it? That is what we ask you to decide and all we ask is that you do justice. Thank you."

While he addressed the jury Palus' back was to Francine. Listening, she felt, for the first time during the trial, anger and a touch of contempt rather than fear. She was watching as the prosecutor, his sincere young face flushed with the effort of his oration, returned to his seat. His eyes met Francine's. He quickly looked away.

Judge Hotchkiss began to instruct the jurors on the possible verdicts from which they could choose. The prosecutor had asked them to find Francine guilty of murder in the first degree. If the jurors believed Palus had proved that the crime was carried out with premeditation and malice, this would be the proper verdict, Hotch-kiss said.

On the other hand, there were other degrees of guilt to be con-sidered. If Francine had acted with malice, but without premedita-tion, the verdict should be murder in the second degree. If she acted in the heat of passion, without either malice or premedita-tion, she had committed manslaughter.

It was also possible, the judge explained, to find her guilty of murder or manslaughter and at the same time mentally ill. Finally, the judge said, if the jurors had found the defense more credible than the prosecution, they could bring back a verdict of not guilty by reason of temporary insanity, or even simply not guilty.

As Francine listened to the judge's quiet, even voice she thought, "He's being fair. He's not trying to influence them one way or the other." She watched the jurors. Their faces, attentive and serious, were turned toward the judge. The married student, a young man named Jeffrey Hill, had been elected foreman. He looked like an ordinary, reasonable young man, but Francine wondered what he could ever have known or felt that resembled her life. The other man, also young, with long blond hair, fitted no standard type, nei-ther hippy nor conservative. His face gave no clue to his feelings. Of the ten women, eight were married and older than Francine; two were young and single. They had all looked shocked by some of the testimony, but that alone was no indication of what they would decide.

The jurors seemed conscientious people who would try to make an honest decision, but Francine still believed it must be impossible for normal people to understand her life. The most likely verdict, she thought, was murder in the second degree. Blunt's testimony that she was incapable of premeditating Mickey's death made a first-degree verdict unlikely, but beyond that she dared not hope.

Judge Hotchkiss concluded his instructions at ten minutes to three. The jurors got to their feet and left the room in single file. When the door closed behind them, Francine for a moment felt giddy with fear. Impulsively she looked toward her family. They were looking in her direction, and Francine felt her eyes brimming. Greydanus took her hand and pressed it as they silently wished each other luck. Then Shelton took her arm. Francine was glad to leave the courtroom quickly, before she broke down.

In silence, Shelton took Francine to the detention cell and locked her in. This time there were no other prisoners. Francine was alone within the black walls etched with graffiti by the despairing women who had preceded her there. She lay down on the steel springs of the bunk and shut her eyes. The bunk began to spin and waves of nausea came over her. She got up and washed her face in the brown water that came from the tap, thinking: "I can't let go now. Not yet. When the verdict comes I have to be ready. I have to hold up my head and take it, whatever it is. I'll be in front of all those people. No matter what happens, I've got to look proud. The kids will be watching. It will hurt them worse if they see me cry!"

Greydanus had prepared Francine for a long wait, probably overnight, and possibly stretching into days. Prisoners are not allowed watches. For Francine it was one of the small cruelties of her situation that she could not estimate the time; sometimes when she fell into a reverie hours passed like minutes; sometimes every hour seemed like a day. Cigarettes—the time it took to smoke one—were a measure of time. Francine had saved a pack for the wait in the cell. She had twenty cigarettes. If she smoked one an hour and managed to sleep that night, the pack would last well into the following day.

Francine walked up and down the cell, looking at the walls, the bars, the gray ghost of daylight on the brick wall outside the window. "I thought, 'My God, this is terrible. This is awful. It's black in here. It's dark. I'm cold and I'm afraid. How long is it going to be?'"

She prayed, "God, you know what is in my heart. You know what happened, and you know why it happened. You know who I am, what kind of person I am; whatever you decide for me, please God, just give me enough strength to be able to take it." She sat down on the bunk and thought, "It doesn't matter how long I wait today. If the verdict is second-degree murder I'll be in prison for ten or fifteen years. Tomorrow I'll be back at the jail, packing my things and leaving, the way I've seen other girls go. What will state prison be like? They say it's worse in some ways, better in others. There's no more uncertainty, no more doubt. You know what you face. Then all you have to do is pray and God will give you the strength to stand it.'"

The door clicked open and Nancy Shelton appeared. "They want you downstairs," she said. Francine thought, "Oh no!" Suddenly she wanted the verdict put off a little longer; she wasn't ready for it after all.

When she reached the defense table the jury was already seated. Jeffrey Hill rose and addressed Judge Hotchkiss. They had not reached a verdict, he said. The spectators groaned in disappointment. The jury wanted further instructions, Hill continued. There was doubt in their minds on the distinctions between the various verdicts. Once again, Judge Hotchkiss explained them. The jury retired and Shelton took Francine back to the cell.

The false alarm had unnerved her and waiting became almost unbearable. When her fear threatened to overwhelm her she paced and prayed.

She had no idea how long she had been in the cell for the second time when Nancy Shelton returned. Her face was without expression. She beckoned, took Francine's arm, and in silence they went down in the elevator, along the corridor, and into the courtroom. Greydanus was already at the table and the jury in the box. The courtroom was hushed. Francine did not look at anyone. She held herself stiffly, concentrating on keeping her self-control. "In a moment it will be all over. Just hold on to yourself, no matter what it is." She did not look at the foreman, Jeffrey Hill, as Hotchkiss asked if the jurors had reached a verdict. She heard him reply that they had. Judge Hotchkiss asked what the verdict was. Hill announced, "Not guilty—by reason of temporary insanity."

For a moment Francine was stunned. Then she burst into tears. She had steeled herself for the worst, but not for the best. She looked at Mr. Greydanus and grabbed his arm, and said, "Thank you—thank you! Oh my God!"

"I looked at my family—the kids, Mom, my sisters. Mom was just sitting there—her face was white and she was staring straight ahead. Joanne told me later that she had to poke her and say 'Mom! Mom! She's free!' Suddenly I realized I could get up. I could go to my kids! Nobody could stop me now; nobody would grab me if I got up. So I jumped up and ran over to them. I hugged them and kissed them. Nothing had ever felt so good in my life. Christy was crying. I said, 'Christy, what's the matter? It's over! You've been so brave. Don't cry now!' She just laid her head on my chest and kept saying, 'I know it, Mom. I know it!' but she couldn't stop. Jimmy and Dana had tears, too. I kissed them until they began to smile.

"Greydanus came and got me. He explained that there were still formalities to go through. Court was still in session. That I'd have to sit back down and that I couldn't go home that night. I'd have to spend one more night in jail. Nicky was clinging to me and wouldn't let go. I gave her my hairbrush, that I had in the pocket of my sweater. I told her to keep it for me so as to help her believe that I was really coming home."

There had been an uproar in the court when the verdict came. When quiet was restored, Hotchkiss thanked the jurors and told them they had done their job well. The jurors were dismissed and the courtroom was cleared. Hotchkiss told Greydanus that on the following morning Francine would be released on bond. Greydanus explained to Francine that though she would be actually free she would be technically under bond until she had been examined once more by a psychiatrist and pronounced sane. Then her release would be complete.

When the courtroom had been cleared, Nancy Shelton and two detectives led Francine out a back way to avoid the reporters and photographers besieging the front door, and took her to a police car for the drive to the Ingham County Jail. Francine discovered it was now after ten o'clock at night. The jury had reached its verdict at 9:15, after a little more than five hours of deliberation—a remarkably short time.

At the jail a number of deputies smilingly congratulated Francine. All the world loves a winner, it seems. In cell #6, there were hugs and kisses from the other women. She was told that when news of her acquittal had been flashed over the TV everyone had screamed with excitement. Assuming that Francine would not return, her friends had packed her things for her and taken the sheets off her bunk. A matron brought new sheets and Francine made her bunk for the last time. Even the matron on duty that night joined in the festive spirit. Bending the rules, she went to the kitchen and got the makings of a party: fried eggs and toast. The women also wanted soda pop and potato chips, two luxuries denied in the jail. One of the male officers gallantly went out and fetched them.

The party went on until late that night. When the others went to sleep Francine lay awake for a long time, wide-eyed, trying to believe that on the following day she would actually be free.

In the morning Deputy Shelton took Francine to court for the last time.

At the Lansing courthouse Francine was again held in the upstairs cell for several hours. Again she paced and smoked, and prayed, but this time she was thanking God. Every time the matron passed, Francine asked what time it was, and the matron would say, "Almost time. Any minute now."

"I was thinking, 'I'm going to be walking out of here. I'm going to walk on the sidewalk. No handcuffs. Nobody holding my arm. I'm going to walk out with my head high. I don't have to be ashamed anymore. I don't have to be afraid!'"

At ten minutes after ten on the morning of November 4, 1977, Judge Hotchkiss pronounced Francine Hughes free.

"When it happened, it felt just like I thought it would. Just exactly! Mr. Greydanus and I were in the courtroom—at the defense table—and there was some legal mumbo-jumbo. Then Judge Hotchkiss said, 'Court dismissed.' I got up. There was a roar of people talking. I didn't hear anything anybody said. I just wanted to walk out the front door.

"There was such a crowd Mr. Greydanus had to fight a way out for the two of us. We had to stop for a couple of minutes outside the courtroom to talk to the reporters and TV people gathered there. Somebody had sent me red roses and Greydanus handed them to me in front of the cameras. I put them to my face to smell them. Their fragrance made me shiver. The card said 'To a battered rose who blooms again,' but there was no name. I looked at the flowers, at their velvety redness, and felt a kind of awe. Then we were out on the sidewalk. The sun hit my face. I heard my feet clicking on the sidewalk. My lungs expanded. I breathed so deep I got dizzy. Even the tears on my cheeks felt good. I wanted to shout. Under my breath I said, 'Thank you.' God had given me back my life."

Epilogue

In the three years since Mickey Hughes' death, Francine has rebuilt a normal life for herself and her children. She lives in a neat and pleasant house in the Jackson area and has supported herself with a series of factory jobs. Unable to find the secretarial work she hoped for, she has enrolled in nursing school. For the first year or more after her release from prison she suffered tremendously from guilt and depression. She reports that gradually her state of mind has improved and she now feels "normal" most of the time. She is still greatly absorbed in her children. All of them are doing well in school and show no signs of permanent damage. Francine is optimistic and tries to avoid thinking about the past. When she is forced to recall it, as she was during certain stages of the preparation of this book, it remains harrowing for her.

Francine still cannot fully understand what happened. She believes that her fault lay in overestimating her strength. "I tried to take too much until my mind snapped." Mickey, and the causes of his behavior, remain as much a mystery to her as ever. She realizes that at the end he was a very sick man. But what about the early years? Was he crazy then? Why was he violent toward her from the very beginning of their relationship?

The question is one whose social importance transcends the tragedy of two individuals. No one knows how many women are currently enduring what Francine endured, but legal experts think that only one of every ten instances of wife-beating is recorded—the

other nine cases fail to become part of the statistics. Family violence had barely been investigated when Richard J. Gelles pub-
lished his now-famous book, *The Violent Home: A Study of Physical Aggression between Husbands and Wives*, in 1974. Gelles began
his research among families in which social workers suspected violence had occurred. Not surprisingly, 55 percent of the husbands
admitted hitting their wives. The more shocking finding was that in
a representative group of families with no known history of violence, one in eight wives had been beaten. Dr. Gelles believes that
there are at least six million abused wives in the United States
today.

The only thing new about wife-beating is that we are beginning
to see it in a new light. An article by Dolores J. Trent in a 1979
issue of *The Women Lawyers Journal* points out that in the Middle
Ages in Europe a man's right to beat his wife was unquestioned,
while a woman who so much as threatened her husband could be
burned alive. In England, as late as 1395, a court confirmed the
right of a husband to inflict extreme punishment on his wife on the
grounds that it was "reasonable and solely for the purpose of re-
ducing her from her errors."

The first judicial opinion suggesting that correction might be
"unreasonable" was voiced in the case of Sir Thomas Seymore in
the early 1600s, who repeatedly beat Lady Seymore. Shortly after,
English law recognized the "Rule of Thumb" which allowed a husband to chastise his wife with a whip no bigger than his thumb.
American common law followed the British tradition and was
upheld in state courts. In North Carolina in 1864, the court declared that even though a husband had choked his wife, "the law
permits him to use such a degree of force as necessary to control an
unruly temper and make her behave herself."

However, a change of opinion was brewing. In Alabama in 1871
a landmark decision stated that the "privilege, ancient though it be,
to beat her with a stick, to pull her hair, choke her, spit in her face
or kick her about the floor . . . is not acknowledged by law." Since
then the privilege of wife-beating has been revoked everywhere.
But the law remains inconsistent, for it still provides virtually no re-
course or protection to the beaten woman.

"Even today," Mrs. Trent writes, "criminal law protection is virtually impossible to invoke. . . . The police are often a direct ob-

stacle to a battered woman who seeks the protection of the law . . . they do not see wife-beating as a crime." The training bulletin of the International Association of Chiefs of Police declares family disputes "personal matters requiring no direct action." What is in fact a felony is covered up by euphemisms—"domestic disturbance" or "family squabble." "If the battered wife succeeds in having her assailant arrested . . . the prosecutor often becomes her next adversary. . . . The burden of proof is on the victim, who must overcome centuries of male bias to convince the prosecutor of the seriousness of her charge. . . . The ultimate adversary of the battered wife is the judge. . . . Few judges will issue a warrant or convict a man on the evidence of just one beating. The woman must show a history of beatings and those she endured before calling the police don't count." As for other remedies, restraining orders and peace bonds, Mrs. Trent dismisses them as "meaningless pieces of paper." In short, she concludes, a battered woman's legal rights are flagrantly denied.

Mrs. Trent's report confirms that Francine Hughes' experience with the law-enforcement agencies was entirely typical and rooted in centuries of custom. As a wife-beater, was Mickey equally typical? Dr. Alan Willoughby of the University of Rhode Island, a clinical psychologist specializing in the treatment of alcoholism and author of *The Alcohol Troubled Person,* was asked to comment on Francine's story and explain, if he could, why Mickey behaved as he did. Dr. Willoughby had this to say:

"What Mickey did to Francine is horrifying, but not surprising. 'Craziness' is not the issue. It is possible that Mickey had some sort of brain damage dating from early in his life and that this exacerbated his rages, but no such explanation is needed to account for his behavior. In some cultures wife-beating is so frequent as to be statistically normal. Mickey reflected a subculture in which male violence is not only accepted but admired. Mickey Hughes enjoyed and sought it. Machismo is sometimes misunderstood as being directed only toward women. In fact the macho code has to do with maintaining territory—as dogs do. In the human male it is not territory in the literal sense, but self-esteem that is physically defended. Apparently Mickey's parents lived by the same code. They did not deplore his violence, though they probably felt it went too far. Francine's own family—her father, her mother, and her brother—

failed to defend her. Mickey and Francine's relationship occurred
against a background in which male violence was tacitly accepted.

"It would be a mistake, however, to believe that wife-beating is
confined to situations in which it is socially tolerated. I am
impressed by the frequency of wife-beating among people to whom
physical violence is ostensibly taboo. I know of judges, lawyers,
businessmen, and doctors, among others, who beat their wives on
occasion. Mickey beat Francine openly. These men beat their wives
in secret. They are angry men who don't dare attack their business
associates and use their wives as safe targets.

"I see several themes shaping Mickey's behavior. In addition to
the cultural theme there is the likelihood that he belonged in the
diagnostic category of the 'inadequate personality.' These are people who have no impairment that you can put your finger on, but
their judgment is poor, their behavior erratic, and they are failure
prone. For them, things invariably go wrong. They are angry, frustrated, and insecure. Mickey's jealousy was born of these feelings;
his fear that someone would take away the attractive woman he
had captured. Ripping her blouse was a statement that he owned
her.

"The inadequate personality feeds on the strength of others. The
moment Mickey married Francine he began to feed on her as he
had previously fed on his mother. There are cannibal tribes who
believe they draw strength by eating the hearts of fallen warriors.
Figuratively that was what Mickey did. By physically dominating a
strong woman he reassured himself that he was stronger and tried,
somehow, to draw her strength into himself.

"A third theme in Mickey's life was alcohol. We must stop thinking of people as being influenced by alcohol only when they are
drunk. Alcohol's effects are much more profound and long-lasting
than has been previously realized. For a number of days after
heavy drinking there are symptoms of anxiety, depression, poor
judgment, irritability, over-reactivity, and suspicion—a syndrome
that resembles paranoia. In Mickey's case, when Francine may have
thought alcohol had no part in an episode, it may actually have
been the precipitating factor.

"Alcohol was critical in Mickey's final deterioration. It is possible
that he sustained some neurological damage in the automobile accident—that we will never know—but even without it, his heavy

K50

drinking added to his defects of personality and, multiplied by frustration and loss of self-esteem after the accident, were quite sufficient to account for his behavior. Mickey was not a sadist. Sadism implies an intertwining of sexual and aggressive impulses. There was no evidence of that in Mickey or of masochism in Francine. At the end, his apparent sadism was a crazy, desperate attempt at control. Alcohol makes people irrational. Even while Mickey was going to AA and presumably sober, his years of drinking were still affecting his thinking.

"It may take months after alcohol is withdrawn for the brain to readjust. In addition, during withdrawal, there can be a lot of anger over being forced to give up this candy. Francine, the children, even the dog, were safe outlets for Mickey's fury.

"The value in the story of Mickey and Francine is that it helps to heighten awareness of the violence all around us. The numbers of people who are being tortured, either physically or psychologically, are horrendous. The victims are not only wives, but children abused by parents, and even parents abused by their children. Such violence is not a new condition, but we are just beginning to perceive its dimensions and its terrible implications. Francine's story makes clear the enormous suffering that it brings about, but we should not write off her case as being entirely extreme or unusual. There are countless Mickeys and countless Francines. We must stop reacting to these cases as isolated and aberrant, but see them as a broad stream in our culture and think of solutions in these terms."